THE POEMS OF
ROBERT HERRICK

Oxford University Press, Amen House, London E.C.4

GLASGOW NEW YORK TORONTO MELBOURNE WELLINGTON
BOMBAY CALCUTTA MADRAS KARACHI LAHORE DACCA
CAPE TOWN SALISBURY NAIROBI IBADAN ACCRA
KUALA LUMPUR HONG KONG

Tempora cinxisset Foliorum densior umbra :
Debetur Genio Laurea Sylva tuo.
Tempora et Illa Tibi mollis redimisset Oliva;
Scilicet excludis Versibus Arma tuis.
Admisces Antiqua Novis, Iucunda Severis :
Hinc Iuvenis discat, Fœmina,Virgo, Senex.
Ut solo minor es Phœbo, sic major es Unus
Omnibus, Ingenio, Mente, Lepore, Stylo.

W. Marshall Fecit.   scripsit I.HC.W.M.

THE POEMS OF

ROBERT HERRICK

EDITED BY

L. C. MARTIN

LONDON

OXFORD UNIVERSITY PRESS

NEW YORK   TORONTO

1965

ROBERT HERRICK

Baptized at St. Vedast's, Foster Lane, London   24 August 1591

Buried at Dean Prior, near Ashburton, Devonshire   15 October 1674

This Oxford Standard Authors edition of The Poems of
Robert Herrick, *edited by L. C. Martin from his Oxford
English Texts edition (Clarendon Press, 1956), was first pub-
lished in 1965*

PRINTED IN GREAT BRITAIN
O. S. A.

INTRODUCTION

ROBERT HERRICK, born in London in 1591, was the seventh child of Nicholas Herrick, goldsmith, who came to London from Leicestershire in 1556 and died in 1592. Where Robert Herrick went to school is not known. At the age of 16 he was apprenticed to Sir William Herrick, his uncle, who like Nicholas was a goldsmith; but in 1613 the apprenticeship was broken off and Herrick went to Cambridge, first to St. John's College and afterwards to Trinity Hall. There was some hesitation about the choice of a career, with a final decision in favour of the Church some time before April 1623, when Herrick was ordained deacon and priest at Peterborough. How he was employed during the next few years has not been ascertained. It seems likely, however, that he was in London forming or extending his acquaintance, some of it probably begun long before, with poets, musicians, and the various citizens and courtiers who are celebrated in his verse. It was apparently during the 1620's that his poetry was most in favour.

In 1627 he was appointed a chaplain to the forces led by the Duke of Buckingham to the Île de Rhé. On the failure and return of this expedition in 1628 Herrick was nominated to the vicarage of Dean Prior in Devonshire, taking up his duties in 1630. In this office he remained until his death in 1674, save for the period 1647–60, when as a Royalist Anglican he was removed from his cure by the Parliamentary Commissioners and was said to have been living in London. He was unmarried.

Herrick's collected poems, *Hesperides*, were published in 1648 in a volume having two sections, secular and religious, the latter with a separate title-page, *His Noble Numbers: or, His Pious Pieces* (see p. 337). According to the main title-page (see p. 1) *Hesperides* covers both categories; but it is often convenient to keep that title for the secular poems alone. The date 1647 on the title-page of the *Noble Numbers* shows that although presumably the printing of both sections was started in that year, only the second and shorter one was then finished. The pagination is continuous throughout the volume but there are separate signatures, A–2C⁸ and Aa–Ee⁸. Already on 29 April 1640 a book of Herrick's poetry had been registered with the Stationers' Company on the application of Andrew Crooke:

> Entred for his Copie vnder the hands of Master Hansley and Master Bourne warden, *The seuerall Poems* written by Master Robert Herrick. vjᵈ. (Arber, *Transcripts of the Registers*, iv. 509.)

Hesperides (including the *Noble Numbers*) contains over 1,400 poems, of which eight had been printed before on various occasions between 1633 and 1647. Three, for instance, together with one poem each by Ben Jonson and Francis Beaumont, had served to fill up the blank leaves of *Poems: Written by Wil. Shake-speare, Gent . . . London . . .* 1640. The text of the eight pieces by Herrick thus published does not always agree with that of 1648 and affords some of the evidence that Herrick was apt to revise what he had written. Thus ll. 11–12 of 'Gather ye rosebuds' (p. 84)

> But being spent, the worse, and worst
> Times still succeed the former.

appear in *The Academy of Complements*, 1646, as

> Expect not then the last and worst,
> Which still succeeds the former.

Herrick's willingness to revise his work can also be illustrated from contemporary manuscripts (not in Herrick's autograph), mostly commonplace-books and a few song-collections. Thus in Bodleian MS. Don. c. 57 the two lines just cited are given as

> Expect not then the last and worst
> Time still succeeds the former.

But as far as is known only 39 of the *Hesperides* and one of the *Noble Numbers* are preserved in manuscript.

Variant readings appear again in different copies of the 1648 volume, owing chiefly to the correction of printer's errors noticed while printing was in progress[1] and to the indiscriminate combination thereafter of corrected and uncorrected sheets. This applies also to three leaves (C7, M8, O8) which were cancelled and set up afresh. In the present edition the readings thus authorized are adopted without record of the errors they

---

[1] In one place (p. 194, l. 4) Herrick, who was presumably at hand in London, made a last-minute revision: 'started' replaces 'played'.

replace. The same applies to further mistakes which were set out in a list of errata drawn up after the printing had been completed.[1] Of the errors which were allowed to remain, some are obvious, like the use of a comma for a full point at the end of a poem, or misprints of the order 'amay' for 'away'; and these small errors are here corrected silently. In a few other places, where the text is more seriously at fault but when on consideration the reading intended is not too hard to discern, this reading appears in the text and the original one in a footnote. With the further exceptions that in this volume 's' replaces 'ſ' and that errors of spacing, wrong founts, and other merely typographical variations are normalized without notice, the present text is intended to give a faithful account of that published in 1648. In this aim it follows the edition of Herrick in the Oxford English Texts as revised in 1956 and reprinted in 1963 (first edition 1915).

In addition to the poems published in 1648 the present volume contains two occasional pieces printed as Herrick's about the same time (pp. 415-16), an epitaph on a mural stone in the church at Dean Prior (p. 419), and a number of poems found in contemporary manuscript collections. The reasons for attributing these poems to him vary in their nature and strength, but generally when his name or initials are attached to a poem and when the poem also shows characteristic turns of thought or style, his authorship, in the absence of conflicting claims, can be provisionally assumed. Such assumption may even on occasion be justified on internal evidence alone, as with the seven poems printed on pp. 440-4. Thus the poem 'Vaile thou thine eyes', besides having the same theme as 'The Lilly in a Chrystal' (p. 75), exactly repeats one of its phrases, 'More gently strokes the sight'; and ll. 21-22 of the Elegy on pp. 443-4 refer clearly enough to two of Herrick's poems in *Hesperides*, 'The Tear sent to her from Stanes' and 'The Primrose'.

Further data suggesting Herrick's authorship of the manuscript poems are provided in the OET edition of 1956. The eighteen poems in that edition (pp. 423-39) drawn from a manuscript

---

[1] The list is introduced in the edition of 1648 (A4ʳ) by the following lines:

> *For these Transgressions which thou here dost see,*
> *Condemne the Printer, Reader, and not me;*
> *Who gave him forth good Grain, though he mistook*
> *The Seed; so sow'd these Tares throughout my Book.*

commonplace-book in the Rosenbach Foundation Library at Philadelphia do not appear again in the present volume, as although they carry Herrick's initials they do not show many of his most distinctive habits of thought or phrasing.

On a first inspection the published poems seem to have been put together with little concern for any kind of order; and yet to some extent, and whether by chance or intention, the order in which they were written seems to have affected the order of presentation. About forty of the secular poems can be dated by the occasions which they commemorate; and with the year 1630 as a dividing-line (when Herrick went into Devonshire) it is found that poems datable before that year are rather more numerous in the first half of *Hesperides* (up to p. 168) than in the second. It is likely, moreover, that his poems would find their way into manuscript collections more easily before 1630 than after; and with only five exceptions out of 39, the pieces common to *Hesperides* and to manuscripts occur in the first half of the volume. (See OET *Herrick*, p. xxviii.) There is also a preponderance of longer poems in the first half and of shorter ones in the second, pointing to the conclusion that he wrote less fluently and more carefully as time went on. Many of the poems most admired today may belong to the years which followed his rustication, since only a few of these are found in manuscripts. Probably also most of the *Noble Numbers* are later than 1630. Some of them appear to have been influenced by George Herbert's *The Temple*, 1633. Several which are concerned with Jewish customs or beliefs seem plainly indebted to J. Gregory's *Notes and Observations vpon some Passages of Scripture*, published in 1646.

Herrick often assured himself that his work would bring him great fame, though perhaps with slow returns at first.

> I make no haste to have my Numbers read.
> *Seldom comes Glorie till a man be dead.*

In fact after the publication of his poems in 1648 he had no glory and very little attention for over 150 years. In 1790 George Ellis included three of Herrick's pieces in *Specimens of the Early English Poets* and he was represented again in Campbell's

Specimens of the British Poets, 1819. A volume devoted to Herrick's work, *Select Poems from the Hesperides* (284 in number), had been published in 1810. *The Works of Robert Herrick*, edited by Thomas Maitland, appeared in 1823. During the last hundred years a great many editions, 'complete' or partial, have been published in response to the widening and deepening appreciation of Herrick's abilities. The chief modern editions aiming at completeness are the following:

1. *Hesperides. The Poems and other Remains of Robert Herrick now first collected*. Edited by W. Carew Hazlitt, London, 1869.

2. *The Complete Works of Robert Herrick*. Edited by the Rev. Alexander B. Grosart. London, 1876.

3. *Robert Herrick. The Hesperides and Noble Numbers*. Edited by Alfred Pollard with a Preface by A. C. Swinburne, London and New York, 1891.

4. *The Poetical Works of Robert Herrick*. Edited by F. W. Moorman (Oxford English Texts), Oxford, 1915. Revised, with additional poems and with a Commentary, by L. C. Martin, 1956 (reprinted 1963). Moorman's text, omitting most of the secular epigrams, was reissued in Oxford English Poets (now Oxford Standard Authors), 1921 (Preface by Percy Simpson). The present edition includes all the epigrams.

In the footnotes and Glossary the poems are numbered according to their order on the pages. *48* = *Hesperides*, 1648; *ed.* = the present editor.

In order that this edition may be used with the *Concordance to the Poems of Robert Herrick* compiled by M. MacLeod (New York: O.U.P., 1936), the pagination up to p. 419 follows that of the O.E.T. editions, to which the Concordance refers.

CONTENTS

HESPERIDES:

OR,

THE WORKS

BOTH

HUMANE & DIVINE

OF

ROBERT HERRICK *Esq.*

OVID.

Effugient avidos Carmina noſtra Rogos.

LONDON,

Printed for *John Williams,* and *Francis Eglesfield,*
and are to be ſold at the Crown and Marygold
in Saint *Pauls* Church-yard. 1648.

TO THE MOST

ILLVSTRIOVS,

AND

Most Hopefull PRINCE,

C H A R L E S,

Prince of *Wales*.

WELL may my Book come forth like Publique Day,
   When such a *Light* as *You* are leads the way:
Who are my Works *Creator*, and alone
The *Flame* of it, and the *Expansion*.
And look how all those heavenly Lamps acquire
Light from the Sun, that *inexhausted Fire:*
So all my *Morne*, and *Evening Stars* from You
Have their *Existence*, and their *Influence* too.
Full is my Book of Glories; but all These
By You become *Immortall Substances*.   10

HESPERIDES

The Argument of his Book

I SING of *Brooks*, of *Blossomes*, *Birds*, and *Bowers*:
Of *April*, *May*, of *June*, and *July*-Flowers.
I sing of *May-poles*, *Hock-carts*, *Wassails*, *Wakes*,
Of *Bride-grooms*, *Brides*, and of their *Bridall-cakes*.
I write of *Youth*, of *Love*, and have Accesse
By these, to sing of cleanly-*Wantonnesse*.
I sing of *Dewes*, of *Raines*, and piece by piece
Of *Balme*, of *Oyle*, of *Spice*, and *Amber-Greece*.
I sing of *Times trans-shifting*; and I write
How *Roses* first came *Red*, and *Lillies White*.   10
I write of *Groves*, of *Twilights*, and I sing
The Court of *Mab*, and of the *Fairie-King*.
I write of *Hell*; I sing (and ever shall)
Of *Heaven*, and hope to have it after all.

To his Muse

WHITHER *Mad maiden* wilt thou roame?
Farre safer 'twere to stay at home:
Where thou mayst sit, and piping please
The poore and private *Cottages*.
Since *Coats*, and *Hamlets*, best agree
With this thy meaner Minstralsie.
There with the Reed, thou mayst expresse
The Shepherds Fleecie happinesse:
And with thy *Eclogues* intermixe
Some smooth, and harmlesse *Beucolicks*.   10
There on a Hillock thou mayst sing
Unto a handsome Shephardling;

Or to a Girle (that keeps the Neat)
With breath more sweet then Violet.
There, there, (perhaps) such Lines as These
May take the simple *Villages*.
But for the Court, the Country wit
Is despicable unto it.
Stay then at home, and doe not goe
Or flie abroad to seeke for woe.   20
Contempts in Courts and Cities dwell;
No *Critick* haunts the Poore mans Cell:
Where thou mayst hear thine own Lines read.
By no one tongue, there, censured.
That man's unwise will search for Ill,
And may prevent it, sitting still.

To his Booke

WHILE thou didst keep thy *Candor* undefil'd,
   Deerely I lov'd thee; as my first-borne child:
But when I saw thee wantonly to roame
From house to house, and never stay at home;
I brake my bonds of Love, and bad thee goe,
Regardlesse whether well thou sped'st, or no.
On with thy fortunes then, what e're they be;
If good I'le smile, if bad I'le sigh for Thee.

Another

TO read my Booke the Virgin shie
   May blush, (while *Brutus* standeth by:)
But when He's gone, read through what's writ,
And never staine a cheeke for it.

Another

WHO with thy leaves shall wipe (at need)
   The place, where swelling *Piles* do breed:
May every Ill, that bites, or smarts,
Perplexe him in his hinder-parts.

To the soure Reader

IF thou dislik'st the Piece thou light'st on first;
Thinke that of All, that I have writ, the worst:
But if thou read'st my Booke unto the end,
And still do'st this, and that verse, reprehend:
O Perverse man! If All disgustfull be,
The Extreame Scabbe take thee, and thine, for me.

To his Booke

COME thou not neere those men, who are like *Bread*
O're-leven'd; or like *Cheese* o're-renetted.

When he would have his verses read

IN sober mornings, doe not thou reherse
The holy incantation of a verse;
But when that men have both well drunke, and fed,
Let my Enchantments then be sung, or read.
When Laurell spirts 'ith fire, and when the Hearth
Smiles to it selfe, and guilds the roofe with mirth;⎯   *A *Javelin*
When up the * *Thyrse* is rais'd, and when the sound   twind with
Of sacred * *Orgies* flyes, A round, A round.   *Ivy.*
When the *Rose* raignes, and locks with ointments shine,   * Songs to
Let rigid *Cato* read these Lines of mine.   *Bacchus.*
       10

Upon Julias Recovery

DROOP, droop no more, or hang the head
Ye *Roses* almost withered;
Now strength, and newer Purple get,
Each here declining *Violet*.
O *Primroses*! let this day be
A Resurrection unto ye;
And to all flowers ally'd in blood,
Or sworn to that sweet Sister-hood:
For Health on *Julia's* cheek hath shed
Clarret, and Creame commingled.   10
And those her lips doe now appeare
As beames of *Corrall*, but more cleare.

    4.3 Now] New *conj. Moorman*

To Silvia *to wed*

L ET us (though late) at last (my *Silvia*) wed;
    And loving lie in one devoted bed.
Thy Watch may stand, my minutes fly poste haste;
No sound calls back the yeere that once is past.
Then sweetest *Silvia*, let's no longer stay;
True love, we know, precipitates delay.
Away with doubts, all scruples hence remove;
No man at one time, can be wise, and love.

The Parliament of Roses to Julia

I DREAMT the Roses one time went
    To meet and sit in Parliament:
The place for these, and for the rest
Of flowers, was thy spotlesse breast:
Over the which a State was drawne
Of Tiffanie, or Cob-web Lawne;
Then in that *Parly*, all those powers
Voted the Rose; the Queen of flowers.
But so, as that her self should be
The maide of Honour unto thee.   10

No bashfulnesse in begging

T O get thine ends, lay bashfulnesse aside;
    Who feares to aske, doth teach to be deny'd.

The Frozen Heart

I FREEZE, I freeze, and nothing dwels
    In me but Snow, and *ysicles.*
For pitties sake give your advice,
To melt this snow, and thaw this ice;
I'le drink down Flames, but if so be
Nothing but love can supple me;
I'le rather keepe this frost, and snow,
Then to be thaw'd, or heated so.

8

To Perilla

AH my *Perilla*! do'st thou grieve to see
Me, day by day, to steale away from thee?
Age cals me hence, and my gray haires bid come,
And haste away to mine eternal home;
'Twill not be long (*Perilla*) after this,
That I must give thee the *supremest* kisse:
Dead when I am, first cast in salt, and bring
Part of the creame from that *Religious Spring*;
With which (*Perilla*) wash my hands and feet;
That done, then wind me in that very sheet   10
Which wrapt thy smooth limbs (when thou didst implore
The Gods protection, but the night before)
Follow me weeping to my Turfe, and there
Let fall a *Primrose*, and with it a teare:
Then lastly, let some weekly-strewings be
Devoted to the memory of me:
Then shall my *Ghost* not walk about, but keep
Still in the coole, and silent shades of sleep.

A Song to the Maskers

1. COME down, and dance ye in the toyle
       Of pleasures, to a Heate;
   But if to moisture, Let the oyle
       Of Roses be your sweat.

2. Not only to your selves assume
       These sweets, but let them fly;
   From this, to that, and so Perfume
       E'ne all the standers by.

3. As Goddesse *Isis* (when she went,
       Or glided through the street)   10
   Made all that touch't her with her scent,
       And whom she touch't, turne sweet.

9

To *Perenna*

WHEN I thy Parts runne o're, I can't espie
In any one, the least indecencie:
But every Line, and Limb diffused thence,
A faire, and unfamiliar excellence:
So, that the more I look, the more I prove,
Ther's still more cause, why I the more should love.

Treason

THE seeds of *Treason* choake up as they spring,
He Acts the Crime, that gives it Cherishing.

Two Things Odious

TWO of a thousand things, are disallow'd,
A lying *Rich* man, and a *Poore* man proud.

To his Mistresses

HELPE me! helpe me! now I call
To my pretty *Witchcrafts* all:
Old I am, and cannot do
That, I was accustom'd to.
Bring your *Magicks, Spels, and Charmes,*
To enflesh my thighs, and armes:
Is there no way to beget
In my limbs their former heat?
Æson had (as *Poets* faine)
Baths that made him young againe: 10
Find that *Medicine* (if you can)
For your drie-decrepid man:
Who would faine his strength renew,
Were it but to pleasure you.

The Wounded Heart

COME bring your *sampler*, and with Art,
Draw in't a wounded Heart:
And dropping here, and there:
Not that I thinke, that any Dart,

Can make your's bleed a teare:
Or peirce it any where;
Yet doe it to this end: that I,
   May by
   This secret see,
  Though you can make   10
That *Heart* to bleed, your's ne'r will ake
   For me.

No Loathsomnesse in love

W HAT I fancy, I approve,
  No Dislike there is in love:
Be my Mistresse short or tall,
And distorted there-withall:
Be she likewise one of those,
That an *Acre* hath of Nose:
Be her forehead, and her eyes
Full of incongruities:
Be her cheeks so shallow too,
As to shew her *Tongue* wag through: 10
Be her lips ill hung, or set,
And her grinders black as jet;
Ha's she thinne haire, hath she none,
She's to me a *Paragon*.

To Anthea

I F, deare *Anthea*, my hard fate it be
 To live some few-sad-howers after thee:
Thy *sacred Corse* with *Odours* I will burne;
And with my *Lawrell* crown thy *Golden Urne*.
Then holding up (there) such religious Things,
As were (time past) thy holy *Filitings*:
Nere to thy *Reverend Pitcher* I will fall
Down dead for grief, and end my woes withall:
So three in one small plat of ground shall ly,
Anthea, *Herrick*, and his *Poetry*. 10

11

The Weeping Cherry

I SAW a *Cherry* weep, and why?
    Why wept it? but for shame,
Because my *Julia's* lip was by,
    And did out-red the same.
But pretty Fondling, let not fall
    A teare at all for that:
Which *Rubies*, *Corralls*, *Scarlets*, all
    For tincture, wonder at.

Soft Musick

THE mellow touch of musick most doth wound
    The soule, when it doth rather sigh, then sound.

The Difference Betwixt Kings and Subiects

TWIXT Kings and Subjects ther's this mighty odds,
    Subjects are taught by *Men*; Kings by the *Gods*.

His Answer to a Question

SOME would know
    Why I so
Long still doe tarry,
    And ask why
    Here that I
Live, and not marry?
    Thus I those
    Doe oppose;
What man would be here,
    Slave to Thrall,   10
    If at all
He could live free here?

Upon Julia's Fall

JULIA was carelesse, and withall,
    She rather took, then got a fall:
The wanton *Ambler* chanc'd to see
Part of her leggs synceritie:

And ravish'd thus, It came to passe,
The Nagge (like to the *Prophets Asse*)
Began to speak, and would have been
A telling what rare sights h'ad seen:
And had told all; but did refraine,
Because his Tongue was ty'd againe.　　10

Expences Exhaust

LIVE with a thrifty, not a needy Fate;
Small shots paid often, waste a vast estate.

Love what it is ✓

LOVE is a circle that doth restlesse move
In the same sweet eternity of love.

Presence and Absence

WHEN what is lov'd, is Present, love doth spring;
But being absent, Love lies languishing.

No Spouse but a Sister

A BACHELOUR I will
Live as I have liv'd still,
And never take a wife
To crucifie my life:
But this I'le tell ye too,
What now I meane to doe;
A Sister (in the stead
Of Wife) about I'le lead;
Which I will keep embrac'd,
And kisse, but yet be chaste.　　10

The Pomander Bracelet

TO me my *Julia* lately sent
A Bracelet richly Redolent:
The Beads I kist, but most lov'd her
That did perfume the Pomander.

The shooe tying

ANTHEA bade me tye her shooe;
I did; and kist the Instep too:
And would have kist unto her knee,
Had not her Blush rebuked me.

The Carkanet

INSTEAD of Orient Pearls, of Jet,
I sent my Love a Karkanet:
About her spotlesse neck she knit
The lace, to honour me, or it:
Then think how wrapt was I to see
My Jet t'enthrall such Ivorie.

His sailing from Julia

WHEN that day comes, whose evening sayes I'm gone
Unto that watrie Desolation:
Devoutly to thy *Closet-gods* then pray,
That my wing'd Ship may meet no *Remora*.
Those Deities which circum-walk the Seas,
And look upon our dreadfull passages,
Will from all dangers, re-deliver me,
For one *drink-offering*, poured out by thee.
Mercie and *Truth* live with thee! and forbeare
(In my short absence) to unsluce a teare: 10
But yet for Loves-sake, let thy lips doe this,
Give my dead picture one engendring kisse:
Work that to life, and let me ever dwell
In thy remembrance (*Julia*.) So farewell.

How the Wall-flower came first, and why so called

WHY this Flower is now call'd so,
List' sweet maids, and you shal know.
Understand, this First-ling was
Once a brisk and bonny Lasse,
Kept as close as *Danae* was:

2.1 Pearls, *ed*.: Pearls *48*

Who a sprightly *Springall* lov'd,
And to have it fully prov'd,
Up she got upon a wall,
Tempting down to slide withall:
But the silken twist unty'd,   10
So she fell, and bruis'd, she dy'd.
Love, in pitty of the deed,
And her loving-lucklesse speed,
Turn'd her to this Plant, we call
Now, *The Flower of the Wall*.

Why Flowers change colour

T HESE fresh beauties (we can prove)
Once were Virgins sick of love,
Turn'd to Flowers. Still in some
Colours goe, and colours come.

To his Mistresse objecting to him neither Toying or Talking

Y OU say I love not, 'cause I doe not play
Still with your curles, and kisse the time away.
You blame me too, because I cann't devise
Some sport, to please those Babies in your eyes:
By *Loves Religion*, I must here confesse it,
The most I love, when I the least expresse it.
Small griefs find tongues: Full Casques are ever found
To give (if any, yet) but little sound.
Deep waters noyse-lesse are; And this we know,
That chiding streams betray small depth below.   10
So when Love speechlesse is, she doth expresse
A depth in love, and that depth, bottomlesse.
Now since my love is tongue-lesse, know me such,
Who speak but little, 'cause I love so much.

Upon the losse of his Mistresses

I HAVE lost, and lately, these
Many dainty Mistresses:
Stately *Julia*, prime of all;
Sapho next, a principall:

Smooth *Anthea*, for a skin
White, and Heaven-like Chrystalline:
Sweet *Electra*, and the choice
Myrha, for the Lute, and Voice.
Next, *Corinna*, for her wit,
And the graceful use of it: 10
With *Perilla:* All are gone;
Onely *Herrick's* left alone,
For to number sorrow by
Their departures hence, and die.

The Dream

ME thought, (last night) love in an anger came,
And brought a rod, so whipt me with the same:
Mirtle the twigs were, meerly to imply;
Love strikes, but 'tis with gentle crueltie.
Patient I was: Love pitifull grew then,
And stroak'd the stripes, and I was whole agen.
Thus like a Bee, *Love-gentle* stil doth bring
Hony to salve, where he before did sting.

The Vine

I DREAM'D this mortal part of mine
Was Metamorphoz'd to a Vine;
Which crawling one and every way,
Enthrall'd my dainty *Lucia.*
Me thought, her long small legs & thighs
I with my *Tendrils* did surprize;
Her Belly, Buttocks, and her Waste
By my soft *Nerv'lits* were embrac'd:
About her head I writhing hung,
And with rich clusters (hid among   }   10
The leaves) her temples I behung:
So that my *Lucia* seem'd to me
Young *Bacchus* ravisht by his tree.
My curles about her neck did craule,
And armes and hands they did enthrall:
So that she could not freely stir,
(All parts there made one prisoner.)

But when I crept with leaves to hide
Those parts, which maids keep unespy'd,
Such fleeting pleasures there I took,   20
That with the fancie I awook;
And found (Ah me!) this flesh of mine
More like a *Stock*, then like a *Vine*.

To Love ✓

I'M free from thee; and thou no more shalt heare
My puling Pipe to beat against thine eare:
Farewell my shackles, (though of pearle they be)
Such precious thraldome ne'r shall fetter me.
He loves his bonds, who when the first are broke,
Submits his neck unto a second yoke.

On himselfe

YOUNG I was, but now am old,
But I am not yet grown cold;
I can play, and I can twine
'Bout a Virgin like a Vine:
In her lap too I can lye
Melting, and in fancie die:
And return to life, if she
Claps my cheek, or kisseth me;
Thus, and thus it now appears
That our love out-lasts our yeeres.   10

Love's play at Push-pin ✓

LOVE and my selfe (beleeve me) on a day
At childish Push-pin (for our sport) did play:
I put, he pusht, and heedless of my skin,
Love prickt my finger with a golden pin:
Since which, it festers so, that I can prove
'Twas but a trick to poyson me with love:
Little the wound was; greater was the smart;
The finger bled, but burnt was all my heart.

The Rosarie

ONE ask'd me where the Roses grew?
    I bade him not goe seek;
But forthwith bade my *Julia* shew
    A bud in either cheek.

Upon Cupid

OLD wives have often told, how they
    Saw *Cupid* bitten by a flea:
And thereupon, in tears half drown'd,
He cry'd aloud, Help, help the wound:
He wept, he sobb'd, he call'd to some
To bring him *Lint*, and *Balsamum*,
To make a *Tent*, and put it in,
Where the *Steletto* pierc'd the skin:
Which being done, the fretfull paine
Asswag'd, and he was well again.   10

The Parcæ, *or,* Three dainty Destinies
The Armilet

THREE lovely Sisters working were
    (As they were closely set)
Of soft and dainty Maiden-haire,
    A curious *Armelet*.
I smiling, ask'd them what they did?
    (Faire *Destinies* all three)
Who told me, they had drawn a thred
    Of Life, and 'twas for me.
They shew'd me then, how fine 'twas spun;
    And I reply'd thereto,   10
I care not now how soone 'tis done,
    Or cut, if cut by you.

Sorrowes succeed

WHEN one is past, another care we have,
    Thus woe succeeds a woe; as wave a wave.

Cherry-pit

JULIA and I did lately sit
  Playing for sport, at Cherry-pit:
She threw; I cast; and having thrown,
I got the Pit, and she the Stone.

To Robin Red-brest

LAID out for dead, let thy last kindnesse be
  With leaves and mosse-work for to cover me:
And while the Wood-nimphs my cold corps inter,
Sing thou my Dirge, sweet-warbling Chorister!
For Epitaph, in Foliage, next write this,
  Here, here the Tomb of Robin Herrick is.

Discontents in Devon

MORE discontents I never had
  Since I was born, then here;
Where I have been, and still am sad,
  In this dull *Devon-shire:*
Yet justly too I must confesse;
  I ne'r invented such
Ennobled numbers for the Presse,
  Then where I loath'd so much.

To his Paternall Countrey

O EARTH! Earth! Earth heare thou my voice, and be
  Loving, and gentle for to cover me:
Banish'd from thee I live; ne'r to return,
Unlesse thou giv'st my small Remains an Urne.

Cherrie-ripe

CHERRIE-Ripe, Ripe, Ripe, I cry,
  Full and faire ones; come and buy:
If so be, you ask me where
They doe grow? I answer, There,

Where my *Julia*'s lips doe smile;
There's the Land, or Cherry-Ile:
Whose Plantations fully show
All the yeere, where Cherries grow.

To his Mistresses

P<small>UT</small> on your silks; and piece by piece
Give them the scent of Amber-Greece:
And for your breaths too, let them smell
Ambrosia-like, or *Nectarell*:
While other Gums their sweets perspire,
By your owne jewels set on fire.

To Anthea

N<small>OW</small> is the time, when all the lights wax dim;
And thou (*Anthea*) must withdraw from him
Who was thy servant. Dearest, bury me
Under that *Holy-oke*, or *Gospel-tree*:
Where (though thou see'st not) thou may'st think upon
Me, when thou yeerly go'st Procession:
Or for mine honour, lay me in that Tombe
In which thy sacred Reliques shall have roome:
For my Embalming (Sweetest) there will be
No Spices wanting, when I'm laid by thee.   10

The Vision to Electra

I <small>DREAM'D</small> we both were in a bed
Of Roses, almost smothered:
The warmth and sweetnes had me there
Made lovingly familiar:
But that I heard thy sweet breath say,
Faults done by night, will blush by day:
I kist thee (panting,) and I call
Night to the Record! that was all.
But ah! if empty dreames so please,
Love give me more such nights as these.   10

Dreames

HERE we are all, by day; By night w'are hurl'd
By dreames, each one, into a sev'rall world.

Ambition

IN Man, Ambition is the common'st thing;
Each one, by nature, loves to be a King.

His request to Julia

JULIA, if I chance to die
Ere I print my Poetry;
I most humbly thee desire
To commit it to the fire:
Better 'twere my Book were dead,
Then to live not perfected.

Money gets the masterie

FIGHT thou with shafts of silver, and o'rcome,
When no force else can get the masterdome.

The Scar-fire

WATER, water I desire,
Here's a house of flesh on fire:
Ope' the fountains and the springs,
And come all to Buckittings:
What ye cannot quench, pull downe;
Spoile a house, to save a towne:
Better tis that one shu'd fall,
Then by one, to hazard all.

Upon Silvia, a Mistresse

WHEN some shall say, Faire once my *Silvia* was;
Thou wilt complaine, False now's thy Looking-glasse:
Which renders that quite tarnisht, which was green;
And Priceless now, what Peerless once had been:
Upon thy Forme more wrinkles yet will fall,
And comming downe, shall make no noise at all.

Cheerfulnesse in Charitie: or, The sweet Sacrifice

'TIS not a thousand Bullocks thies
    Can please those Heav'nly Deities,
If the Vower don't express
In his Offering, Cheerfulness.

Once poore, still penurious

GOES the world now, it will with thee goe hard:
    The fattest Hogs we grease the more with Lard.
To him that has, there shall be added more;
Who is penurious, he shall still be poore.

Sweetnesse in Sacrifice

'TIS not greatness they require,
    To be offer'd up by fire:
But 'tis sweetness that doth please
Those Eternall Essences.

Steame in Sacrifice

IF meat the Gods give, I the steame
    High-towring wil devote to them:
Whose easie natures like it well,
If we the roste have, they the smell.

Upon Julia's Voice

SO smooth, so sweet, so silv'ry is thy voice,
    As, could they hear, the Damn'd would make no noise,
But listen to thee, (walking in thy chamber)
Melting melodious words, to Lutes of Amber.

Againe

WHEN I thy singing next shall heare,
    Ile wish I might turne all to eare,
To drink in Notes, and Numbers; such
As blessed soules cann't heare too much:

Then melted down, there let me lye
Entranc'd, and lost confusedly:
And by thy Musique strucken mute,
Die, and be turn'd into a Lute.

All things decay and die

ALL *things decay with Time*: The Forrest sees
The growth, and down-fall of her aged trees:
That Timber tall, which three-score *lusters* stood
The proud *Dictator* of the State-like wood:
I meane (the Soveraigne of all Plants) the Oke
Droops, dies, and falls without the cleavers stroke.

The succession of the foure sweet months

FIRST, *April*, she with mellow showrs
Opens the way for early flowers;
Then after her comes smiling *May*,
In a more rich and sweet aray:
Next enters *June*, and brings us more
Jems, then those two, that went before:
Then (lastly) *July* comes, and she
More wealth brings in, then all those three.

No Shipwrack of Vertue. To a friend

THOU sail'st with others, in this *Argus* here;
Nor wrack, or *Bulging* thou hast cause to feare:
But trust to this, my noble passenger;
Who swims with Vertue, he shall still be sure
(*Ulysses*-like) all tempests to endure;
And 'midst a thousand gulfs to be secure.

Upon his Sister-in-Law, Mistresse
Elizab: Herrick

FIRST, for Effusions due unto the dead,
My solemne Vowes have here accomplished:
Next, how I love thee, that my griefe must tell,
Wherein thou liv'st for ever. Deare farewell.

Of Love. A Sonet

H OW Love came in, I do not know,
Whether by th'eye, or eare, or no:
Or whether with the soule it came
(At first) infused with the same:
Whether in part 'tis here or there,
Or, like the soule, whole every where:
This troubles me: but I as well
As any other, this can tell;
That when from hence she does depart,
The out-let then is from the heart.   10

To Anthea

A H my *Anthea!* Must my heart still break?
(*Love makes me write, what shame forbids to speak.*)
Give me a kisse, and to that kisse a score;
Then to that twenty, adde an hundred more:
A thousand to that hundred: so kisse on,
To make that thousand up a million.
Treble that million, and when that is done,
Let's kisse afresh, as when we first begun.
But yet, though Love likes well such Scenes as these,
There is an Act that will more fully please: 10
Kissing and glancing, soothing, all make way
But to the acting of this private Play:
Name it I would; but being blushing red,
The rest Ile speak, when we meet both in bed.

The Rock of Rubies: and
The quarrie of Pearls

S OME ask'd me where the *Rubies* grew?
And nothing I did say:
But with my finger pointed to
The lips of *Julia.*
Some ask'd how *Pearls* did grow, and where?
Then spoke I to my Girle,
To part her lips, and shew'd them there
The Quarelets of Pearl.

Conformitie

CONFORMITY was ever knowne
A foe to Dissolution:
Nor can we that a ruine call,
Whose crack gives crushing unto all.

T O   T H E   K I N G,

Upon his comming with his
Army into the West

WELCOME, most welcome to our Vowes and us,
Most great, and universall *Genius!*
The Drooping West, which hitherto has stood
As one, in long-lamented-widow-hood;
Looks like a Bride now, or a bed of flowers,
Newly refresh't, both by the Sun, and showers.
War, which before was horrid, now appears
Lovely in you, brave Prince of Cavaliers!
A deale of courage in each bosome springs
By your accesse; (*O you the best of Kings!*)   10
Ride on with all white *Omens*; so, that where
Your Standard's up, we fix a Conquest there.

Upon Roses

UNDER a Lawne, then skyes more cleare,
Some ruffled Roses nestling were:
And snugging there, they seem'd to lye
As in a flowrie Nunnery:
They blush'd, and look'd more fresh then flowers
Quickned of late by Pearly showers;
And all, because they were possest
But of the heat of *Julia's* breast:
Which as a warme, and moistned spring,
Gave them their ever flourishing.   10

To the King and Queene, upon
their unhappy distances

WOE, woe to them, who (by a ball of strife)
Doe, and have parted here a Man and Wife:
CHARLS the best Husband, while MARIA strives
To be, and is, the very best of Wives:
Like Streams, you are divorc'd; but 'twill come, when
These eyes of mine shall see you mix agen.
Thus speaks the *Oke*, here; *C.* and *M.* shall meet,
Treading on *Amber*, with their silver-feet:
Nor wil't be long, ere this accomplish'd be;
The words found true, *C. M.* remember me.   10

Dangers wait on Kings

AS oft as Night is banish'd by the Morne,
So oft, we'll think, we see a King new born.

The Cheat of Cupid: Or,
The ungentle guest

ONE silent night of late,
  When every creature rested,
Came one unto my gate,
  And knocking, me molested.

Who's that (said I) beats there,
  And troubles thus the Sleepie?
Cast off (said he) all feare,
  And let not Locks thus keep ye.

For I a Boy am, who
  By Moonlesse nights have swerved;   10
And all with showrs wet through,
  And e'en with cold half starved.

I pittifull arose,
  And soon a Taper lighted;
And did my selfe disclose
  Unto the lad benighted.

I saw he had a Bow,
    And Wings too, which did shiver;
And looking down below,
    I spy'd he had a Quiver.   20

I to my Chimney's shine
    Brought him, (as Love professes)
And chaf'd his hands with mine,
    And dry'd his dropping Tresses:

But when he felt him warm'd,
    Let's try this bow of ours,
And string if they be harm'd,
    Said he, with these late showrs.

Forthwith his bow he bent,
    And wedded string and arrow,   30
And struck me that it went
    Quite through my heart and marrow.

Then laughing loud, he flew
    Away, and thus said flying,
Adieu, mine Host, Adieu,
    Ile leave thy heart a dying.

To the reverend shade of his religious Father

THAT for seven *Lusters* I did never come
    To doe the *Rites* to thy Religious Tombe:
That neither haire was cut, or true teares shed
By me, o'r thee, (*as justments to the dead*)
Forgive, forgive me; since I did not know
Whether thy bones had here their Rest, or no.
But now 'tis known, Behold; behold, I bring
Unto thy Ghost, th'Effused Offering:
And look, what Smallage, Night-shade, Cypresse, Yew,
Unto the shades have been, or now are due,   10
Here I devote; And something more then so;
I come to pay a Debt of Birth I owe.
Thou gav'st me life, (but Mortall;) For that one
Favour, Ile make full satisfaction;
For my life mortall, Rise from out thy Herse,
And take a life immortall from my Verse.

27

Delight in Disorder

A SWEET disorder in the dresse
Kindles in cloathes a wantonnesse:
A Lawne about the shoulders thrown
Into a fine distraction:
An erring Lace, which here and there
Enthralls the Crimson Stomacher:
A Cuffe neglectfull, and thereby
Ribbands to flow confusedly:
A winning wave (deserving Note)
In the tempestuous petticote: 10
A carelesse shooe-string, in whose tye
I see a wilde civility:
Doe more bewitch me, then when Art
Is too precise in every part.

To his Muse

WERE I to give thee *Baptime*, I wo'd chuse
To *Christen* thee, the *Bride*, the *Bashfull Muse*,
Or *Muse* of *Roses:* since that name does fit
Best with those *Virgin-Verses* thou hast writ:
Which are so cleane, so chast, as none may feare
Cato the *Censor*, sho'd he scan each here.

Upon Love ✓

LOVE scorch'd my finger, but did spare
The burning of my heart:
To signifie, in Love my share
    Sho'd be a little part.

Little I love; but if that he
    Wo'd but that heat recall:
That joynt to ashes burnt sho'd be,
    Ere I wo'd love at all.

3.7 burnt sho'd be *Witt's Recreations 1663*: sho'd be burnt *48*

To Dean-bourn, *a rude River in* Devon, *by which sometimes he lived*

DEAN-BOURN, farewell; I never look to see
Deane, or thy warty incivility.
Thy rockie bottome, that doth teare thy streams,
And makes them frantick, ev'n to all extreames;
To my content, I never sho'd behold,
Were thy streames silver, or thy rocks all gold.
Rockie thou art; and rockie we discover
Thy men; and rockie are thy wayes all over.
O men, O manners; Now, and ever knowne
To be *A Rockie Generation!* 10
A people currish; churlish as the seas;
And rude (almost) as rudest Salvages.
With whom I did, and may re-sojourne when
Rockes turn to Rivers, Rivers turn to Men.

Kissing Usurie

BIANCHA, Let
Me pay the debt
I owe thee for a kisse
Thou lend'st to me;
And I to thee
Will render ten for this:

If thou wilt say,
Ten will not pay
For that so rich a one;
Ile cleare the summe, 10
If it will come
Unto a Million.

By this I guesse,
Of happinesse
Who has a little measure:
He must of right,
To th'utmost mite,
Make payment for his pleasure.

To Julia

How rich and pleasing thou my *Julia* art
In each thy dainty, and peculiar part!
First, for thy *Queen-ship* on thy head is set
Of flowers a sweet commingled Coronet:
About thy neck a Carkanet is bound,
Made of the *Rubie*, *Pearle* and *Diamond:*
A golden ring, that shines upon thy thumb:
About thy wrist, the rich * *Dardanium.*   *A Bracelet, from Darda- nus so call'd*
Between thy Breasts (then Doune of Swans
more white)
There playes the *Saphire* with the *Chrysolite.*   10
No part besides must of thy selfe be known,
But by the *Topaz*, *Opal*, *Calcedon.*

To Laurels

A FUNERALL stone,
Or Verse I covet none;
But onely crave
Of you, that I may have
A sacred Laurel springing from my grave:
Which being seen,
Blest with perpetuall greene,
May grow to be
Not so much call'd a tree,
As the eternall monument of me.   ·   10

His Cavalier

GIVE me that man, that dares bestride
The active Sea-horse, & with pride,
Through that huge field of waters ride:

Who, with his looks too, can appease
The ruffling winds and raging Seas,
In mid'st of all their outrages.
This, this a virtuous man can doe,
Saile against Rocks, and split them too;
I! and a world of Pikes passe through.

Zeal required in Love

I'LE doe my best to win, when'ere I wooe:
That man loves not, who is not zealous too.

The Bag of the Bee

ABOUT the sweet bag of a Bee,
    Two *Cupids* fell at odds;
And whose the pretty prize shu'd be,
    They vow'd to ask the Gods.

Which *Venus* hearing; thither came,
    And for their boldness stript them:
And taking thence from each his flame;
    With rods of *Mirtle* whipt them.

Which done, to still their wanton cries,
    When quiet grown sh'ad seen them,   10
She kist, and wip'd thir dove-like eyes;
    And gave the Bag between them.

Love kill'd by Lack

LET me be warme; let me be fully fed:
    Luxurious Love by Wealth is nourished.
Let me be leane, and cold, and once grown poore,
I shall dislike, what once I lov'd before.

To his Mistresse

CHOOSE me your Valentine;
    Next, let us marry:
Love to the death will pine,
    If we long tarry.

Promise, and keep your vowes,
    Or vow ye never:
Loves doctrine disallowes
    Troth-breakers ever.

You have broke promise twice
    (Deare) to undoe me;   10
If you prove faithlesse thrice,
    None then will wooe ye.

To the generous Reader

SEE, and not see; and if thou chance t'espie
  Some Aberrations in my Poetry;
Wink at small faults, the greater, ne'rthelesse
Hide, and with them, their Fathers nakedness.
Let's doe our best, our Watch and Ward to keep:
Homer himself, in a long work, may sleep.

To Criticks

ILE write, because Ile give
  You Criticks means to live:
For sho'd I not supply
The Cause, th'effect wo'd die.

Duty to Tyrants

GOOD Princes must be pray'd for: for the bad
  They must be borne with, and in rev'rence had.
Doe they first pill thee, next, pluck off thy skin?
Good children kisse the rods, that punish sin.
Touch not the Tyrant; Let the Gods alone
To strike him dead, that but usurps a Throne.

Being once blind, his request to Biancha

WHEN Age or Chance has made me blind,
  So that the path I cannot find:
And when my falls and stumblings are
More then the stones i'th'street by farre:

l. 12 ye *ed.*: you *48*

Goe thou afore; and I shall well
Follow thy Perfumes by the smell:
Or be my guide; and I shall be
Led by some light that flows from thee.
Thus held, or led by thee, I shall
In wayes confus'd, nor slip or fall.   **10**

Upon Blanch

BLANCH swears her Husband's lovely; when a scald
Has blear'd his eyes: Besides, his head is bald.
Next, his wilde eares, like Lethern wings full spread,
Flutter to flie, and beare away his head.

No want where there's little

To Bread and Water none is poore;
And having these, what need of more?
Though much from out the Cess be spent,
Nature with little is content.

Barly-Break: or, Last in Hell

WE two are last in Hell: what may we feare
To be tormented, or kept Pris'ners here?
Alas! If kissing be of plagues the worst,
We'll wish, in Hell we had been Last and First.

The Definition of Beauty

BEAUTY, no other thing is, then a Beame
Flasht out between the Middle and Extreame.

To Dianeme

DEARE, though to part it be a Hell,
Yet *Dianeme* now farewell:
Thy frown (last night) did bid me goe;
But whither, onely Grief do's know.
I doe beseech thee, ere we part,
(If mercifull, as faire thou art;

Or else desir'st that Maids sho'd tell
Thy pitty by Loves-Chronicle)
O *Dianeme*, rather kill
Me, then to make me languish stil!   10
'Tis cruelty in thee to'th'height,
Thus, thus to wound, not kill out-right:
Yet there's a way found (if thou please)
By sudden death to give me ease:
And thus devis'd, doe thou but this,
Bequeath to me one parting kisse:
So sup'rabundant joy shall be
The Executioner of me.

To Anthea *lying in bed*

So looks *Anthea*, when in bed she lyes,
Orecome, or halfe betray'd by Tiffanies:
Like to a Twi-light, or that simpring Dawn,
That Roses shew, when misted o're with Lawn.
Twilight is yet, till that her Lawnes give way;
Which done, that Dawne, turnes then to perfect day.

To Electra

More white then whitest Lillies far,
Or Snow, or whitest Swans you are:
More white then are the whitest Creames,
Or Moone-light tinselling the streames:
More white then *Pearls*, or *Juno's* thigh;
Or *Pelops* Arme of *Yvorie*.
True, I confesse; such Whites as these
May me delight, not fully please:
Till, like *Ixion's* Cloud you be
White, warme, and soft to lye with me.   10

A Country life: To his Brother,
M. Tho: Herrick

Thrice, and above, blest (my soules halfe) art thou,
In thy both Last, and Better Vow:

Could'st leave the City, for exchange, to see
    The Countries sweet simplicity:
And it to know, and practice; with intent
    To grow the sooner innocent:
By studying to know vertue; and to aime
    More at her nature, then her name:
The last is but the least; the first doth tell
    Wayes lesse to live, then to live well: 10
And both are knowne to thee, who now can'st live
    Led by thy conscience; to give
Justice to soone-pleas'd nature; and to show,
    Wisdome and she together goe,
And keep one Centre: This with that conspires,
    To teach Man to confine desires:
And know, that Riches have their proper stint,
    In the contented mind, not mint.
And can'st instruct, that those who have the itch
    Of craving more, are never rich.   20
These things thou know'st to'th'height, and dost prevent
    That plague; because thou art content
With that Heav'n gave thee with a warie hand,
    (More blessed in thy Brasse, then Land)
To keep cheap Nature even, and upright;
    To coole, not cocker Appetite.
Thus thou canst tearcely·live to satisfie
    The belly chiefly; not the eye:
Keeping the barking stomach wisely quiet,
    Lesse with a neat, then needfull diet.   30
But that which most makes sweet thy country life,
    Is, the fruition of a wife:
Whom (Stars consenting with thy Fate) thou hast
    Got, not so beautifull, as chast:
By whose warme side thou dost securely sleep
    (While Love the Centinell doth keep)
With those deeds done by day, which n'er affright
    Thy silken slumbers in the night.
Nor has the darknesse power to usher in
    Feare to those sheets, that know no sin.   40
But still thy wife, by chast intentions led,
    Gives thee each night a Maidenhead.
The Damaskt medowes, and the peebly streames
    Sweeten, and make soft your dreames:

35

The Purling springs, groves, birds, and well-weav'd Bowrs,
    With fields enameled with flowers,
Present their shapes; while fantasie discloses
    Millions of *Lillies* mixt with *Roses.*
Then dream, ye heare the Lamb by many a bleat
    Woo'd to come suck the milkie Teat: 50
While *Faunus* in the Vision comes to keep,
    From rav'ning wolves, the fleecie sheep.
With thousand such enchanting dreams, that meet
    To make sleep not so sound, as sweet:
Nor can these figures so thy rest endeare,
    As not to rise when *Chanticlere*
Warnes the last Watch; but with the Dawne dost rise
    To work, but first to sacrifice;
Making thy peace with heav'n, for some late fault,
    With Holy-meale, and spirting-salt.   60
Which done, thy painfull Thumb this sentence tells us,
    Jove for our labour all things sells us.
Nor are thy daily and devout affaires
    Attended with those desp'rate cares,
Th'industrious Merchant has; who for to find
    Gold, runneth to the Western Inde,
And back again, (tortur'd with fears) doth fly,
    Untaught, to suffer Poverty.
But thou at home, blest with securest ease,
    Sitt'st, and beleev'st that there be seas,   70
And watrie dangers; while thy whiter hap,
    But sees these things within thy Map.
And viewing them with a more safe survey,
    Mak'st easie Feare unto thee say,
A heart thrice wall'd with Oke, and Brasse, that man
    Had, first, durst plow the Ocean.
But thou at home without or tyde or gale,
    Canst in thy Map securely saile:
Seeing those painted Countries; and so guesse
    By those fine Shades, their Substances: 80
And from thy Compasse taking small advice,
    Buy'st Travell at the lowest price.
Nor are thine eares so deafe, but thou canst heare
    (Far more with wonder, then with feare)
Fame tell of States, of Countries, Courts, and Kings;
    And beleeve there be such things:

When of these truths, thy happyer knowledge lyes,
    More in thine eares, then in thine eyes.
And when thou hear'st by that too-true-Report,
    Vice rules the Most, or All at Court: 90
Thy pious wishes are, (though thou not there)
    Vertue had, and mov'd her Sphere.
But thou liv'st fearlesse; and thy face ne'r shewes
    Fortune when she comes, or goes.
But with thy equall thoughts, prepar'd dost stand,
    To take her by the either hand:
Nor car'st which comes the first, the foule or faire;
    A wise man ev'ry way lies square.
And like a surly *Oke* with storms perplext;
    Growes still the stronger, strongly vext.   100
Be so, bold spirit; Stand Center-like, unmov'd;
    And be not onely thought, but prov'd
To be what I report thee; and inure
    Thy selfe, if want comes to endure:
And so thou dost: for thy desires are
    Confin'd to live with private *Larr:*
Not curious whether Appetite be fed,
    Or with the first, or second bread.
Who keep'st no proud mouth for delicious cates:
    Hunger makes coorse meats, delicates.   110
Can'st, and unurg'd, forsake that Larded fare,
    Which Art, not Nature, makes so rare;
To taste boyl'd Nettles, Colworts, Beets, and eate
    These, and sowre herbs, as dainty meat?
While soft Opinion makes thy *Genius* say,
    Content makes all Ambrosia.
Nor is it, that thou keep'st this stricter size
    So much for want, as exercise:
To numb the sence of Dearth, which sho'd sinne haste it,
    Thou might'st but onely see't, not taste it.   120
Yet can thy humble roofe maintaine a Quire
    Of singing Crickits by thy fire:
And the brisk Mouse may feast her selfe with crums,
    Till that the green-ey'd Kitling comes.
Then to her Cabbin, blest she can escape
    The sudden danger of a Rape.
And thus thy little-well-kept-stock doth prove,
    Wealth cannot make a life, but Love.

Nor art thou so close-handed, but can'st spend
    (Counsell concurring with the end)   130
As well as spare: still conning o'r this Theame,
    To shun the first, and last extreame.
Ordaining that thy small stock find no breach,
    Or to exceed thy Tether's reach:
But to live round, and close, and wisely true
    To thine owne selfe; and knowne to few.
Thus let thy Rurall Sanctuary be
    Elizium to thy wife and thee;
There to disport your selves with golden measure:
    For seldome use commends the pleasure.   140
Live, and live blest; thrice happy Paire; Let Breath,
    But lost to one, be th'others death.
And as there is one Love, one Faith, one Troth,
    Be so one Death, one Grave to both.
Till when, in such assurancè live, ye may
    Nor feare, or wish your dying day.

Divination by a Daffadill

WHEN a Daffadill I see,
    Hanging down his head t'wards me;
Guesse I may, what I must be:
First, I shall decline my head;
Secondly, I shall be dead;
Lastly, safely buryed.

To the Painter, to draw him a Picture

COME, skilfull *Lupo*, now, and take
    Thy *Bice*, thy *Umber*, *Pink*, and *Lake*;
And let it be thy Pensils strife,
To paint a Bridgeman to the life:
Draw him as like too, as you can,
An old, poore, lying, flatt'ring man:
His cheeks be-pimpled, red and blue;
His nose and lips of mulbrie hiew.

Then for an easie fansie; place
A Burling iron for his face: 10
Next, make his cheeks with breath to swell,
And for to speak, if possible:
But do not so; for feare, lest he
Sho'd by his breathing, poyson thee.

Upon Cuffe. *Epig.*

CUFFE comes to Church much; but he keeps his bed
 Those Sundayes onely, when as Briefs are read.
This makes *Cuffe* dull; and troubles him the most,
Because he cannot sleep i'th'Church, free-cost.

Upon Fone *a School-master*. Epig.

FONE sayes, those mighty whiskers he do's weare,
 Are twigs of Birch, and willow, growing there:
If so, we'll think too, (when he do's condemne
Boyes to the lash) that he do's whip with them.

A Lyrick to Mirth

WHILE the milder Fates consent,
 Let's enjoy our merryment:
Drink, and dance, and pipe, and play;
Kisse our *Dollies* night and day:
Crown'd with clusters of the Vine;
Let us sit, and quaffe our wine.
Call on *Bacchus*; chaunt his praise;
Shake the *Thyrse*, and bite the *Bayes*:
Rouze *Anacreon* from the dead;
And return him drunk to bed: 10
Sing o're *Horace*; for ere long
Death will come and mar the song:
Then shall *Wilson* and *Gotiere*
Never sing, or play more here.

To the Earle of *Westmerland*

WHEN my date's done, and my gray age must die;
Nurse up, great Lord, this my posterity:
Weak though it be; long may it grow, and stand,
Shor'd up by you, (*Brave Earle of Westmerland.*)

Against Love ✓

WHEN ere my heart, Love's warmth, but entertaines,
O Frost! O Snow! O Haile forbid the Banes.
One drop now deads a spark; but if the same
Once gets a force, Floods cannot quench the flame.
Rather then love, let me be ever lost;
Or let me 'gender with eternall frost.

Upon Julia's *Riband*

AS shews the Aire, when with a Rain-bow grac'd;
So smiles that Riband 'bout my *Julia's* waste:
Or like——Nay 'tis that *Zonulet* of love,
Wherein all pleasures of the world are wove.

The frozen Zone: or, Julia *disdainfull*

WHITHER? Say, whither shall I fly,
To slack these flames wherein I frie?
To the Treasures, shall I goe,
Of the Raine, Frost, Haile, and Snow?
Shall I search the under-ground,
Where all Damps, and Mists are found?
Shall I seek (for speedy ease)
All the floods, and frozen seas?
Or descend into the deep,
Where eternall cold does keep?   10
These may coole; but there's a Zone
Colder yet then any one:
That's my *Julia's* breast; where dwels
Such destructive Ysicles;
As that the Congelation will
Me sooner starve, then those can kill.

An Epitaph upon a sober Matron

WITH blamelesse carriage, I liv'd here,
To'th' (almost) sev'n and fortieth yeare.
Stout sons I had, and those twice three;
One onely daughter lent to me:
The which was made a happy Bride,
But thrice three Moones before she dy'd.
My modest wedlock, that was known
Contented with the bed of one.

To the Patron of Poets,
M. End: Porter

LET there be Patrons; Patrons like to thee,
Brave *Porter!* Poets ne'r will wanting be:
Fabius, and *Cotta, Lentulus,* all live
In thee, thou Man of Men! who here do'st give
Not onely subject-matter for our wit,
But likewise Oyle of Maintenance to it:
For which, before thy Threshold, we'll lay downe
Our Thyrse, for Scepter; and our Baies for Crown.
For to say truth, all Garlands are thy due;
The *Laurell, Mirtle, Oke,* and *Ivie* too.   10

The sadnesse of things for Sapho's *sicknesse*

LILLIES will languish; Violets look ill;
Sickly the Prim-rose: Pale the Daffadill:
That gallant Tulip will hang down his head,
Like to a Virgin newly ravished.
Pansies will weep; and Marygolds will wither;
And keep a Fast, and Funerall together,
If *Sapho* droop; Daisies will open never,
But bid Good-night, and close their lids for ever.

Leanders *Obsequies*

WHEN as *Leander* young was drown'd,
No heart by love receiv'd a wound;
But on a Rock himselfe sate by,
There weeping sup'rabundantly.
Sighs numberlesse he cast about,
And all his Tapers thus put out:
His head upon his hand he laid;
And sobbing deeply, thus he said,
Ah cruell Sea! and looking on't,
Wept as he'd drowne the Hellespont.   10
And sure his tongue had more exprest,
But that his teares forbad the rest.

Hope heartens

NONE goes to warfare, but with this intent;
The gaines must dead the feare of detriment.

Foure things make us happy here

HEALTH is the first good lent to men;
A gentle disposition then:
Next, to be rich by no by-wayes;
Lastly, with friends t'enjoy our dayes.

His parting from Mrs Dorothy Keneday

WHEN I did goe from thee, I felt that smart,
Which Bodies do, when Souls from them depart.
Thou did'st not mind it; though thou then might'st see
Me turn'd to tears; yet did'st not weep for me.
'Tis true, I kist thee; but I co'd not heare
Thee spend a sigh, t'accompany my teare.
Me thought 'twas strange, that thou so hard sho'dst prove,
Whose heart, whose hand, whose ev'ry part spake love.
Prethee (lest Maids sho'd censure thee) but say
Thou shed'st one teare, when as I went away;   10
And that will please me somewhat: though I know,
And Love will swear't, my Dearest did not so.

The Teare sent to her from Stanes

1. GLIDE gentle streams, and beare
   Along with you my teare
      To that coy Girle;
      Who smiles, yet slayes
      Me with delayes;
   And strings my tears as Pearle.

2. See! see she's yonder set,
   Making a Carkanet
      Of Maiden-flowers!
      There, there present   10
      This Orient,
   And Pendant Pearle of ours.

3. Then say, I've sent one more
   Jem to enrich her store;
      And that is all
      Which I can send,
      Or vainly spend,
   For tears no more will fall.

4. Nor will I seek supply
   Of them, the spring's once drie;   20
      But Ile devise,
      (Among the rest)
      A way that's best
   How I may save mine eyes.

5. Yet say; sho'd she condemne
   Me to surrender them;
      Then say; my part
      Must be to weep
      Out them, to keep
   A poore, yet loving heart.   30

6. Say too, She wo'd have this;
   She shall: Then my hope is,
      That when I'm poore,
      And nothing have
      To send, or save;
   I'm sure she'll ask no more.

Upon one Lillie, *who marryed with a maid call'd* Rose

WHAT times of sweetnesse this faire day fore-shows,
  When as the Lilly marries with the Rose!
What next is lookt for? but we all sho'd see
To spring from these a sweet Posterity.

An Epitaph upon a child

VIRGINS promis'd when I dy'd,
  That they wo'd each Primrose-tide,
Duely, Morne and Ev'ning, come,
And with flowers dresse my Tomb.
Having promis'd, pay your debts,
Maids, and here strew Violets.

Upon Scobble. *Epig.*

SCOBBLE for Whoredome whips his wife; and cryes,
  He'll slit her nose; But blubb'ring, she replyes,
Good Sir, make no more cuts i'th'outward skin,
One slit's enough to let Adultry in.

The Houre-glasse

THAT Houre-glasse, which there ye see
  With Water fill'd, (Sirs, credit me)
The humour was, (as I have read)
But Lovers tears inchristalled.
Which, as they drop by drop doe passe
From th'upper to the under-glasse,
Do in a trickling manner tell,
(By many a watrie syllable)
That Lovers tears in life-time shed,
Do restless run when they are dead.   10

His fare-well to Sack

FAREWELL thou Thing, time-past so knowne, so deare
To me, as blood to life and spirit: Neare,
Nay, thou more neare then kindred, friend, man, wife,
Male to the female, soule to body: Life
To quick action, or the warme soft side
Of the resigning, yet resisting Bride.
The kisse of Virgins; First-fruits of the bed;
Soft speech, smooth touch, the lips, the Maiden-head:
These, and a thousand sweets, co'd never be
So neare, or deare, as thou wast once to me.   10
O thou the drink of Gods, and Angels! Wine
That scatter'st Spirit and Lust; whose purest shine,
More radiant then the Summers Sun-beams shows;
Each way illustrious, brave; and like to those
Comets we see by night; whose shagg'd portents
Fore-tell the comming of some dire events:
Or some full flame, which with a pride aspires,
Throwing about his wild, and active fires.
'Tis thou, above Nectar, O Divinest soule!
(Eternall in thy self) that canst controule   20
That, which subverts whole nature, grief and care;
Vexation of the mind, and damn'd Despaire.
'Tis thou, alone, who with thy Mistick Fan,
Work'st more then Wisdome, Art, or Nature can,
To rouze the sacred madnesse; and awake
The frost-bound-blood, and spirits; and to make
Them frantick with thy raptures, flashing through
The soule, like lightning, and as active too.
'Tis not *Apollo* can, or those thrice three
Castalian Sisters, sing, if wanting thee.   30
Horace, *Anacreon* both had lost their fame,
Had'st thou not fill'd them with thy fire and flame.
Phœbean splendour! and thou *Thespian* spring!
Of which, sweet Swans must drink, before they sing
Their true-pac'd-Numbers, and their Holy-Layes,
Which makes them worthy *Cedar*, and the *Bayes*.
But why? why longer doe I gaze upon
Thee with the eye of admiration?

Since I must leave thee; and enforc'd, must say
To all thy witching beauties, Goe, Away.   40
But if thy whimpring looks doe ask me why?
Then know, that Nature bids thee goe, not I.
'Tis her erroneous self has made a braine
Uncapable of such a Soveraigne,
As is thy powerfull selfe. Prethee not smile;
Or smile more inly; lest thy looks beguile
My vowes denounc'd in zeale, which thus much show thee,
That I have sworn, but by thy looks to know thee.
Let others drink thee freely; and desire
Thee and their lips espous'd; while I admire,   50
And love thee; but not taste thee. Let my Muse
Faile of thy former helps; and onely use
Her inadult'rate strength: what's done by me
Hereafter, shall smell of the Lamp, not thee.

Upon Glasco. *Epig.*

G*LASCO* had none, but now some teeth has got;
Which though they furre, will neither ake, or rot.
Six teeth he has, whereof twice two are known
Made of a Haft, that was a Mutton-bone.
Which not for use, but meerly for the sight,
He weares all day, and drawes those teeth at night.

Upon Mrs. Eliz: Wheeler, *under the name of Amarillis*

S WEET *Amarillis*, by a Spring's
Soft and soule-melting murmurings,
Slept; and thus sleeping, thither flew
A *Robin-Red-brest*; who at view,
Not seeing her at all to stir,
Brought leaves and mosse to cover her:
But while he, perking, there did prie
About the Arch of either eye;
The lid began to let out day;
At which poore *Robin* flew away: 10
And seeing her not dead, but all disleav'd;
He chirpt for joy, to see himself disceav'd.

The Custard

FOR second course, last night, a Custard came
  To th'board, so hot, as none co'd touch the same:
Furze, three or foure times with his cheeks did blow
Upon the Custard, and thus cooled so:
It seem'd by this time to admit the touch;
But none co'd eate it, 'cause it stunk so much.

To Myrrha *hard-hearted*

FOLD now thine armes; and hang the head,
  Like to a Lillie withered:
Next, look thou like a sickly Moone;
Or like *Jocasta* in a swoone.
Then weep, and sigh, and softly goe,
Like to a widdow drown'd in woe:
Or like a Virgin full of ruth,
For the lost sweet-heart of her youth:
And all because, Faire Maid, thou art
Insensible of all my smart;   10
And of those evill dayes that be
Now posting on to punish thee.
The Gods are easie, and condemne
All such as are not soft like them.

The Eye

MAKE me a heaven; and make me there
  Many a lesse and greater spheare.
Make me the straight, and oblique lines;
The Motions, Lations, and the Signes.
Make me a Chariot, and a Sun;
And let them through a Zodiac run:
Next, place me Zones, and Tropicks there;
With all the Seasons of the Yeare.
Make me a Sun-set; and a Night:
And then present the Mornings-light   10
Cloath'd in her Chamlets of Delight.
To these, make Clouds to poure downe raine;
With weather foule, then faire againe.

And when, wise Artist, that thou hast,
With all that can be, this heaven grac't;
Ah! what is then this curious skie,
But onely my *Corinna's* eye?

Upon the much lamented, *Mr.* J. Warr

WHAT Wisdome, Learning, Wit, or Worth,
Youth, or sweet Nature, co'd bring forth,
Rests here with him; who was the Fame,
The Volumne of himselfe, and Name.
If, Reader, then thou wilt draw neere,
And doe an honour to thy teare;
Weep then for him, for whom laments
Not one, but many Monuments.

Upon Gryll

GRYLL eates, but ne're sayes Grace; To speak the troth,
Gryll either keeps his breath to coole his broth;
Or else because *Grill's* roste do's burn his Spit,
Gryll will not therefore say a Grace for it.

The suspition upon his over-much familiarity with a Gentlewoman

AND must we part, because some say,
Loud is our love, and loose our play,
And more then well becomes the day?
Alas for pitty! and for us
Most innocent, and injur'd thus.
Had we kept close, or play'd within,
Suspition now had been the sinne,
And shame had follow'd long ere this,
T'ave plagu'd, what now unpunisht is.
But we as fearlesse of the Sunne,   10
As faultlesse; will not wish undone,
What now is done: since *where no sin*
Unbolts the doore, no shame comes in.

Then comely and most fragrant Maid,
Be you more warie, then afraid
Of these Reports; because you see
The fairest most suspected be.
The common formes have no one eye,
Or eare of burning jealousie
To follow them: but chiefly, where   20
Love makes the cheek, and chin a sphere
To dance and play in: (Trust me) there
Suspicion questions every haire. `
Come, you are faire; and sho'd be seen
While you are in your sprightfull green:
And what though you had been embrac't
By me, were you for that unchast?
No, no, no more then is yond' Moone,
Which shining in her perfect Noone;
In all that great and glorious light,   30
Continues cold, as is the night.
Then, beauteous Maid, you may retire;
And as for me, my chast desire
Shall move t'wards you; although I see
Your face no more: So live you free
From Fames black lips, as you from me.

Single life most secure

SUSPICION, Discontent, and Strife,
Come in for Dowrie with a Wife.

The Curse. A Song

GOE perjur'd man; and if thou ere return
To see the small remainders in mine Urne:
When thou shalt laugh at my Religious dust;
And ask, Where's now the colour, forme and trust
Of Womans beauty? and with hand more rude
Rifle the Flowers which the Virgins strew'd:
Know, I have pray'd to Furie, that some wind
May blow my ashes up, and strike thee blind.

49

The wounded Cupid. *Song*

CUPID as he lay among
   Roses, by a Bee was stung.
Whereupon in anger flying
To his Mother, said thus crying;
Help! O help! your Boy's a dying.
And why, my pretty Lad, said she?
Then blubbering, replyed he,
A winged Snake has bitten me,
Which Country people call a Bee.
At which she smil'd; then with her hairs   10
And kisses drying up his tears:
Alas! said she, my Wag! if this
Such a pernicious torment is:
Come, tel me then, how great's the smart
Of those, thou woundest with thy Dart!

To Dewes. A Song

I BURN, I burn; and beg of you
   To quench, or coole me with your Dew.
I frie in fire, and so consume,
Although the Pile be all perfume.
Alas! the heat and death's the same;
Whether by choice, or common flame:
To be in Oyle of *Roses* drown'd,
Or water; where's the comfort found?
Both bring one death; and I die here,
Unlesse you coole me with a Teare: 10
Alas! I call; but ah! I see
Ye coole, and comfort all, but me.

Some comfort in calamity

To conquer'd men, some comfort 'tis to fall
   By th'hand of him who is the Generall.

The Vision

SITTING alone (as one forsook)
  Close by a Silver-shedding Brook;
With hands held up to Love, I wept;
And after sorrowes spent, I slept:
Then in a Vision I did see
A glorious forme appeare to me:
A Virgins face she had; her dresse
Was like a sprightly *Spartanesse*.
A silver bow with green silk strung,
Down from her comely shoulders hung: 10
And as she stood, the wanton Aire
Dandled the ringlets of her haire.
Her legs were such *Diana* shows,
When tuckt up she a hunting goes;
With Buskins shortned to descrie
The happy dawning of her thigh:
Which when I saw, I made accesse
To kisse that tempting nakednesse:
But she forbad me, with a wand
Of Mirtle she had in her hand: 20
And chiding me, said, Hence, Remove,
Herrick, thou art too coorse to love.

Love me little, love me long

YOU say, to me-wards your affection's strong;
  Pray love me little, so you love me long.
Slowly goes farre: The meane is best: Desire
Grown violent, do's either die, or tire.

Upon a Virgin kissing a Rose

'TWAS but a single *Rose*,
  Till you on it did breathe;
But since (me thinks) it shows
  Not so much *Rose*, as Wreathe.

Upon a Wife that dyed mad with Jealousie

IN this little Vault she lyes,
Here, with all her jealousies:
Quiet yet; but if ye make
Any noise, they both will wake,
And such spirits raise, 'twill then
Trouble Death to lay agen.

Upon the Bishop of Lincolne's Imprisonment

NEVER was Day so over-sick with showres,
But that it had some intermitting houres.
Never was Night so tedious, but it knew
The Last Watch out, and saw the Dawning too.
Never was Dungeon so obscurely deep,
Wherein or Light, or Day, did never peep.
Never did Moone so ebbe, or seas so wane,
But they left Hope-seed to fill up againe.
So you, my Lord, though you have now your stay,.
Your Night, your Prison, and your Ebbe; you may   10
Spring up afresh; when all these mists are spent,
And Star-like, once more, guild our Firmament.
Let but That Mighty *Cesar* speak, and then,
All bolts, all barres, all gates shall cleave; as when
That Earth-quake shook the house, and gave the stout
Apostles, way (unshackled) to goe out.
This, as I wish for, so I hope to see;
Though you (my Lord) have been unkind to me:
To wound my heart, and never to apply
(When you had power) the meanest remedy: 20
Well; though my griefe by you was gall'd, the more;
Yet I bring Balme and Oile to heal your sore.

Disswasions from Idlenesse

CYNTHIUS pluck ye by the eare,
That ye may good doctrine heare.
Play not with the maiden-haire;
For each Ringlet there's a snare.
Cheek, and eye, and lip, and chin;
These are traps to take fooles in.

Armes, and hands, and all parts else,
Are but Toiles, or Manicles
Set on purpose to enthrall
Men, but Slothfulls most of all.   10
Live employ'd, and so live free
From these fetters; like to me
Who have found, and still can prove,
The lazie man the most doth love.

Upon Strut

S *TRUT*, once a Fore-man of a Shop we knew;
But turn'd a Ladies Usher now, ('tis true:)
Tell me, has *Strut* got ere a title more?
No; he's but Fore-man, as he was before.

An Epithalamie to Sir Thomas Southwell *and his Ladie*

I

N OW, now's the time; so oft by truth
Promis'd sho'd come to crown your youth.
   Then Faire ones, doe not wrong
   Your joyes, by staying long:
   Or let Love's fire goe out,
   By lingring thus in doubt:
   But learn, that Time once lost,
   Is ne'r redeem'd by cost.
Then away; come, *Hymen* guide
To the bed, the bashfull Bride.   10

II

Is it (sweet maid) your fault these holy
Bridall-Rites goe on so slowly?
   Deare, is it this you dread,
   The losse of Maiden-head?
   Beleeve me; you will most
   Esteeme it when 'tis lost:
   Then it no longer keep,
   Lest Issue lye asleep.
Then away; come, *Hymen* guide
To the bed, the bashfull Bride.   20

III

These Precious-Pearly-Purling teares,
But spring from ceremonious feares.
    And 'tis but Native shame,
    That hides the loving flame:
    And may a while controule
    The soft and am'rous soule;
    But yet, Loves fire will wast
    Such bashfulnesse at last.
Then away; come, *Hymen* guide
To the bed, the bashfull Bride.   30

IV

Night now hath watch'd her self half blind;
Yet not a Maiden-head resign'd!
    'Tis strange, ye will not flie
    To Love's sweet mysterie.
    Might yon Full-Moon the sweets
    Have, promis'd to your sheets;
    She soon wo'd leave her spheare,
    To be admitted there.
Then away; come, *Hymen* guide
To the bed, the bashfull Bride.   40

V

On, on devoutly, make no stay;
While *Domiduca* leads the way:
    And *Genius* who attends
    The bed for luckie ends:
    With *Juno* goes the houres,
    And Graces strewing flowers.
    And the boyes with sweet tunes sing,
    Hymen, O *Hymen* bring
Home the Turtles; *Hymen* guide
To the bed, the bashfull Bride.   50

VI

Behold! how *Hymens* Taper-light
Shews you how much is spent of night.
    See, see the Bride-grooms Torch
    Halfe wasted in the porch.

And now those Tapers five,
That shew the womb shall thrive:
    Their silv'rie flames advance,
    To tell all prosp'rous chance
Still shall crown the happy life
Of the good man and the wife.   60

VII

Move forward then your Rosie feet,
And make, what ere they touch, turn sweet.
    May all, like flowrie Meads
    Smell, where your soft foot treads;
    And every thing assume
    To it, the like perfume:
    As *Zephirus* when he 'spires
    Through *Woodbine*, and *Sweet-bryers*.
Then away; come *Hymen*, guide
To the bed the bashfull Bride.   70

VIII

And now the yellow Vaile, at last,
Over her fragrant cheek is cast.
    Now seems she to expresse
    A bashfull willingnesse:
    Shewing a heart consenting;
    As with a will repenting.
    Then gently lead her on
    With wise suspicion:
For that, Matrons say, a measure
Of that Passion sweetens Pleasure.   80

IX

You, you that be of her neerest kin,
Now o're the threshold force her in.
    But to avert the worst;
    Let her, her fillets first
    Knit to the posts: this point
    Remembring, to anoint
    The sides: for 'tis a charme
    Strong against future harme:
And the evil deads, the which
There was hidden by the Witch.   90

X

O *Venus!* thou, to whom is known
The best way how to loose the Zone
 Of Virgins! Tell the Maid,
 She need not be afraid:
 And bid the Youth apply
 Close kisses, if she cry:
 And charge, he not forbears
 Her, though she wooe with teares.
Tel them, now they must adventer,
Since that Love and Night bid enter.   100

XI

No Fatal Owle the Bedsted keeps,
With direful notes to fright your sleeps:
 No Furies, here about,
 To put the Tapers out,
 Watch, or did make the bed:
 'Tis *Omen* full of dread:
 But all faire signs appeare
 Within the Chamber here.
Juno here, far off, doth stand
Cooling sleep with charming wand.   110

XII

Virgins, weep not; 'twill come, when,
As she, so you'l be ripe for men.
 Then grieve her not, with saying
 She must no more a Maying:
 Or by Rose-buds devine,
 Who'l be her Valentine.
 Nor name those wanton reaks
 Y'ave had at Barly-breaks.
But now kisse her, and thus say,
Take time Lady while ye may.   120

XIII

Now barre the doors, the Bride-groom puts
The eager Boyes to gather Nuts.
 And now, both Love and Time
 To their full height doe clime:

O! give them active heat
And moisture, both compleat:
    Fit Organs for encrease,
    To keep, and to release
That, which may the honour'd Stem
Circle with a Diadem.   130

XIV

And now, Behold! the Bed or Couch
That ne'r knew Brides, or Bride-grooms touch,
    Feels in it selfe a fire;
    And tickled with Desire,
    Pants with a Downie brest,
    As with a heart possest:
    Shrugging as it did move,
    Ev'n with the soule of love.
And (oh!) had it but a tongue,
Doves, 'two'd say, yee bill too long.   140

XV

O enter then! but see ye shun
A sleep, untill the act be done.
    Let kisses, in their close,
    Breathe as the Damask Rose:
    Or sweet, as is that gumme
    Doth from *Panchaia* come.
    Teach Nature now to know,
    Lips can make Cherries grow
Sooner, then she, ever yet,
In her wisdome co'd beget.   150

XVI

On your minutes, hours, dayes, months, years,
Drop the fat blessing of the sphears.
    That good, which Heav'n can give
    To make you bravely live;
    Fall, like a spangling dew,
    By day, and night on you.
    May Fortunes Lilly-hand
    Open at your command;
With all luckie Birds to side
With the Bride-groom, and the Bride.   160

XVII

Let bounteous Fate your spindles full
Fill, and winde up with whitest wooll.
 Let them not cut the thred
 Of life, untill ye bid.
 May Death yet come at last;
 And not with desp'rate hast:
 But when ye both can say,
 Come, Let us now away.
Be ye to the Barn then born,
Two, like two ripe shocks of corn.   170

Teares are Tongues

WHEN *Julia* chid, I stood as mute the while,
 As is the fish, or tonguelesse Crocadile.
Aire coyn'd to words, my *Julia* co'd not heare;
But she co'd see each eye to stamp a teare:
By which, mine angry Mistresse might descry,
Teares are the noble language of the eye.
And when true love of words is destitute,
The Eyes by tears speak, while the Tongue is mute.

Upon a young mother of many children

LET all chaste Matrons, when they chance to see
 My num'rous issue: Praise, and pitty me.
Praise me, for having such a fruitfull wombe;
Pity me too, who found so soone a Tomb.

To Electra

ILE come to thee in all those shapes
 As *Jove* did, when he made his rapes:
 Onely, Ile not appeare to thee,
 As he did once to *Semele*.
 Thunder and Lightning Ile lay by,
 To talk with thee familiarly.
 Which done, then quickly we'll undresse
 To one and th'others nakednesse.

And ravisht, plunge into the bed,
(Bodies and souls commingled)   10
And kissing, so as none may heare,
We'll weary all the Fables there.

His wish

IT is sufficient if we pray
To *Jove*, who gives, and takes away:
Let him the Land and Living finde;
Let me alone to fit the mind.

His Protestation *to* Perilla.

NOONE-day and Midnight shall at once be seene:
Trees, at one time, shall be both sere and greene:
Fire and water shall together lye
In one-self-sweet-conspiring sympathie:
Summer and Winter shall at one time show
Ripe eares of corne, and up to th'eares in snow:
Seas shall be sandlesse; Fields devoid of grasse;
Shapelesse the world, (as when all *Chaos* was)
Before, my deare *Perilla*, I will be
False to my vow, or fall away from thee.   10

Love perfumes all parts

IF I kisse *Anthea's* brest,
There I smell the Phenix nest:
If her lip, the most sincere
Altar of Incense, I smell there.
Hands, and thighs, and legs, are all
Richly Aromaticall.
Goddesse *Isis* cann't transfer
Musks and Ambers more from her:
Nor can *Juno* sweeter be,
When she lyes with *Jove*, then she.   10

To Julia

Permit me, *Julia*, now to goe away;
 Or by thy love, decree me here to stay.
If thou wilt say, that I shall live with thee;
Here shall my endless Tabernacle be:
If not, (as banisht) I will live alone
There, where no language ever yet was known.

On himselfe

Love-sick I am, and must endure
 A desp'rate grief, that finds no cure.
Ah me! I try; and trying, prove,
No Herbs have power to cure Love.
Only one Soveraign salve, I know,
And that is Death, the end of Woe.

Vertue is sensible of suffering

Though a wise man all pressures can sustaine;
 His vertue still is sensible of paine:
Large shoulders though he has, and well can beare,
He feeles when Packs do pinch him; and the where.

The cruell Maid

And Cruell Maid, because I see
 You scornfull of my love, and me:
Ile trouble you no more; but goe
My way, where you shall never know
What is become of me: there I
Will find me out a path to die;
Or learne some way how to forget
You, and your name, for ever: yet
Ere I go hence; know this from me,
What will, in time, your Fortune be: 10
This to your coynesse I will tell;
And having spoke it once, Farewell.
The Lillie will not long endure;
Nor the Snow continue pure:

The Rose, the Violet, one day
See, both these Lady-flowers decay:
And you must fade, as well as they.
And it may chance that Love may turn,
And (like to mine) make your heart burn
And weep to see't; yet this thing doe,   20
That my last Vow commends to you:
When you shall see that I am dead,
For pitty let a teare be shed;
And (with your Mantle o're me cast)
Give my cold lips a kisse at last:
If twice you kisse, you need not feare,
That I shall stir, or live more here.
Next, hollow out a Tombe to cover
Me; me, the most despised Lover:
And write thereon, *This, Reader, know,*   30
Love kill'd this man. No more but so.

To Dianeme

SWEET, be not proud of those two eyes,
Which Star-like sparkle in their skies:
Nor be you proud, that you can see
All hearts your captives; yours, yet free:
Be you not proud of that rich haire,
Which wantons with the Love-sick aire:
When as that *Rubie*, which you weare,
Sunk from the tip of your soft eare,
Will last to be a precious Stone,
When all your world of Beautie's gone.   10

TO THE KING,

To cure the Evill

To find that Tree of Life, whose Fruits did feed,
And Leaves did heale, all sick of humane seed:
To finde *Bethesda*, and an Angel there,
Stirring the waters, I am come; and here,
At last, I find, (after my much to doe)
The Tree, Bethesda, and the Angel too:

And all in Your Blest Hand, which has the powers
Of all those suppling-healing herbs and flowers.
To that soft *Charm*, that *Spell*, that *Magick Bough*,
That high Enchantment I betake me now: 10
And to that Hand, (the Branch of Heavens faire Tree)
I kneele for help; O! lay that hand on me,
Adored *Cesar*! and my Faith is such,
I shall be heal'd, if that my *KING* but touch.
The Evill is not Yours: my sorrow sings,
Mine is the Evill, but the Cure, the KINGS.

His misery in a Mistresse

WATER, Water I espie:
  Come, and coole ye; all who frie
In your loves; but none as I.

Though a thousand showres be
Still a falling, yet I see
Not one drop to light on me.

Happy you, who can have seas
For to quench ye, or some ease
From your kinder Mistresses.

I have one, and she alone,   10
Of a thousand thousand known,
Dead to all compassion.

Such an one, as will repeat
Both the cause, and make the heat
More by Provocation great.

Gentle friends, though I despaire
Of my cure, doe you beware
Of those Girles, which cruell are.

Upon Jollies *wife*

FIRST, *Jollies* wife is lame; then next, loose-hipt:
  Squint-ey'd, hook-nos'd; and lastly, Kidney-lipt.

To a Gentlewoman, objecting to him his gray haires

Aᴍ I despis'd, because you say,
  And I dare sweare, that I am gray?
Know, Lady, you have but your day:
And time will come when you shall weare
Such frost and snow upon your haire:
And when (though long it comes to passe)
You question with your Looking-glasse;
And in that sincere *Christall* seek,
But find no Rose-bud in your cheek:
Nor any bed to give the shew   10
Where such a rare Carnation grew.
Ah! then too late, close in your chamber keeping,
          It will be told
          That you are old;
By those true teares y'are weeping.

To Cedars

Iꜰ 'mongst my many Poems, I can see
  One, onely, worthy to be washt by thee:
I live for ever; let the rest all lye
In dennes of Darkness, or condemn'd to die.

Upon Cupid

Lᴏᴠᴇ, like a Gypsie, lately came;
  And did me much importune
To see my hand; that by the same
  He might fore-tell my Fortune.

He saw my Palme; and then, said he,
  I tell thee, by this score here;
That thou, within few months, shalt be
  The youthfull Prince *D'Amour* here.

I smil'd; and bade him once more prove,
    And by some crosse-line show it;   10
That I co'd ne'r be Prince of Love,
    Though here the Princely Poet.

How Primroses came green.

VIRGINS, time-past, known were these,
    Troubled with Green-sicknesses,
Turn'd to flowers: Stil the hieu,
Sickly Girles, they beare of you.

To Jos: *Lo: Bishop of* Exeter

WHOM sho'd I feare to write to, if I can
    Stand before you, my learn'd *Diocesan?*
And never shew blood-guiltinesse, or feare
To see my Lines *Excathedrated* here.
Since none so good are, but you may condemne;
Or here so bad, but you may pardon them.
If then, (my Lord) to sanctifie my Muse
One onely Poem out of all you'l chuse;
And mark it for a Rapture nobly writ,
'Tis Good Confirm'd; for you have Bishop't it.   10

Upon a black Twist, rounding the Arme of the Countesse of Carlile

I SAW about her spotlesse wrist,
    Of blackest silk, a curious twist;
Which, circumvolving gently, there
Enthrall'd her Arme, as Prisoner.
Dark was the Jayle; but as if light
Had met t'engender with the night;
Or so, as Darknesse made a stay
To shew at once, both night and day.
I fancie none! but if there be
Such Freedome in Captivity;   10
I beg of Love, that ever I
May in like Chains of Darknesse lie.

3.9 none *ed.*: more *48.* 'I fancie more' is almost certainly erroneous. The
emendation 'One fancie more' is hardly an improvement. 'I fancie none'
suits the context and agrees with Herrick's occasional claims to wholeness of
heart (e.g. in 12.4 and 17.1). Contemporary printers often confused 'n'
with 'm' and 'r'.

On himselfe

I FEARE no Earthly Powers;
But care for crowns of flowers:
And love to have my Beard
With Wine and Oile besmear'd.
This day Ile drowne all sorrow;
Who knowes to live to morrow?

Upon Pagget

PAGGET, a School-boy, got a Sword, and then
He vow'd Destruction both to Birch, and Men:
Who wo'd not think this Yonker fierce to fight?
Yet comming home, but somewhat late, (last night)
Untrusse, his Master bade him; and that word
Made him take up his shirt, lay down his sword.

A Ring presented to Julia

JULIA, I bring
To thee this Ring,
Made for thy finger fit;
To shew by this,
That our love is
(Or sho'd be) like to it.

Close though it be,
The joynt is free:
So when Love's yoke is on,
It must not gall,
Or fret at all
With hard oppression.

But it must play
Still either way;
And be, too, such a yoke,
As not too wide,
To over-slide;
Or be so strait to choak.

10

So we, who beare,
This beame, must reare   20
Our selves to such a height:
As that the stay
Of either may
Create the burden light.

And as this round
Is no where found
To flaw, or else to sever:
So let our love
As endless prove;
And pure as Gold for ever.   30

To the Detracter

WHERE others love, and praise my Verses; still
   Thy long-black-Thumb-nail marks 'em out for ill:
A fellon take it, or some Whit-flaw come
For to unslate, or to untile that thumb!
But cry thee Mercy: Exercise thy nailes
To scratch or claw, so that thy tongue not railes:
Some numbers prurient are, and some of these
Are wanton with their itch; scratch, and 'twill please.

Upon the same

I ASK'T thee oft, what Poets thou hast read,
   And lik'st the best? Still thou reply'st, The dead.
I shall, ere long, with green turfs cover'd be;
Then sure thou't like, or thou wilt envie me.

Julia's *Petticoat*

THY Azure Robe, I did behold,
   As ayrie as the leaves of gold;
Which erring here, and wandring there,
Pleas'd with transgression ev'ry where:
Sometimes 'two'd pant, and sigh, and heave,
As if to stir it scarce had leave:

But having got it; thereupon,
'Two'd make a brave expansion.
And pounc't with Stars, it shew'd to me
Like a *Celestiall Canopie.*   10
Sometimes 'two'd blaze, and then abate,
Like to a flame growne moderate:
Sometimes away 'two'd wildly fling;
Then to thy thighs so closely cling,
That some conceit did melt me downe,
As Lovers fall into a swoone:
And all confus'd, I there did lie
Drown'd in Delights; but co'd not die.
That Leading Cloud, I follow'd still,
Hoping t'ave seene of it my fill;   20
But ah! I co'd not: sho'd it move
To Life Eternal, I co'd love.

To Musick

BEGIN to charme, and as thou stroak'st mine eares
With thy enchantment, melt me into tears.
Then let thy active hand scu'd o're thy Lyre:
And make my spirits frantick with the fire.
That done, sink down into a silv'rie straine;
And make me smooth as Balme, and Oile againe.

Distrust

TO safe-guard Man from wrongs, there nothing must
Be truer to him, then a wise Distrust.
And to thy selfe be best this sentence knowne,
Heare all men speak; but credit few or none.

Corinna's *going a Maying*

GET up, get up for shame, the Blooming Morne
Upon her wings presents the god unshorne.
See how *Aurora* throwes her faire
Fresh-quilted colours through the aire:
Get up, sweet-Slug-a-bed, and see
The Dew-bespangling Herbe and Tree.

Each Flower has wept, and bow'd toward the East,
Above an houre since; yet you not drest,
  Nay! not so much as out of bed?
  When all the Birds have Mattens seyd,   10
  And sung their thankfull Hymnes: 'tis sin,
  Nay, profanation to keep in,
When as a thousand Virgins on this day,
Spring, sooner then the Lark, to fetch in May.

Rise; and put on your Foliage, and be seene
To come forth, like the Spring-time, fresh and greene;
  And sweet as *Flora*. Take no care
  For Jewels for your Gowne, or Haire:
  Feare not; the leaves will strew
  Gemms in abundance upon you: 20
Besides, the childhood of the Day has kept,
Against you come, some *Orient Pearls* unwept:
  Come, and receive them while the light
  Hangs on the Dew-locks of the night:
  And *Titan* on the Eastern hill
  Retires himselfe, or else stands still
Till you come forth. Wash, dresse, be briefe in praying:
Few Beads are best, when once we goe a Maying.

Come, my *Corinna*, come; and comming, marke
How each field turns a street; each street a Parke   30
  Made green, and trimm'd with trees: see how
  Devotion gives each House a Bough,
  Or Branch: Each Porch, each doore, ere this,
  An Arke a Tabernacle is
Made up of white-thorn neatly enterwove;
As if here were those cooler shades of love.
  Can such delights be in the street,
  And open fields, and we not see't?
  Come, we'll abroad; and let's obay
  The Proclamation made for May: 40
And sin no more, as we have done, by staying;
But my *Corinna*, come, let's goe a Maying.

There's not a budding Boy, or Girle, this day,
But is got up, and gone to bring in May.
    A deale of Youth, ere this, is come
    Back, and with *White-thorn* laden home.
    Some have dispatcht their Cakes and Creame,
    Before that we have left to dreame:
And some have wept, and woo'd, and plighted Troth,
And chose their Priest, ere we can cast off sloth: 50
    Many a green-gown has been given;
    Many a kisse, both odde and even:
    Many a glance too has been sent
    From out the eye, Loves Firmament:
Many a jest told of the Keyes betraying
This night, and Locks pickt, yet w'are not a Maying.

Come, let us goe, while we are in our prime;
And take the harmlesse follie of the time.
    We shall grow old apace, and die
    Before we know our liberty.   60
    Our life is short; and our dayes run
    As fast away as do's the Sunne:
And as a vapour, or a drop of raine
Once lost, can ne'r be found againe:
    So when or you or I are made
    A fable, song, or fleeting shade;
    All love, all liking, all delight
    Lies drown'd with us in endlesse night.
Then while time serves, and we are but decaying;
Come, my *Corinna*, come, let's goe a Maying.   70

On Julia's *breath*

BREATHE, *Julia*, breathe, and Ile protest,
    Nay more, Ile deeply sweare,
That all the Spices of the East
    Are circumfused there.

Upon a Child. An Epitaph

BUT borne, and like a short Delight,
    I glided by my Parents sight.
That done, the harder Fates deny'd
My longer stay, and so I dy'd.

If pittying my sad Parents Teares,
You'l spil a tear, or two with theirs:
And with some flowrs my grave bestrew,
Love and they'l thank you for't. Adieu.

A Dialogue betwixt Horace *and* Lydia, *Translated* Anno 1627. *and set by Mr.* Ro: Ramsey

Hor. WHILE, *Lydia*, I was lov'd of thee,
        Nor any was preferr'd 'fore me
To hug thy whitest neck: Then I,
The Persian King liv'd not more happily.

Lyd. While thou no other didst affect,
    Nor *Cloe* was of more respect;
Then *Lydia*, far-fam'd *Lydia*,
I flourish't more then Roman *Ilia*.

Hor. Now *Thracian Cloe* governs me,
    Skilfull i'th'Harpe, and Melodie: 10
For whose affection, *Lydia*, I
(So Fate spares her) am well content to die.

Lyd. My heart now set on fire is
    By *Ornithes* sonne, young *Calais*;
For whose commutuall flames here I
(To save his life) twice am content to die.

Hor. Say our first loves we sho'd revoke,
    And sever'd, joyne in brazen yoke:
Admit I *Cloe* put away,
And love againe love-cast-off *Lydia*?   20

Lyd. Though mine be brighter then the Star;
    Thou lighter then the Cork by far:
Rough as th'*Adratick sea*, yet I
Will live with thee, or else for thee will die.

The captiv'd Bee: or,
The little Filcher

As *Julia* once a slumb'ring lay,
   It chanc't a Bee did flie that way,
(After a dew, or dew-like shower)
To tipple freely in a flower.
For some rich flower, he took the lip
Of *Julia*, and began to sip;
But when he felt he suckt from thence
Hony, and in the quintessence:
He drank so much he scarce co'd stir;
So *Julia* took the Pilferer.   10
And thus surpriz'd (as Filchers use)
He thus began himselfe t'excuse:
Sweet *Lady-Flower*, I never brought
Hither the least one theeving thought:
But taking those rare lips of yours
For some fresh, fragrant, luscious flowers:
I thought I might there take a taste,
Where so much sirrop ran at waste.
Besides, know this, I never sting
The flower that gives me nourishing: 20
But with a kisse, or thanks, doe pay
For Honie, that I beare away.
This said, he laid his little *scrip*
Of hony, 'fore her Ladiship:
And told her, (as some tears did fall)
That, that he took, and that was all.
At which she smil'd; and bade him goe
And take his bag; but thus much know,
When next he came a pilfring so,
He sho'd from her full lips derive,   30
Hony enough to fill his hive.

Upon Prig

Prig now drinks Water, who before drank Beere:
   What's now the cause? we know the case is cleere:
Look in *Prig's* purse, the chev'rell there tells you
Prig mony wants, either to buy, or brew.

2.3 *Prig's* ed.: *Prigs's* 48

Upon Batt

Batt he gets children, not for love to reare 'em;
But out of hope his wife might die to beare 'em.

An Ode to Master Endymion Porter, *upon his Brothers death*

Not all thy flushing Sunnes are set,
   Herrick, as yet:
Nor doth this far-drawn Hemisphere
Frown, and look sullen ev'ry where.
Daies may conclude in nights; and Suns may rest,
  As dead, within the West;
Yet the next Morne, re-guild the fragrant East.

Alas for me! that I have lost
   E'en all almost:
Sunk is my sight; set is my Sun;   10
And all the loome of life undone:
The staffe, the Elme, the prop, the shelt'ring wall
  Whereon my Vine did crawle,
Now, now, blowne downe; needs must the old stock fall.

Yet, *Porter*, while thou keep'st alive,
   In death I thrive:
And like a *Phenix* re-aspire
From out my *Narde*, and Fun'rall fire:
And as I prune my feather'd youth, so I
  Doe mar'l how I co'd die,   20
When I had Thee, my chiefe Preserver, by.

I'm up, I'm up, and blesse that hand,
   Which makes me stand
Now as I doe; and but for thee,
I must confesse, I co'd not be.
The debt is paid: for he who doth resigne
  Thanks to the gen'rous Vine;
Invites fresh Grapes to fill his Presse with Wine.

To his dying Brother, *Master* William Herrick

LIFE of my life, take not so soone thy flight,
  But stay the time till we have bade Good night.
Thou hast both Wind and Tide with thee; Thy way
As soone dispatcht is by the Night, as Day.
Let us not then so rudely henceforth goe
Till we have wept, kist, sigh't, shook hands, or so.
There's paine in parting; and a kind of hell,
When once true-lovers take their last Fare-well.
What? shall we two our endlesse leaves take here
Without a sad looke, or a solemne teare?   10
He knowes not Love, that hath not this truth proved,
Love is most loth to leave the thing beloved.
Pay we our Vowes, and goe; yet when we part,
Then, even then, I will bequeath my heart
Into thy loving hands: For Ile keep none
To warme my Breast, when thou my Pulse art gone.
No, here Ile last, and walk (a harmless shade)
About this Urne, wherein thy Dust is laid,
To guard it so, as nothing here shall be
Heavy, to hurt those sacred seeds of thee.   20

The Olive Branch

SADLY I walk't within the field,
  To see what comfort it wo'd yeeld:
And as I went my private way,
An Olive-branch before me lay:
And seeing it, I made a stay.
And took it up, and view'd it; then
Kissing the *Omen*, said Amen:
Be, be it so, and let this be
A Divination unto me:
That in short time my woes shall cease;   10
And Love shall crown my End with Peace.

Upon Much-more. *Epig.*

MUCH-MORE, provides, and hoords up like an Ant;
  Yet *Much-more* still complains he is in want.
Let *Much-more* justly pay his tythes; then try
How both his Meale and Oile will multiply.

To Cherry-blossomes

YE may simper, blush, and smile,
  And perfume the aire a while:
But (sweet things) ye must be gone;
Fruit, ye know, is comming on:
Then, Ah! Then, where is your grace,
When as Cherries come in place?

How Lillies came white

WHITE though ye be; yet, Lillies, know,
  From the first ye were not so:
      But Ile tell ye
      What befell ye;
Cupid and his Mother lay
In a Cloud; while both did play,
He with his pretty finger prest
The rubie niplet of her breast;
Out of the which, the creame of light,
      Like to a Dew,   10
      Fell downe on you,
      And made ye white.

To Pansies

AH, cruell Love! must I endure
  Thy many scorns, and find no cure?
Say, are thy medicines made to be
Helps to all others, but to me?
Ile leave thee, and to Pansies come;
Comforts you'l afford me some:
You can ease my heart, and doe
What Love co'd ne'r be brought unto.

On Gelli-flowers begotten

WHAT was't that fell but now
  From that warme kisse of ours?
Look, look, by Love I vow
    They were two Gelli-flowers.

Let's kisse, and kisse agen;
    For if so be our closes
Make Gelli-flowers, then
    I'm sure they'l fashion Roses.

The Lilly in a Christal

Y OU have beheld a smiling *Rose*
    When Virgins hands have drawn
      O'r it a Cobweb-Lawne:
And here, you see, this Lilly shows,
    Tomb'd in a *Christal* stone,
More faire in this transparent case,
    Then when it grew alone;
    And had but single grace.

You see how *Creame* but naked is;
    Nor daunces in the eye   10
      Without a Strawberrie:
Or some fine tincture, like to this,
    Which draws the sight thereto,
More by that wantoning with it;
    Then when the paler hieu
    No mixture did admit.

You see how *Amber* through the streams
    More gently stroaks the sight,
      With some conceal'd delight;
Then when he darts his radiant beams   20
    Into the boundlesse aire:
Where either too much light his worth
    Doth all at once impaire,
    Or set it little forth.

Put Purple Grapes, or Cherries in-
    To Glasse, and they will send
      More beauty to commend
Them, from that cleane and subtile skin,
    Then if they naked stood,
And had no other pride at all,   30
    But their own flesh and blood,
    And tinctures naturall.

Thus Lillie, Rose, Grape, Cherry, Creame,
    And Straw-berry do stir
      More love, when they transfer
A weak, a soft, a broken beame;

Then if they sho'd discover
At full their proper excellence;
Without some Scean cast over,
To juggle with the sense.   40

Thus let this *Christal'd Lillie* be
A Rule, how far to teach,
Your nakednesse must reach:
And that, no further, then we see
Those glaring colours laid
By Arts wise hand, but to this end
They sho'd obey a shade;
Lest they too far extend.

So though y'are white as Swan, or Snow,
And have the power to move   50
A world of men to love:
Yet, when your Lawns & Silks shal flow;
And that white cloud divide
Into a doubtful Twi-light; then,
Then will your hidden Pride
Raise greater fires in men.

To his Booke

LIKE to a Bride, come forth my Book, at last,
With all thy richest jewels over-cast:
Say, if there be 'mongst many jems here; one
Deservelesse of the name of *Paragon*:
Blush not at all for that; since we have set
Some *Pearls* on *Queens*, that have been counterfet.

Upon some women

THOU who wilt not love, doe this;
Learne of me what Woman is.
Something made of thred and thrumme;
A meere Botch of all and some.
Pieces, patches, ropes of haire;
In-laid Garbage ev'ry where.
Out-side silk, and out-side Lawne;
Sceanes to cheat us neatly drawne.

False in legs, and false in thighes;
False in breast, teeth, haire, and eyes: 10
False in head, and false enough;
Onely true in shreds and stuffe.

Supreme fortune falls soonest

WHILE leanest Beasts in Pastures feed,
    The fattest Oxe the first must bleed.

The Welcome to Sack

SO soft streams meet, so springs with gladder smiles
  Meet after long divorcement by the Iles:
When Love (the child of likenesse) urgeth on
Their Christal natures to an union.
So meet stolne kisses, when the Moonie nights
Call forth fierce Lovers to their wisht Delights:
So *Kings* & *Queens* meet, when Desire convinces
All thoughts, but such as aime at getting Princes,
As I meet thee. Soule of my life, and fame!
Eternall Lamp of Love! whose radiant flame   10
Out-glares the Heav'ns *Osiris*; and thy gleams   * The Sun
Out-shine the splendour of his mid-day beams.
Welcome, O welcome my illustrious Spouse;
Welcome as are the ends unto my Vowes:
I! far more welcome then the happy soile,
The Sea-scourg'd Merchant, after all his toile,
Salutes with tears of joy; when fires betray
The smoakie chimneys of his *Ithaca.*
Where hast thou been so long from my embraces,
Poore pittyed Exile? Tell me, did thy Graces   20
Flie discontented hence, and for a time
Did rather choose to blesse another clime?
Or went'st thou to this end, the more to move me,
By thy short absence, to desire and love thee?
Why frowns my Sweet? Why won't my Saint confer
Favours on me, her fierce Idolater?
Why are Those Looks, Those Looks the which have been
Time-past so fragrant, sickly now drawn in
Like a dull Twi-light? Tell me; and the fault
Ile expiate with Sulphur, Haire, and Salt: 30

And with the Christal humour of the spring,
Purge hence the guilt, and kill this quarrelling.
Wo't thou not smile, or tell me what's amisse?
Have I been cold to hug thee, too remisse,
Too temp'rate in embracing? Tell me, ha's desire
To thee-ward dy'd i'th'embers, and no fire
Left in this rak't-up Ash-heap, as a mark
To testifie the glowing of a spark?
Have I divorc't thee onely to combine
In hot Adult'ry with another Wine?   40
True, I confesse I left thee, and appeale
'Twas done by me, more to confirme my zeale,
And double my affection on thee; as doe those,
Whose love growes more enflam'd, by being Foes.
But to forsake thee ever, co'd there be
A thought of such like possibilitie?
When thou thy selfe dar'st say, thy Iles shall lack
Grapes, before *Herrick* leaves Canarie Sack.
Thou mak'st me ayrie, active to be born,
Like *Iphyclus*, upon the tops of Corn.   50
Thou mak'st me nimble, as the winged howers,
To dance and caper on the heads of flowers,
And ride the Sun-beams. Can there be a thing
Under the heavenly **Isis*, that can bring   * The Moon
More love unto my life, or can present
My *Genius* with a fuller blandishment?
Illustrious Idoll! co'd th'*Ægyptians* seek
Help from the *Garlick*, *Onyon*, and the *Leek*,
And pay no vowes to thee? who wast their best
God, and far more transcendent then the rest?   60
Had *Cassius*, that weak Water-drinker, known
Thee in thy Vine, or had but tasted one
Small Chalice of thy frantick liquor; He
As the wise *Cato* had approv'd of thee.
Had not **Joves* son, that brave *Tyrinthian* Swain,   * Hercules
(Invited to the *Thesbian* banquet) ta'ne
Full goblets of thy gen'rous blood; his spright
Ne'r had kept heat for fifty Maids that night.
Come, come and kisse me; Love and lust commends
Thee, and thy beauties; kisse, we will be friends   70
Too strong for Fate to break us: Look upon
Me, with that full pride of complexion,

As *Queenes*, meet *Queenes*; or come thou unto me,
As *Cleopatra* came to *Anthonie*;
When her high carriage did at once present
To the *Triumvir*, Love and Wonderment.
Swell up my nerves with spirit; let my blood
Run through my veines, like to a hasty flood.
Fill each part full of fire, active to doe
What thy commanding soule shall put it to.　　　　　80
And till I turne Apostate to thy love,
Which here I vow to serve, doe not remove
Thy Fiers from me; but *Apollo*'s curse
Blast these-like actions, or a thing that's worse;
When these Circumstants shall but live to see
The time that I prevaricate from thee.
Call me *The sonne of Beere*, and then confine
Me to the Tap, the Tost, the Turfe; Let Wine
Ne'r shine upon me; May my Numbers all
Run to a sudden Death, and Funerall.　　　　　90
And last, when thee (deare Spouse) I disavow,
Ne'r may Prophetique *Daphne* crown my Brow.

Impossibilities to his friend

M Y faithful friend, if you can see
　　The Fruit to grow up, or the Tree:
If you can see the colour come
Into the blushing Peare, or Plum:
If you can see the water grow
To cakes of Ice, or flakes of Snow:
If you can see, that drop of raine
Lost in the wild sea, once againe:
If you can see, how Dreams do creep
Into the Brain by easie sleep:　　　　　10
Then there is hope that you may see
Her love me once, who now hates me.

Upon Luggs. *Epig.*

L UGGS, by the Condemnation of the Bench,
　　Was lately whipt for lying with a Wench.
Thus Paines and Pleasures turne by turne succeed:
He smarts at last, who do's not first take heed.

1.2 up, or] (?) upon

Upon Gubbs. *Epig.*

G UBBS call's his children *Kitlings:* and wo'd bound
(Some say) for joy, to see those Kitlings drown'd.

To live merrily, and to trust to Good Verses

N OW is the time for mirth,
Nor cheek, or tongue be dumbe:
For with the flowrie earth,
The golden pomp is come.

The golden Pomp is come;
For now each tree do's weare
(Made of her Pap and Gum)
Rich beads of *Amber* here.

Now raignes the *Rose*, and now
Th'*Arabian* Dew besmears   10
My uncontrolled brow,
And my retorted haires.

Homer, this Health to thee,
In Sack of such a kind,
That it wo'd make thee see,
Though thou wert ne'r so blind.

Next, *Virgil*, Ile call forth,
To pledge this second Health
In Wine, whose each cup's worth
An Indian Common-wealth.   20

A Goblet next Ile drink
To *Ovid*; and suppose,
Made he the pledge, he'd think
The world had all *one Nose.*

Then this immensive cup
Of *Aromatike* wine,
Catullus, I quaffe up
To that Terce Muse of thine.

Wild I am now with heat;
　　O *Bacchus!* coole thy Raies!　　　　30
Or frantick I shall eate
　　Thy *Thyrse*, and bite the *Bayes*.

Round, round, the roof do's run;
　　And being ravisht thus,
Come, I will drink a Tun
　　To my *Propertius*.

Now, to *Tibullus*, next,
　　This flood I drink to thee:
But stay; I see a Text,
　　That this presents to me.　　　　40

Behold, *Tibullus* lies
　　Here burnt, whose smal return
Of ashes, scarce suffice
　　To fill a little Urne.

Trust to good Verses then;
　　They onely will aspire,
When Pyramids, as men,
　　Are lost, i'th'funerall fire.

And when all Bodies meet
　　In *Lethe* to be drown'd;　　　　50
Then onely Numbers sweet,
　　With endless life are crown'd.

Faire dayes: or, *Dawnes deceitfull*

FAIRE was the Dawne; and but e'ne now the Skies
　　Shew'd like to Creame, enspir'd with Strawberries:
But on a sudden, all was chang'd and gone
That smil'd in that first-sweet complexion.
Then Thunder-claps and Lightning did conspire
To teare the world, or set it all on fire.
What trust to things below, when as we see,
As Men, the Heavens have their Hypocrisie?

　　　　1.7 things below, *ed.*: things, below *48*

Lips Tonguelesse

FOR my part, I never care
    For those lips, that tongue-ty'd are:
Tell-tales I wo'd have them be
Of my Mistresse, and of me.
Let them prattle how that I
Sometimes freeze, and sometimes frie:
Let them tell how she doth move
Fore- or backward in her love:
Let them speak by gentle tones,
One and th'others passions: 10
How we watch, and seldome sleep;
How by Willowes we doe weep:
How by stealth we meet, and then
Kisse, and sigh, so part agen.
This the lips we will permit
For to tell, not publish it.

To the Fever, not to trouble Julia

TH'AST dar'd too farre; but Furie now forbeare
    To give the least disturbance to her haire:
But lesse presume to lay a Plait upon
Her skins most smooth, and cleare expansion.
'Tis like a Lawnie-Firmament as yet
Quite dispossest of either fray, or fret.
Come thou not neere that Filmne so finely spred,
Where no one piece is yet unlevelled.
This if thou dost, woe to thee Furie, woe,
Ile send such Frost, such Haile, such Sleet, and Snow,   10
Such Flesh-quakes, Palsies, and such fears as shall
Dead thee to th'most, if not destroy thee all.
And thou a thousand thousand times shalt be
More shak't thy selfe, then she is scorch't by thee.

To Violets

1. WELCOME Maids of Honour,
    You doe bring
        In the Spring;
And wait upon her.

2. She has Virgins many,
    Fresh and faire;
        Yet you are
More sweet then any.

3. Y'are the Maiden Posies,
    And so grac't,
        To be plac't,
'Fore Damask Roses.

10

4. Yet though thus respected,
    By and by
        Ye doe lie,
Poore Girles, neglected.

Upon Bunce. Epig.

MONY thou ow'st me; Prethee fix a day
    For payment promis'd, though thou never pay:
Let it be Doomes-day; nay, take longer scope;
Pay when th'art honest; let me have some hope.

To Carnations. A Song

1. STAY while ye will, or goe;
    And leave no scent behind ye:
Yet trust me, I shall know
    The place, where I may find ye.

2. Within my *Lucia*'s cheek,
    (Whose Livery ye weare)
Play ye at *Hide* or *Seek*,
    I'm sure to find ye there.

To the Virgins, to make much of Time

1. GATHER ye Rose-buds while ye may,
   Old Time is still a flying:
   And this same flower that smiles to day,
   To morrow will be dying.

2. The glorious Lamp of Heaven, the Sun,
   The higher he's a getting;
   The sooner will his Race be run,
   And neerer he's to Setting.

3. That Age is best, which is the first,
   When Youth and Blood are warmer;
   But being spent, the worse, and worst
   Times, still succeed the former.

10

4. Then be not coy, but use your time;
   And while ye may, goe marry:
   For having lost but once your prime,
   You may for ever tarry.

Safety to look to ones selfe

FOR my neighbour Ile not know,
   Whether high he builds or no:
Onely this Ile look upon,
Firm be my foundation.
Sound, or unsound, let it be;
'Tis the lot ordain'd for me.
He who to the ground do's fall,
Has not whence to sink at all.

To his Friend, on the untuneable Times

PLAY I co'd once; but (gentle friend) you see
   My Harp hung up, here on the Willow tree.
Sing I co'd once; and bravely too enspire
(With luscious Numbers) my melodious Lyre.
Draw I co'd once (although not stocks or stones,
Amphion-like) men made of flesh and bones,
Whether I wo'd; but (ah!) I know not how,
I feele in me, this transmutation now.
Griefe, (my deare friend) has first my Harp unstrung;
Wither'd my hand, and palsie-struck my tongue.

10

His Poetrie his Pillar

1. ONELY a little more
  I have to write,
   Then Ile give o're,
And bid the world Good-night.

2. 'Tis but a flying minute,
  That I must stay,
   Or linger in it;
And then I must away.

3. O time that cut'st down all!
  And scarce leav'st here   10
   Memoriall
Of any men that were.

4. How many lye forgot
  In Vaults beneath?
   And piece-meale rot
Without a fame in death?

5. Behold this living stone,
  I reare for me,
   Ne'r to be thrown
Downe, envious Time by thee.   20

6. Pillars let some set up,
  (If so they please)
   Here is my hope,
And my *Pyramides*.

Safety on the Shore

WHAT though the sea be calme? Trust to the shore:
Ships have been drown'd, where late they danc't before.

A Pastorall upon the birth of Prince Charles, *Presented to the King, and Set by* Mr. Nic: Laniere

The Speakers, Mirtillo, Amintas, *and* Amarillis.

Amin. GOOD day, *Mirtillo. Mirt.* And to you no lesse:
  And all faire Signs lead on our Shepardesse.
Amar. With all white luck to you. *Mirt.* But say, What news
Stirs in our Sheep-walk? *Amin.* None, save that my Ewes,

My Weathers, Lambes, and wanton Kids are well,
Smooth, faire, and fat, none better I can tell:
Or that this day *Menalchas* keeps a feast
For his Sheep-shearers. *Mir*. True, these are the least.
But dear *Amintas*, and sweet *Amarillis*,
Rest but a while here, by this bank of Lillies.   10
And lend a gentle eare to one report
The Country has. *Amint*. From whence? *Amar*. From whence?
    Mir. The Court.
Three dayes before the shutting in of *May*,
(With whitest Wool be ever crown'd that day!)
To all our joy, a sweet-fac't child was borne,
More tender then the childhood of the Morne.
Chor. Pan pipe to him, and bleats of lambs and sheep,
Let Lullaby the pretty Prince asleep!
Mirt. And that his birth sho'd be more singular,
At Noone of Day, was seene a silver Star,   20
Bright as the Wise-mens Torch, which guided them
To Gods sweet Babe, when borne at *Bethlehem*;
While Golden Angels (some have told to me)
Sung out his Birth with Heav'nly Minstralsie.
Amint. O rare! But is't a trespasse if we three
Sho'd wend along his Baby-ship to see?
Mir. Not so, not so. *Chor*. But if it chance to prove
At most a fault, 'tis but a fault of love.
Amar. But deare *Mirtillo*, I have heard it told,
Those learned men brought *Incense*, *Myrrhe*, and *Gold*,   30
From Countries far, with store of Spices, (sweet)
And laid them downe for Offrings at his feet.
Mirt. 'Tis true indeed; and each of us will bring
Unto our smiling, and our blooming King,
A neat, though not so great an Offering.
Amar. A Garland for my Gift shall be
Of flowers, ne'r suckt by th'theeving Bee:
And all most sweet; yet all lesse sweet then he.
Amint. And I will beare along with you
Leaves dropping downe the honyed dew,   40
With oaten pipes, as sweet, as new.
Mirt. And I a Sheep-hook will bestow,
To have his little King-ship know,
As he is Prince, he's Shepherd too.
Chor. Come let's away, and quickly let's be drest,

86

And quickly give, *The swiftest Grace is best.*
And when before him we have laid our treasures,
We'll blesse the Babe, Then back to Countrie pleasures.

To the Lark

G OOD speed, for I this day
  Betimes my Mattens say:
    Because I doe
    Begin to wooe:
    Sweet singing Lark,
    Be thou the Clark,
    And know thy when
    To say, *Amen.*
    And if I prove
    Blest in my love;   10
    Then thou shalt be
    High-Priest to me,
    At my returne,
    To Incense burne;
  And so to solemnize
  Love's, and my Sacrifice.

The Bubble. A Song

T o my revenge, and to her desp'rate feares,
  Flie thou madd Bubble of my sighs, and tears.
In the wild aire, when thou hast rowl'd about,
And (like a blasting Planet) found her out;
Stoop, mount, passe by to take her eye, then glare
Like to a dreadfull Comet in the Aire:
Next, when thou dost perceive her fixed sight,
For thy revenge to be most opposite;
Then like a Globe, or Ball of Wild-fire, flie,
And break thy self in shivers on her eye.   10

A Meditation for his Mistresse

1. Y OU are a *Tulip* seen to day,
  But (Dearest) of so short a stay;
  That where you grew, scarce man can say.

2.2 madd *MSS.*: made *48*

2. You are a lovely *July-flower*,
   Yet one rude wind, or ruffling shower,
   Will force you hence, (and in an houre.)

3. You are a sparkling *Rose* i'th'bud,
   Yet lost, ere that chast flesh and blood
   Can shew where you or grew, or stood.

4. You are a full-spread faire-set Vine,   10
   And can with Tendrills love intwine,
   Yet dry'd, ere you distill your Wine.

5. You are like Balme inclosed (well)
   In *Amber*, or some *Chrystall* shell,
   Yet lost ere you transfuse your smell.

6. You are a dainty *Violet*,
   Yet wither'd, ere you can be set
   Within the Virgins Coronet.

7. You are the *Queen* all flowers among,
   But die you must (faire Maid) ere long,   20
   As He, the maker of this Song.

The bleeding hand: or, The sprig of Eglantine given to a maid

FROM this bleeding hand of mine,
  Take this sprig of *Eglantine*.
Which (though sweet unto your smell)
Yet the fretfull bryar will tell,
He who plucks the sweets shall prove
Many thorns to be in Love.

Lyrick for Legacies

GOLD I've none, for use or show,
  Neither Silver to bestow
At my death; but thus much know,
That each Lyrick here shall be
Of my love a Legacie,
Left to all posterity.
Gentle friends, then doe but please,
To accept such coynes as these;
As my last Remembrances.

A Dirge upon the Death of the Right Valiant Lord, Bernard Stuart

1. HENCE, hence, profane; soft silence let us have;
   While we this *Trentall* sing about thy Grave.

2.   Had Wolves or Tigers seen but thee,
       They wo'd have shew'd civility;
       And in compassion of thy yeeres,
       Washt those thy purple wounds with tears.
       But since th'art slaine; and in thy fall,
       The drooping Kingdome suffers all.

Chor.   This we will doe; we'll daily come
       And offer Tears upon thy Tomb: 10
       And if that they will not suffice,
       Thou shalt have soules for sacrifice.

Sleepe in thy peace, while we with spice perfume thee,
And *Cedar* wash thee, that no times consume thee.

3.   Live, live thou dost, and shalt; for why?
       Soules doe not with their bodies die:
       Ignoble off-springs, they may fall
       Into the flames of Funerall:
       When as the chosen seed shall spring
       Fresh, and for ever flourishing.   20

Cho. And times to come shall, weeping, read thy glory,
      Lesse in these Marble stones, then in thy story.

To Perenna, *a Mistresse*

DEARE *Perenna*, prethee come,
   And with *Smallage* dresse my Tomb:
Adde a *Cypresse*-sprig thereto,
With a teare; and so *Adieu.*

Great boast, small rost

OF Flanks and Chines of Beefe doth *Gorrell* boast
   He has at home; but who tasts boil'd or rost?
Look in his Brine-tub, and you shall find there
Two stiffe-blew-Pigs-feet, and a sow's cleft eare.

Upon a Bleare-ey'd woman

WITHER'D with yeeres, and bed-rid *Mumma* lyes;
Dry-rosted all, but raw yet in her eyes.

The Fairie Temple: or, Oberons *Chappell.*
Dedicated to Mr. John Merrifield,
Counsellor at Law

RARE Temples thou hast seen, I know,
And rich for in and outward show:
Survey this Chappell, built, alone,
Without or Lime, or Wood, or Stone:
Then say, if one th'ast seene more fine
Then this, the Fairies once, now *Thine.*

The Temple

AWAY enchac't with glasse & beads
There is, that to the Chappel leads:
Whose structure (for his holy rest)
Is here the *Halcion's* curious nest:
Into the which who looks shall see
His *Temple of Idolatry:*
Where he of *God-heads* has such store,
As *Rome's Pantheon* had not more.
His house of *Rimmon,* this he calls,
Girt with small bones, instead of walls.   10
First, in a *Neech,* more black then jet,
His Idol-Cricket there is set:
Then in a Polisht Ovall by
There stands his *Idol-Beetle-flie:*
Next in an Arch, akin to this,
His *Idol-Canker* seated is:
Then in a Round, is plac't by these,
His golden god, *Cantharides.*
So that where ere ye look, ye see,
No *Capitoll,* no *Cornish* free,   20
Or *Freeze,* from this fine Fripperie.

Now this the Fairies wo'd have known,
Theirs is a mixt Religion.
And some have heard the Elves it call
Part Pagan, part Papisticall.
If unto me all Tongues were granted,
I co'd not speak the Saints here painted.
Saint *Tit*, Saint *Nit*, Saint *Is*, Saint *Itis*,
Who 'gainst *Mabs-state* plac't here right is.
Saint *Will o'th' Wispe* (of no great bignes)   30
But *alias* call'd here *Fatuus ignis*.
Saint *Frip*, Saint *Trip*, Saint *Fill*, S. *Fillie*,
Neither those other-Saint-ships will I
Here goe about for to recite
Their number (almost) infinite,
Which one by one here set downe are
In this most curious Calendar.
First, at the entrance of the gate,
A little-Puppet-Priest doth wait,
Who squeaks to all the commers there,   40
Favour your tongues, who enter here.
Pure hands bring hither, without staine.
A second pules, *Hence, hence, profane.*
Hard by, i'th'shell of halfe a nut,
The Holy-water there is put:
A little brush of Squirrils haires,
(Compos'd of odde, not even paires)
Stands in the Platter, or close by,
To purge the Fairie Family.
Neere to the Altar stands the Priest,   50
There off'ring up the Holy-Grist:
Ducking in Mood, and perfect Tense,
With (much-good-do't him) reverence.
The Altar is not here foure-square,
Nor in a forme Triangular;
Nor made of glasse, or wood, or stone,
But of a little Transverce bone;
Which boyes, and Bruckel'd children call
(Playing for Points and Pins) *Cockall*.
Whose Linnen-Drapery is a thin   60
Subtile and ductile Codlin's skin;
Which o're the board is smoothly spred,
With little Seale-work Damasked.

The Fringe that circumbinds it too,
Is Spangle-work of trembling dew,
Which, gently gleaming, makes a show,
Like Frost-work glitt'ring on the Snow.
Upon this fetuous board doth stand
Something for *Shew-bread*, and at hand
(Just in the middle of the Altar)   70
Upon an end, the *Fairie-Psalter*,
Grac't with the Trout-flies curious wings,
Which serve for watched Ribbanings.
Now, we must know, the Elves are led
Right by the Rubrick, which they read.
And if Report of them be true,
They have their Text for what they doe;
I, and their Book of Canons too.
And, as Sir *Thomas Parson* tells,
They have their Book of Articles: 80
And if that Fairie Knight not lies,
They have their Book of Homilies:
And other Scriptures, that designe
A short, but righteous discipline.
The Bason stands the board upon
To take the Free-Oblation:
A little Pin-dust; which they hold
More precious, then we prize our gold:
Which charity they give to many
Poore of the Parish, (if there's any)   90
Upon the ends of these neat Railes
(Hatcht, with the Silver-light of snails)
The Elves, in formall manner, fix
Two pure, and holy *Candlesticks:*
In either which a small tall bent
Burns for the Altars ornament.
For sanctity, they have, to these,
Their curious *Copes* and *Surplices*
Of cleanest *Cobweb*, hanging by
In their *Religious Vesterie*.   100
They have their *Ash-pans*, & their *Brooms*
To purge the Chappel and the rooms:
Their many *mumbling Masse-priests* here,
And many a dapper *Chorister*.
Their ush'ring *Vergers*, here likewise,

Their *Canons*, and their *Chaunteries:*
Of *Cloyster-Monks* they have enow,
I, and their *Abby-Lubbers* too:
And if their Legend doe not lye,
They much affect the *Papacie:*   110
And since the last is dead, there's hope,
Elve Boniface shall next be Pope.
They have their *Cups* and *Chalices*;
Their *Pardons* and *Indulgences:*
Their *Beads* of Nits, *Bels*, *Books*, & *Wax*
Candles (forsooth) and other knacks:
Their *Holy Oyle*, their *Fasting-Spittle*;
Their *sacred Salt* here, (not a little.)
Dry *chips*, old *shooes*, *rags*, *grease*, & *bones*;
Beside their *Fumigations*,   120
To drive the Devill from the Cod-piece
Of the Fryar, (of work an odde-piece.)
Many a trifle too, and trinket,
And for what use, scarce man wo'd think it.
Next, then, upon the *Chanters* side
An *Apples-core* is hung up dry'd,
With ratling Kirnils, which is rung
To call to Morn, and Even-Song.
The Saint, to which the most he prayes
And offers *Incense* Nights and dayes,   130
The *Lady* of the *Lobster* is,
Whose foot-pace he doth stroak & kisse;
And, humbly, chives of Saffron brings,
For his most cheerfull offerings.
When, after these, h'as paid his vows,
He lowly to the Altar bows:
And then he dons the Silk-worms shed,
(Like a *Turks Turbant* on his head)
And reverently departeth thence,
Hid in a cloud of *Frankincense:*   140
And by the glow-worms light wel guided,
Goes to the Feast that's now provided.

To *Mistresse* Katherine Bradshaw, *the lovely, that crowned him with Laurel*

MY Muse in Meads has spent her many houres,
Sitting, and sorting severall sorts of flowers,
To make for others garlands; and to set
On many a head here, many a Coronet:
But, amongst All encircled here, not one
Gave her a day of Coronation;
Till you (sweet Mistresse) came and enterwove
A *Laurel* for her, (ever young as love)
You first of all crown'd her; she must of due,
Render for that, a crowne of life to you.   10

The Plaudite, or end of life

IF after rude and boystrous seas,
My wearyed Pinnace here finds ease:
If so it be I've gain'd the shore
With safety of a faithful Ore:
If having run my Barque on ground,
Ye see the aged Vessell crown'd:
What's to be done? but on the Sands
Ye dance, and sing, and now clap hands.
The first Act's doubtfull, (but we say)
It is the last commends the Play.   10

To the most *vertuous Mistresse* Pot, *who many times entertained him*

WHEN I through all my many Poems look,
And see your selfe to beautifie my Book;
Me thinks that onely lustre doth appeare
A Light ful-filling all the Region here.
Guild still with flames this Firmament, and be
A Lamp Eternall to my Poetrie.
Which if it now, or shall hereafter shine,
'Twas by your splendour (Lady) not by mine.
The Oile was yours; and that I owe for yet:
He payes the halfe, who do's confesse the Debt.   10

To Musique, to becalme his Fever

1. CHARM me asleep, and melt me so
    With thy Delicious Numbers;
That being ravisht, hence I goe
    Away in easie slumbers.
      Ease my sick head,
      And make my bed,
Thou Power that canst sever
      From me this ill:
      And quickly still:
      Though thou not kill   10
      My Fever.

2. Thou sweetly canst convert the same
    From a consuming fire,
Into a gentle-licking flame,
    And make it thus expire.
      Then make me weep
      My paines asleep;
And give me such reposes,
      That I, poore I,
      May think, thereby,   20
      I live and die
        'Mongst Roses.

3. Fall on me like a silent dew,
    Or like those Maiden showrs,
Which, by the peepe of day, doe strew
    A Baptime o're the flowers.
      Melt, melt my paines,
      With thy soft straines;
That having ease me given,
      With full delight,   30
      I leave this light;
      And take my flight
      For Heaven

Upon a Gentlewoman with a sweet Voice

So long you did not sing, or touch your Lute,
We knew 'twas Flesh and Blood, that there sate mute.
But when your Playing, and your Voice came in,
'Twas no more you then, but a *Cherubin*.

Upon Cupid

As lately I a Garland bound,
'Mongst Roses, I there *Cupid* found:
I took him, put him in my cup,
And drunk with Wine, I drank him up.
Hence then it is, that my poore brest
Co'd never since find any rest.

Upon Julia's *breasts*

DISPLAY thy breasts, my *Julia*, there let me
Behold that circummortall purity:
Betweene whose glories, there my lips Ile lay,
Ravisht, in that faire *Via Lactea*.

Best to be merry

FOOLES are they, who never know
How the times away doe goe:
But for us, who wisely see
Where the bounds of black Death be:
Let's live merrily, and thus
Gratifie the *Genius*.

The Changes to Corinna

BE not proud, but now encline
Your soft eare to Discipline.
You have changes in your life,
Sometimes peace, and sometimes strife:
You have ebbes of face and flowes,
As your health or comes, or goes;
You have hopes, and doubts, and feares
Numberlesse, as are your haires.
You have Pulses that doe beat
High, and passions lesse of heat.

10

You are young, but must be old,
And, to these, ye must be told,
Time, ere long, will come and plow
Loathed Furrowes in your brow:
And the dimnesse of your eye
Will no other thing imply,
But you must die
As well as I.

No Lock against Letcherie

BARRE close as you can, and bolt fast too your doore,
To keep out the Letcher, and keep in the whore:
Yet, quickly you'l see by the turne of a pin,
The Whore to come out, or the Letcher come in.

Neglect

ART quickens Nature; Care will make a face:
Neglected beauty perisheth apace.

Upon himselfe

MOP-EY'D I am, as some have said,
Because I've liv'd so long a maid:
But grant that I sho'd wedded be,
Sho'd I a jot the better see?
No, I sho'd think, that Marriage might,
Rather then mend, put out the light.

Upon a Physitian

THOU cam'st to cure me (Doctor) of my cold,
And caught'st thy selfe the more by twenty fold:
Prethee goe home; and for thy credit be
First.cur'd thy selfe; then come and cure me.

Upon Sudds *a Laundresse*

SUDDS Launders Bands in pisse; and starches them
Both with her Husband's, and her own tough fleame.

To the Rose. Song

1. GOE happy Rose, and enterwove
   With other Flowers, bind my Love.
   Tell her too, she must not be,
   Longer flowing, longer free,
   That so oft has fetter'd me.

2. Say (if she's fretfull) I have bands
   Of Pearle, and Gold, to bind her hands:
   Tell her, if she struggle still,
   I have Mirtle rods, (at will)
   For to tame, though not to kill.   10

3. Take thou my blessing, thus, and goe,
   And tell her this, but doe not so,
   Lest a handsome anger flye,
   Like a Lightning, from her eye,
   And burn thee'up, as well as I.

Upon Guesse. *Epig.*

GUESSE cuts his shooes, and limping, goes about
To have men think he's troubled with the Gout:
But 'tis no Gout (beleeve it) but hard Beere,
Whose acrimonious humour bites him here.

To his Booke

THOU art a plant sprung up to wither never,
But like a Laurell, to grow green for ever.

Upon a painted Gentlewoman

MEN say y'are faire; and faire ye are, 'tis true;
But (Hark!) we praise the Painter now, not you.

Upon a crooked Maid

CROOKED you are, but that dislikes not me;
So you be straight, where Virgins straight sho'd be.

Draw Gloves

AT Draw-Gloves we'l play,
And prethee, let's lay
A wager, and let it be this;
Who first to the Summe
Of twenty shall come,
Shall have for his winning a kisse.

To Musick, to becalme a sweet-sick-youth

CHARMS, that call down the moon from out her sphere,
On this sick youth work your enchantments here:
Bind up his senses with your numbers, so,
As to entrance his paine, or cure his woe.
Fall gently, gently, and a while him keep
Lost in the civill Wildernesse of sleep:
That done, then let him, dispossest of paine,
Like to a slumbring Bride, awake againe.

To the High and Noble Prince, GEORGE, Duke, Marquesse, and Earle of Buckingham

NEVER my Book's perfection did appeare,
Til I had got the name of VILLARS here.
Now 'tis so full, that when therein I look,
I see a Cloud of Glory fills my Book.
Here stand it stil to dignifie our Muse,
Your sober Hand-maid; who doth wisely chuse,
Your Name to be a *Laureat Wreathe* to Hir,
Who doth both love and feare you *Honour'd Sir.*

His Recantation

LOVE, I recant,
　And pardon crave,
That lately I offended,
　　But 'twas,
　　Alas,
　To make a brave,
But no disdaine intended.

　No more Ile vaunt,
　For now I see,
Thou onely hast the power,
　　To find,
　　And bind
　A heart that's free,
And slave it in an houre.

The comming of good luck

SO Good-luck came, and on my roofe did light,
　Like noyse-lesse Snow; or as the dew of night:
Not all at once, but gently, as the trees
Are, by the Sun-beams, tickel'd by degrees.

The Present: or, *The Bag of the Bee*

FLY to my Mistresse, pretty pilfring Bee,
　And say, thou bring'st this Hony-bag from me:
When on her lip, thou hast thy sweet dew plac't,
Mark, if her tongue, but slily, steale a taste.
If so, we live; if not, with mournfull humme,
Tole forth my death; next, to my buryall come.

On Love

LOVE bade me aske a gift,
　And I no more did move,
But this, that I might shift
　Still with my clothes, my Love:
That favour granted was;
　Since which, though I love many,
Yet so it comes to passe,
　That long I love not any.

The Hock-cart, or Harvest home:
To the Right Honourable,
Mildmay, Earle of
Westmorland

COME Sons of Summer, by whose toile,
  We are the Lords of Wine and Oile:
By whose tough labours, and rough hands,
We rip up first, then reap our lands.
Crown'd with the eares of corne, now come,
And, to the Pipe, sing Harvest home.
Come forth, my Lord, and see the Cart
Drest up with all the Country Art.
See, here a *Maukin*, there a sheet,
As spotlesse pure, as it is sweet: 10
The Horses, Mares, and frisking Fillies,
(Clad, all, in Linnen, white as Lillies.)
The Harvest Swaines, and Wenches bound
For joy, to see the *Hock-cart* crown'd.
About the Cart, heare, how the Rout
Of Rurall Younglings raise the shout;
Pressing before, some coming after,
Those with a shout, and these with laughter.
Some blesse the Cart; some kisse the sheaves;
Some prank them up with Oaken leaves: 20
Some crosse the Fill-horse; some with great
Devotion, stroak the home-borne wheat:
While other Rusticks, lesse attent
To Prayers, then to Merryment,
Run after with their breeches rent.
Well, on, brave boyes, to your Lords Hearth,
Glitt'ring with fire; where, for your mirth,
Ye shall see first the large and cheefe
Foundation of your Feast, Fat Beefe:
With Upper Stories, Mutton, Veale   30
And Bacon, (which makes full the meale)
With sev'rall dishes standing by,
As here a Custard, there a Pie,
And here all tempting Frumentie.
And for to make the merry cheere,
If smirking Wine be wanting here,
There's that, which drowns all care, stout Beere;

Which freely drink to your Lords health,
Then to the Plough, (the Common-wealth)
Next to your Flailes, your Fanes, your Fatts;   40
Then to the Maids with Wheaten Hats:
To the rough Sickle, and crookt Sythe,
Drink frollick boyes, till all be blythe.
Feed, and grow fat; and as ye eat,
Be mindfull, that the lab'ring Neat
(As you) may have their fill of meat.
And know, besides, ye must revoke
The patient Oxe unto the Yoke,
And all goe back unto the Plough
And Harrow, (though they'r hang'd up now.)   50
And, you must know, your Lords word's true,
Feed him ye must, whose food fils you.
And that this pleasure is like raine,
Not sent ye for to drowne your paine,
But for to make it spring againe.

The Perfume

To morrow, *Julia*, I betimes must rise,
    For some small fault, to offer sacrifice:
The Altar's ready; Fire to consume
The fat; breathe thou, and there's the rich perfume.

Upon her Voice

Let but thy voice engender with the string,
    And Angels will be borne, while thou dost sing.

Not to love

He that will not love, must be
    My Scholar, and learn this of me:
There be in Love as many feares,
As the Summers Corne has eares:
Sighs, and sobs, and sorrowes more
Then the sand, that makes the shore:
Freezing cold, and firie heats,
Fainting swoones, and deadly sweats;

Now an Ague, then a Fever,
Both tormenting Lovers ever.   10
Wod'st thou know, besides all these,
How hard a woman 'tis to please?
How crosse, how sullen, and how soone
She shifts and changes like the Moone.
How false, how hollow she's in heart;
And how she is her owne least part:
How high she's priz'd, and worth but small;
Little thou't love, or not at all.

To Musick. A Song

MUSICK, thou *Queen of Heaven*, Care-charming-spel,
   That strik'st a stilnesse into hell:
Thou that tam'st *Tygers*, and fierce storms (that rise)
   With thy soule-melting Lullabies:
Fall down, down, down, from those thy chiming spheres,
To charme our soules, as thou enchant'st our eares.

To the Western wind

1. SWEET Western Wind, whose luck it is,
      (Made rivall with the aire)
   To give *Perenn'as* lip a kisse,
      And fan her wanton haire.

2. Bring me but one, Ile promise thee,
      Instead of common showers,
   Thy wings shall be embalm'd by me,
      And all beset with flowers.

Upon the death of his Sparrow.
An Elegie

WHY doe not all fresh maids appeare
   To work Love's Sampler onely here,
Where spring-time smiles throughout the yeare?
Are not here *Rose-buds*, *Pinks*, all flowers,
Nature begets by th'Sun and showers,
Met in one Hearce-cloth, to ore-spred
The body of the under-dead?

Phill, the late dead, the late dead Deare,
O! may no eye distill a Teare
For you once lost, who weep not here!   10
Had *Lesbia* (too-too-kind) but known
This Sparrow, she had scorn'd her own:
And for this dead which under-lies,
Wept out her heart, as well as eyes.
But endlesse Peace, sit here, and keep
My *Phill*, the time he has to sleep,
And thousand Virgins come and weep,
To make these flowrie Carpets show
Fresh, as their blood; and ever grow,
Till passengers shall spend their doome,   20
Not *Virgil's* Gnat had such a Tomb.

To Primroses fill'd with morning-dew

1. WHY doe ye weep, sweet Babes? can Tears
                    Speak griefe in you,
               Who were but borne
          Just as the modest Morne
          Teem'd her refreshing dew?
Alas you have not known that shower,
               That marres a flower;
               Nor felt th'unkind
          Breath of a blasting wind;
          Nor are ye worne with yeares;   10
                    Or warpt, as we,
               Who think it strange to see,
Such pretty flowers, (like to Orphans young)
To speak by Teares, before ye have a Tongue.

2. Speak, whimp'ring Younglings, and make known
                    The reason, why
               Ye droop, and weep;
          Is it for want of sleep?
          Or childish Lullabie?
Or that ye have not seen as yet   20
               The *Violet?*
               Or brought a kisse
          From that Sweet-heart, to this?
          No, no, this sorrow shown

By your teares shed,
Wo'd have this Lecture read,
That things of greatest, so of meanest worth,
Conceiv'd with grief are, and with teares brought forth.

How Roses came red

1. ROSES at first were white,
    Till they co'd not agree,
  Whether my *Sapho's* breast,
    Or they more white sho'd be.

2. But being vanquisht quite,
    A blush their cheeks bespred;
  Since which (beleeve the rest)
    The *Roses* first came red.

Comfort to a Lady upon the Death of her Husband

DRY your sweet cheek, long drown'd with sorrows raine;
Since Clouds disperst, Suns guild the Aire again.
Seas chafe and fret, and beat, and over-boile;
But turne soone after calme, as Balme, or Oile.
Winds have their time to rage; but when they cease,
The leavie-trees nod in a still-born peace.
Your storme is over; Lady, now appeare
Like to the peeping-spring-time of the yeare.
Off then with grave clothes; put fresh colours on;
And flow, and flame, in your *Vermillion*.   10
Upon your cheek sate *Ysicles* awhile;
Now let the Rose raigne like a Queene, and smile.

How Violets came blew

LOVE on a day (wise Poets tell)
    Some time in wrangling spent,
  Whether the Violets sho'd excell,
    Or she, in sweetest scent.

But *Venus* having lost the day,
    Poore Girles, she fell on you;
  And beat ye so, (as some dare say)
    Her blowes did make ye blew.

Upon Groynes. *Epig*

G*ROYNES*, for his fleshly *Burglary* of late,
  Stood in the *Holy-Forum Candidate*:
The word is *Roman*; but in English knowne:
Penance, and standing so, are both but one.

To the Willow-tree

1. T<small>HOU</small> art to all lost love the best,
     The onely true plant found,
   Wherewith young men and maids distrest,
     And left of love, are crown'd.

2. When once the Lovers Rose is dead,
     Or laid aside forlorne;
   Then Willow-garlands, 'bout the head,
     Bedew'd with teares, are worne.

3. When with Neglect, (the Lovers bane)
     Poore Maids rewarded be,   10
   For their love lost; their onely gaine
     Is but a Wreathe from thee.

4. And underneath thy cooling shade,
     (When weary of the light)
   The love-spent Youth, and love-sick Maid,
     Come to weep out the night.

Mrs. Eliz. Wheeler, *under the name of the lost Shepardesse*

A<small>MONG</small> the *Mirtles*, as I walkt,
  Love and my sighs thus intertalkt:
Tell me, said I, in deep distresse,
Where I may find my Shepardesse.
Thou foole, said Love, know'st thou not this?
In every thing that's sweet, she is.
In yond' *Carnation* goe and seek,
There thou shalt find her lip and cheek:

In that ennamel'd *Pansie* by,
There thou shalt have her curious eye:⠀⠀⠀⠀⠀10
In bloome of *Peach*, and *Roses* bud,
There waves the Streamer of her blood.
'Tis true, said I, and thereupon
I went to pluck them one by one,
To make of parts an union;
But on a sudden all were gone.
At which I stopt; Said Love, these be
The true resemblances of thee;
For as these flowers, thy joyes must die,
And in the turning of an eye;⠀⠀⠀⠀⠀⠀20
And all thy hopes of her must wither,
Like those short sweets ere knit together.

TO THE KING

IF when these Lyricks (CESAR) You shall heare,
And that *Apollo* shall so touch Your eare,
As for to make this, that, or any one
Number, Your owne, by free Adoption;
That Verse, of all the Verses here, shall be
The Heire to This *great Realme of Poetry*.

TO THE QUEENE

GODDESSE *of Youth, and Lady of the Spring,*
(*Most fit to be the Consort to a King*)
Be pleas'd to rest you in *This Sacred Grove*,
Beset with *Mirtles*; whose each leafe drops Love.
Many a sweet-fac't *Wood-Nymph* here is seene,
Of which chast *Order You* are now the *Queene*:
Witness their *Homage*, when they come and strew
Your Walks with Flowers, and give their Crowns to you.
Your Leavie-Throne (with *Lilly*-work) possesse;
And be both *Princesse* here, and *Poetresse*.⠀⠀⠀⠀10

The Poets good wishes for the most hopefull and handsome Prince, the Duke of Yorke

MAY his pretty Duke-ship grow
    Like t'a Rose of *Jericho*:
Sweeter far, then ever yet
Showrs or Sun-shines co'd beget.
May the Graces, and the Howers
Strew his hopes, and Him with flowers:
And so dresse him up with Love,
As to be the Chick of *Jove*.
May the thrice-three-Sisters sing
Him the Soveraigne of their Spring: 10
And entitle none to be
Prince of *Hellicon*, but He.
May his soft foot, where it treads,
Gardens thence produce and Meads:
And those Meddowes full be set
With the Rose, and Violet.
May his ample Name be knowne
To the last succession:
And his actions high be told
Through the world, but writ in gold.   20

To Anthea, *who may command him any thing*

BID me to live, and I will live
    Thy Protestant to be:
Or bid me love, and I will give
    A loving heart to thee.

2. A heart as soft, a heart as kind,
    A heart as sound and free,
As in the whole world thou canst find,
    That heart Ile give to thee.

3. Bid that heart stay, and it will stay,
    To honour thy Decree: 10
Or bid it languish quite away,
    And't shall doe so for thee.

4. Bid me to weep, and I will weep,
   While I have eyes to see:
And having none, yet I will keep
   A heart to weep for thee.

5. Bid me despaire, and Ile despaire,
   Under that *Cypresse* tree:
Or bid me die, and I will dare
   E'en Death, to die for thee.

6. Thou art my life, my love, my heart,
   The very eyes of me:
And hast command of every part,
   To live and die for thee.

20

Prevision, or Provision

THAT *Prince takes soone enough the Victors roome,*
Who first provides, not to be overcome.

Obedience in Subjects

THE *Gods to Kings the Judgement give to sway:*
The Subjects onely glory to obay.

More potent, lesse peccant

HE *that may sin, sins least; Leave to transgresse*
Enfeebles much the seeds of wickednesse.

Upon a maid that dyed the day
she was marryed

THAT Morne which saw me made a Bride,
   The Ev'ning witnest that I dy'd.
Those holy lights, wherewith they guide
Unto the bed the bashfull Bride;
Serv'd, but as Tapers, for to burne,
And light my Reliques to their Urne.
This *Epitaph*, which here you see,
Supply'd the *Epithalamie.*

Upon Pink *an ill-fac'd Painter. Epig.*

To paint the Fiend, *Pink* would the Devill see;
    And so he may, if he'll be rul'd by me:
Let but *Pink*'s face i'th'Looking-glasse be showne,
And *Pink* may paint the Devill's by his owne.

Upon Brock. *Epig.*

To clense his eyes, *Tom Brock* makes much adoe,
    But not his mouth (the fouler of the two.)
A clammie Reume makes loathsome both his eyes:
His mouth worse furr'd with oathes and blasphemies.

To Meddowes

1. Ye have been fresh and green,
        Ye have been fill'd with flowers:
    And ye the Walks have been
        Where Maids have spent their houres.

2. You have beheld, how they
        With *Wicker Arks* did come
    To kisse, and beare away
        The richer Couslips home.

3. Y'ave heard them sweetly sing,
        And seen them in a Round:
    Each Virgin, like a Spring,
        With Hony-succles crown'd.

4. But now, we see, none here,
        Whose silv'rie feet did tread,
    And with dishevell'd Haire,
        Adorn'd this smoother Mead.

5. Like Unthrifts, having spent,
        Your stock, and needy grown,
    Y'are left here to lament
        Your poore estates, alone.

Crosses

Though good things answer many good intents;
    Crosses doe still bring forth the best events.

Miseries

THOUGH hourely comforts from the Gods we see,
No life is yet life-proofe from miserie.

Laugh and lie downe

Y'AVE laught enough (sweet) vary now your Text;
And laugh no more; or laugh, and lie down next.

To his Houshold gods

RISE, Houshold-gods, and let us goe;
But whither, I my selfe not know.
First, let us dwell on rudest seas;
Next, with severest Salvages;
Last, let us make our best abode,
Where humane foot, as yet, ne'r trod:
Search worlds of Ice; and rather there
Dwell, then in lothed *Devonshire.*

To the Nightingale, and Robin-Red-brest

WHEN I departed am, ring thou my knell,
Thou pittifull, and pretty *Philomel:*
And when I'm laid out for a Corse; then be
Thou *Sexton* (*Red-brest*) for to cover me.

To the Yew and Cypresse to grace his Funerall

1.   BOTH you two have
Relation to the grave:
And where
The *Fun'rall-Trump* sounds, you are there.

2.   I shall be made
Ere long a fleeting shade:
Pray come,
And doe some honour to my Tomb.

3.   Do not deny
My last request; for I
Will be
Thankfull to you, or friends, for me.

10

I call and I call

I CALL, I call, who doe ye call?
 The Maids to catch this Cowslip-ball:
But since these Cowslips fading be,
Troth, leave the flowers, and Maids, take me.
Yet, if that neither you will doe,
Speak but the word, and Ile take you.

On a perfum'd Lady

YOU say y'are sweet; how sho'd we know
 Whether that you be sweet or no?
From *Powders* and *Perfumes* keep free;
Then we shall smell how sweet you be.

A Nuptiall Song, or Epithalamie, on Sir Clipseby Crew *and his Lady*

1. WHAT'S that we see from far? the spring of Day
 Bloom'd from the East, or faire Injewel'd May
 Blowne out of April; or some New-
 Star fill'd with glory to our view,
  Reaching at heaven,
To adde a nobler Planet to the seven?
  Say, or doe we not descrie
Some Goddesse, in a cloud of Tiffanie
  To move, or rather the
 Emergent *Venus* from the Sea?   10

2. 'Tis she! 'tis she! or else some more Divine
Enlightned substance; mark how from the Shrine
  Of holy Saints she paces on,
  Treading upon *Vermilion*
   And *Amber*; Spice-
ing the Chafte Aire with fumes of Paradise.
 Then come on, come on, and yeeld
A savour like unto a blessed field,
  When the bedabled Morne
 Washes the golden eares of corne.   20

3. See where she comes; and smell how all the street
Breathes Vine-yards and Pomgranats: O how sweet!
    As a fir'd Altar, is each stone,
    Perspiring pounded Cynamon.
        The Phenix nest,
Built up of odours, burneth in her breast.
    Who therein wo'd not consume
His soule to Ash-heaps in that rich perfume?
        Bestroaking Fate the while
He burnes to Embers on the Pile.   30

4. *Himen, O Himen!* Tread the sacred ground;
Shew thy white feet, and head with Marjoram crown'd:
    Mount up thy flames, and let thy Torch
    Display the Bridegroom in the porch,
        In his desires
More towring, more disparkling then thy fires:
    Shew her how his eyes do turne
And roule about, and in their motions burne
        Their balls to Cindars: haste,
Or else to ashes he will waste.   40

5. Glide by the banks of Virgins then, and passe
The Shewers of Roses, lucky-foure-leav'd grasse:
    The while the cloud of younglings sing,
    And drown yee with a flowrie Spring:
        While some repeat
Your praise, and bless you, sprinkling you with Wheat:
    While that others doe divine;
Blest is the Bride, on whom the Sun doth shine;
        And thousands gladly wish
You multiply, as doth a Fish.   50

6. And beautious Bride we do confess y'are wise,
In dealing forth these bashfull jealousies:
    In Lov's name do so; and a price
    Set on your selfe, by being nice:
        But yet take heed;
What now you seem, be not the same indeed,
    And turne *Apostate*: Love will
Part of the way be met; or sit stone-still.
        On then, and though you slow-
ly go, yet, howsoever, go.   60

7. And now y'are enter'd; see the Codled Cook
Runs from his *Torrid Zone*, to prie, and look,
  And blesse his dainty Mistresse: see,
  The Aged point out, This is she,
    Who now must sway
The House (Love shield her) with her Yea and Nay:
  And the smirk Butler thinks it
Sin, in's Nap'rie, not to express his wit;
    Each striving to devise
  Some gin, wherewith to catch your eyes.   70

8. To bed, to bed, kind Turtles, now, and write
This the short'st day, and this the longest night;
  But yet too short for you: 'tis we,
  Who count this night as long as three,
    Lying alone,
Telling the Clock strike Ten, Eleven, Twelve, One.
  Quickly, quickly then prepare;
And let the Young-men and the Bride-maids share
    Your Garters; and their joynts
  Encircle with the Bride-grooms Points.   80

9. By the Brides eyes, and by the teeming life
Of her green hopes, we charge ye, that no strife
  (Farther then Gentlenes tends) gets place
  Among ye, striving for her lace:
    O doe not fall
Foule in these noble pastimes, lest ye call
  Discord in, and so divide
The youthfull Bride-groom, and the fragrant Bride:
    Which Love fore-fend; but spoken,
  Be't to your praise, no peace was broken.   90

10. Strip her of Spring-time, tender-whimpring-maids,
Now *Autumne*'s come, when all those flowrie aids
  Of her Delayes must end; Dispose
  That *Lady-smock*, that *Pansie*, and that *Rose*
    Neatly apart;
But for *Prick-madam*, and for *Gentle-heart*;
  And soft-*Maidens-blush*, the Bride
Makes holy these, all others lay aside:
    Then strip her, or unto her
  Let him come, who dares undo her.   100

11. And to enchant yee more, see every where
About the Roofe a *Syren* in a Sphere;
     (As we think) singing to the dinne
     Of many a warbling *Cherubin*:
          O marke yee how
The soule of Nature melts in numbers: now
     See, a thousand *Cupids* flye,
To light their Tapers at the Brides bright eye.
       To Bed; or her they'l tire,
     Were she an Element of fire.   110

12. And to your more bewitching, see, the proud
Plumpe Bed beare up, and swelling like a cloud,
     Tempting the too too modest; can
     Yee see it brusle like a Swan,
          And you be cold
To meet it, when it woo's and seemes to fold
     The Armes to hugge you? throw, throw
Your selves into the mighty over-flow
        Of that white Pride, and Drowne
     The night, with you, in floods of Downe.   120

13. The bed is ready, and the maze of Love
Lookes for the treaders; every where is wove
     Wit and new misterie; read, and
     Put in practise, to understand
          And know each wile,
Each hieroglyphick of a kisse or smile;
     And do it to the full; reach
High in your own conceipt, and some way teach
        Nature and Art, one more
     Play, then they ever knew before.   130

14. If needs we must for Ceremonies-sake,
Blesse a *Sack-posset*; Luck go with it; take
     The Night-Charme quickly; you have spells,
     And magicks for to end and hells,
         To passe; but such
And of such Torture as no one would grutch
     To live therein for ever: Frie
And consume, and grow again to die,
        And live, and in that case,
     Love the confusion of the place.   140

l. 104 *Cherubin MSS.*: *Cherubim 48*   l. 113 too too *MSS.*: two too *48*
l. 117 you *MSS.*: it *48*

15. But since It must be done, dispatch, and sowe
Up in a sheet your Bride, and what if so
   It be with Rock, or walles of Brasse,
   Ye Towre her up, as *Danae* was;
     Thinke you that this,
Or hell it selfe a powerfull Bulwarke is?
   I tell yee no; but like a
Bold bolt of thunder he will make his way,
    And rend the cloud, and throw
   The sheet about, like flakes of snow.   150

16. All now is husht in silence; *Midwife-moone*,
With all her *Owle-ey'd* issue begs a boon
   Which you must grant; that's entrance; with
   Which extract, all we can call pith
     And quintiscence
Of Planetary bodies; so commence
   All faire *Constellations*
Looking upon yee, that two Nations
    Springing from two such Fires,
   May blaze the vertue of their Sires.   160

The silken Snake

FOR sport my *Julia* threw a Lace
 Of silke and silver at my face:
Watchet the silke was; and did make
A shew, as if't'ad been a snake:
The suddenness did me affright;
But though it scar'd, it did not bite.

Upon himselfe

I AM Sive-like, and can hold
 Nothing hot, or nothing cold.
Put in Love, and put in too
Jealousie, and both will through:
Put in Feare, and hope, and doubt;
What comes in, runnes quickly out:
Put in secrecies withall,
What ere enters, out it shall:

l. 158 that two *some copies of 48*: that, That *other copies*

116

But if you can stop the Sive,
For mine own part I'de as lieve,   10
Maides sho'd say, or Virgins sing,
Herrick keeps, as holds nothing.

Upon Love

LOVE'S a thing, (as I do heare)
Ever full of pensive feare;
Rather then to which I'le fall,
Trust me, I'le not like at all:
If to love I should entend,
Let my haire then stand an end:
And that terrour likewise prove,
Fatall to me in my love.
But if horrour cannot slake
Flames, which wo'd an entrance make;   10
Then the next thing I desire,
Is to love, and live i'th fire.

Reverence to Riches

LIKE to the Income must be our expence;
Mans Fortune must be had in reverence.

Devotion makes the Deity

WHO *formes a Godhead out of Gold or Stone,*
Makes not a God; but he that prayes to one.

To all young men that love

I COULD wish you all, who love,
That ye could your thoughts remove
From your Mistresses, and be,
Wisely wanton (like to me.)
I could wish you dispossest
Of that *Fiend that marres your rest*;
And with Tapers comes to fright
Your weake senses in the night.
I co'd wish, ye all, who frie
Cold as Ice, or coole as I.   10

But if flames best like ye, then
Much good do't ye Gentlemen.
I a merry heart will keep,
While you wring your hands and weep.

The Eyes

'TIS a known principle in War,
The eies be first, that conquer'd are.

No fault in women

No fault in women to refuse
The offer, which they most wo'd chuse.
No fault in women, to confesse
How tedious they are in their dresse.
No fault in women, to lay on
The tincture of *Vermillion:*
And there to give the cheek a die
Of white, where nature doth deny.
No fault in women, to make show
Of largeness, when th'are nothing so: 10
(When true it is, the out-side swels
With inward Buckram, little else.)
No fault in women, though they be
But seldome from suspition free:
No fault in womankind, at all,
If they but slip, and never fall.

Upon Shark. *Epig.*

SHARK, when he goes to any publick feast,
Eates to ones thinking, of all there, the least.
What saves the master of the House thereby?
When if the servants search, they may descry
In his wide Codpeece, (dinner being done)
Two Napkins cram'd up, and a silver Spoone.

Oberons *Feast*

SHAPCOT! To thee the Fairy State
I with discretion, dedicate.
Because thou prizest things that are
Curious, and un-familiar.
Take first the feast; these dishes gone;
Wee'l see the Fairy-Court *anon.*

A LITTLE mushroome table spred,
　　After short prayers, they set on bread;
A Moon-parcht grain of purest wheat,
With some small glit'ring gritt, to eate　　　10
His choyce bitts with; then in a trice
They make a feast lesse great then nice.
But all this while his eye is serv'd,
We must not thinke his eare was sterv'd:
But that there was in place to stir
His Spleen, the chirring Grashopper;
The merry Cricket, puling Flie,
The piping Gnat for minstralcy.
And now, we must imagine first,
The Elves present to quench his thirst　　　20
A pure seed-Pearle of Infant dew,
Brought and besweetned in a blew
And pregnant violet; which done,
His kitling eyes begin to runne
Quite through the table, where he spies
The hornes of paperie Butterflies,
Of which he eates, and tastes a little
Of that we call the Cuckoes spittle.
A little Fuz-ball-pudding stands
By, yet not blessed by his hands,　　　30
That was too coorse; but then forthwith
He ventures boldly on the pith
Of sugred Rush, and eates the sagge
And well bestrutted Bees sweet bagge:
Gladding his pallat with some store
Of Emits eggs; what wo'd he more?
But Beards of Mice, a Newt's stew'd thigh,
A bloated Earewig, and a Flie;

With the Red-capt worme, that's shut
Within the concave of a Nut,   40
Browne as his Tooth. A little Moth,
Late fatned in a piece of cloth:
With withered cherries; Mandrakes eares;
Moles eyes; to these, the slain-Stags teares:
The unctuous dewlaps of a Snaile;
The broke-heart of a Nightingale
Ore-come in musicke; with a wine,
Ne're ravisht from the flattering Vine,
But gently prest from the soft side
Of the most sweet and dainty Bride,   50
Brought in a dainty daizie, which
He fully quaffs up to bewitch
His blood to height; this done, commended
Grace by his Priest; *The feast is ended.*

Event of things not in our power

BY Time, and Counsell, doe the best we can,
Th'event is never in the power of man.

Upon her blush

WHEN *Julia* blushes, she do's show
Cheeks like to Roses, when they blow.

Merits make the man

OUR Honours, and our Commendations be
Due to the Merits, not Authoritie.

To Virgins

HEARE ye Virgins, and Ile teach,
What the times of old did preach.
Rosamond was in a Bower
Kept, as *Danae* in a Tower:
But yet Love (who subtile is)
Crept to that, and came to this.
Be ye lockt up like to these,
Or the rich *Hesperides*;

Or those Babies in your eyes,
In their Christall Nunneries;
Notwithstanding Love will win,
Or else force a passage in:
And as coy be, as you can,
Gifts will get ye, or the man.

Vertue

EACH must, in vertue, strive for to excell;
That man lives twice, that lives the first life well.

The Bell-man

FROM noise of Scare-fires rest ye free,
From Murders *Benedicitie.*
From all mischances, that may fright
Your pleasing slumbers in the night:
Mercie secure ye all, and keep
The Goblin from ye, while ye sleep.
Past one aclock, and almost two,
My Masters all, *Good day to you.*

Bashfulnesse

OF all our parts, the eyes expresse
The sweetest kind of bashfulnesse.

To the most accomplisht Gentleman, Master Edward Norgate, Clark of the Signet to His Majesty. Epig.

FOR one so rarely tun'd to fit all parts;
For one to whom espous'd are all the Arts;
Long have I sought for: but co'd never see
Them all concenter'd in one man, but Thee.
Thus, thou, that man art, whom the Fates conspir'd
To make but One (and that's thy selfe) admir'd.

Upon Prudence Baldwin *her sicknesse*

PRUE, my dearest Maid, is sick,
  Almost to be Lunatick:
Æsculapius! come and bring
Means for her recovering;
And a gallant Cock shall be
Offer'd up by Her, to Thee.

To Apollo. *A short Hymne*

PHŒBUS! when that I a Verse,
  Or some numbers more rehearse;
Tune my words, that they may fall,
Each way smoothly Musicall:
For which favour, there shall be
Swans devoted unto thee.

A Hymne to Bacchus

BACCHUS, let me drink no more;
  Wild are Seas, that want a shore.
When our drinking has no stint,
There is no one pleasure in't.
I have drank up for to please
Thee, that great cup *Hercules:*
Urge no more; and there shall be
Daffadills g'en up to Thee.

Upon Bungie

BUNGIE do's fast; looks pale; puts Sack-cloth on;
  Not out of Conscience, or Religion:
Or that this Yonker keeps so strict a Lent,
Fearing to break the Kings Commandement:
But being poore, and knowing Flesh is deare,
He keeps not one, but many Lents i'th'yeare.

On himselfe

Here down my wearyed limbs Ile lay;
My Pilgrims staffe; my weed of gray:
My Palmers hat; my Scallops shell;
My Crosse; my Cord; and all farewell.
For having now my journey done,
(Just at the setting of the Sun)
Here I have found a Chamber fit,
(God and good friends be thankt for it)
Where if I can a lodger be
A little while from Tramplers free;   10
At my up-rising next, I shall,
If not requite, yet thank ye all.
Meane while, the *Holy-Rood* hence fright
The fouler Fiend, and evill Spright,
From scaring you or yours this night.

Casualties

Good things, that come of course, far lesse doe please,
Then those, which come by sweet contingences.

Bribes and Gifts get all

Dead falls the Cause, if once the Hand be mute;
But let that speak, the Client gets the suit.

The end

If well thou hast begun, goe on fore-right;
It is the End that crownes us, not the Fight.

Upon a child that dyed

Here she lies, a pretty bud,
Lately made of flesh and blood:
Who, as soone, fell fast asleep,
As her little eyes did peep.
Give her strewings; but not stir
The earth, that lightly covers her.

Upon Sneape. *Epig.*

SNEAPE has a face so brittle, that it breaks
Forth into blushes, whensoere he speaks.

Content, not cates

'TIS not the food, but the content
That makes the Tables merriment.
Where Trouble serves the board, we eate
The Platters there, as soone as meat.
A little Pipkin with a bit
Of Mutton, or of Veale in it,
Set on my Table, (Trouble-free)
More then a Feast contenteth me.

The Entertainment: or, *Porch-verse, at the Marriage of Mr.* Hen. Northly, *and the most witty Mrs.* Lettice Yard

WEELCOME! but yet no entrance, till we blesse
First you, then you, and both for white successe.
Profane no Porch young man and maid, for fear
Ye wrong the *Threshold-god*, that keeps peace here:
Please him, and then all good-luck will betide
You, the brisk Bridegroome, you the dainty Bride.
Do all things sweetly, and in comely wise;
Put on your Garlands first, then Sacrifice:
That done; when both of you have seemly fed,
We'll call on Night, to bring ye both to Bed: 10
Where being laid, all Faire signes looking on,
Fish-like, encrease then to a million:
And millions of spring-times may ye have,
Which spent, one death, bring to ye both one Grave.

The good-night or Blessing

BLESSINGS, in abundance come,
To the Bride, and to her Groome;
May the Bed, and this short night,
Know the fulness of delight!

3.14 one death *ed.*: on death *48*

Pleasures, many here attend ye,
And ere long, a Boy Love send ye
Curld and comely, and so trimme,
Maides (in time) may ravish him.
Thus a dew of Graces fall
On ye both; Goodnight to all.   10

Upon Leech

L EECH boasts, he has a Pill, that can alone,
With speed give sick men their salvation:
'Tis strange, his Father long time has been ill,
And credits Physick, yet not trusts his Pill:
And why? he knowes he must of Cure despaire,
Who makes the slie Physitian his Heire.

To Daffadills

1. F AIRE Daffadills, we weep to see
You haste away so soone:
As yet the early-rising Sun
Has not attain'd his Noone.
Stay, stay,
Untill the hasting day
Has run
But to the Even-song;
And, having pray'd together, we
Will goe with you along.   10

2. We have short time to stay, as you,
We have as short a Spring;
As quick a growth to meet Decay,
As you, or any thing.
We die,
As your hours doe, and drie
Away,
Like to the Summers raine;
Or as the pearles of Mornings dew
Ne'r to be found againe.   20

To a Maid

Y OU say, you love me; that I thus must prove;
If that you lye, then I will sweare you love.

Upon a Lady that dyed in child-bed, and left a daughter behind her

A s Gilly flowers do but stay
To blow, and seed, and so away;
So you sweet Lady (sweet as May)
The gardens-glory liv'd a while,
To lend the world your scent and smile.
But when your own faire print was set
Once in a Virgin *Flosculet*,
(Sweet as your selfe, and newly blown)
To give that life, resign'd your own:
But so, as still the mothers power   10
Lives in the pretty Lady-flower.

A New-yeares gift sent to Sir Simeon Steward

N o newes of Navies burnt at Seas;
No noise of late spawn'd *Tittyries*:
No closset plot, or open vent,
That frights men with a Parliament:
No new devise, or late found trick,
To read by th'Starres, the Kingdoms sick:
No ginne to catch the State, or wring
The free-born Nosthrills of the King,
We send to you; but here a jolly
Verse crown'd with *Yvie*, and with *Holly*:   10
That tels of Winters Tales and Mirth,
That Milk-maids make about the hearth,
Of Christmas sports, the *Wassell-boule*,
That's tost up, after *Fox-i'th'hole*:
Of *Blind-man-buffe*, and of the care
That young men have to shooe the *Mare*:

3.14 That's] That *48* (cf. 231, l. 57)

Of Twelf-tide Cakes, of Pease, and Beanes
Wherewith ye make those merry Sceanes,
When as ye chuse your King and Queen,
And cry out, *Hey, for our town green.*   20
Of Ash-heapes, in the which ye use
Husbands and Wives by streakes to chuse:
Of crackling Laurell, which fore-sounds,
A Plentious harvest to your grounds:
Of these, and such like things, for shift,
We send in stead of New-yeares gift.
Read then, and when your faces shine
With bucksome meat and capring Wine:
Remember us in Cups full crown'd,
And let our Citie-health go round,   30
Quite through the young maids and the men,
To the ninth number, if not tenne;
Untill the fired Chesnuts leape
For joy, to see the fruits ye reape,
From the plumpe Challice, and the Cup,
That tempts till it be tossed up:
Then as ye sit about your embers,
Call not to mind those fled Decembers;
But think on these, that are t'appeare,
As Daughters to the instant yeare: 40
Sit crown'd with Rose-buds, and carouse,
Till *Liber Pater* twirles the house
About your eares; and lay upon
The yeare (your cares) that's fled and gon.
And let the russet Swaines the Plough
And Harrow hang up resting now;
And to the Bag-pipe all addresse;
Till sleep takes place of wearinesse.
And thus, throughout, with Christmas playes
Frolick the full twelve Holy-dayes.   50

Mattens, or morning Prayer

WHEN with the Virgin morning thou do'st rise,
  Crossing thy selfe; come thus to sacrifice:
First wash thy heart in innocence, then bring
Pure hands, pure habits, pure, pure every thing.

Next to the Altar humbly kneele, and thence,
Give up thy soule in clouds of frankinsence.
Thy golden Censors fil'd with odours sweet,
Shall make thy actions with their ends to meet.

Evensong

BEGINNE with *Jove*; then is the worke halfe done;
And runnes most smoothly, when tis well begunne.
Jove's is the first and last: The Morn's his due,
The midst is thine; But *Joves* the Evening too;
As sure as *Mattins* do's to him belong,
So sure he layes claime to the *Evensong*.

The Bracelet to Julia

WHY I tye about thy wrist,
  Julia, this my silken twist;
For what other reason is't,
But to shew thee how in part,
Thou my pretty Captive art?
But thy Bondslave is my heart:
'Tis but silke that bindeth thee,
Knap the thread, and thou art free:
But 'tis otherwise with me;
I am bound, and fast bound so,   10
That from thee I cannot go;
If I co'd, I wo'd not so.

The Christian Militant

A MAN prepar'd against all ills to come,
  That dares to dead the fire of martirdome:
That sleeps at home; and sayling there at ease,
Feares not the fierce sedition of the Seas:
That's counter-proofe against the Farms mis-haps,
Undreadfull too of courtly thunderclaps:
That weares one face (like heaven) and never showes
A change, when Fortune either comes, or goes:
That keepes his own strong guard, in the despight
Of what can hurt by day, or harme by night: 10

2 (*title*) Bracelet *ed.*: Braclet 48

128

That takes and re-delivers every stroake
Of Chance, (as made up all of rock, and oake:)
That sighs at others death; smiles at his own
Most dire and horrid crucifixion.
Who for true glory suffers thus; we grant
Him to be here our *Christian militant.*

A short Hymne to Larr

THOUGH I cannot give thee fires
   Glit'ring to my free desires:
These accept, and Ile be free,
Offering *Poppy* unto thee.

Another to Neptune

MIGHTY *Neptune*, may it please
   Thee, the *Rector* of the Seas,
That my Barque may safely runne
Through thy watrie-region;
And a *Tunnie-fish* shall be
Offer'd up, with thanks to thee.

Upon Greedy. *Epig*

AN old, old widow *Greedy* needs wo'd wed,
   Not for affection to her, or her Bed;
But in regard, 'twas often said, this old
Woman wo'd bring him more then co'd be told,
He tooke her; now the jest in this appeares,
So old she was, that none co'd tell her yeares.

His embalming to Julia

FOR my embalming, *Julia*, do but this,
   Give thou my lips but their supreamest kiss:
Or else trans-fuse thy breath into the chest,
Where my small reliques must for ever rest:
That breath the *Balm*, the *myrrh*, the *Nard* shal be,
To give an *incorruption* unto me.

Gold, before Goodnesse

HOW rich a man is, all desire to know;
But none enquires if good he be, or no.

The Kisse. A Dialogue

1. AMONG thy Fancies, tell me this,
What is the thing we call a kisse?
2. I shall resolve ye, what it is.

It is a creature born and bred
Between the lips, (all cherrie-red,)
By love and warme desires fed,
Chor. And makes more soft the Bridall Bed.

2. It is an active flame, that flies,
First, to the Babies of the eyes;
And charmes them there with lullabies;   10
Chor. And stils the Bride too, when she cries.

2. Then to the chin, the cheek, the eare,
It frisks, and flyes, now here, now there,
'Tis now farre off, and then tis nere;
Chor. And here, and there, and every where.

1. Ha's it a speaking virtue? 2. Yes;
1. How speaks it, say? 2. Do you but this,
Part your joyn'd lips, then speaks your kisse;
Chor. And this loves sweetest language is.

1. Has it a body? 2. I, and wings   20
With thousand rare encolourings:
And as it flyes, it gently sings,
Chor. Love, honie yeelds; but never stings

The admonition

SEEST thou those *Diamonds* which she weares
In that rich Carkanet;
Or those on her dishevel'd haires,
Faire *Pearles* in order set?

Beleeve young man all those were teares
    By wretched Wooers sent,
In mournfull *Hyacinths* and *Rue*,
    That figure discontent;
Which when not warmed by her view,
    By cold neglect, each one,   10
Congeal'd to Pearle and stone;
    Which precious spoiles upon her,
    She weares as trophees of her honour.
Ah then consider! What all this implies;
She that will weare thy teares, wo'd weare thine eyes.

To his honoured kinsman Sir William Soame. *Epig.*

I CAN but name thee, and methinks I call
  All that have been, or are canonicall
For love and bountie, to come neare, and see,
Their many vertues volum'd up in thee;
In thee Brave Man! Whose incorrupted fame,
Casts forth a light like to a Virgin flame:
And as it shines, it throwes a scent about,
As when a Rain-bow in perfumes goes out.
So vanish hence, but leave a name, as sweet,
As *Benjamin*, and *Storax*, when they meet.   10

On himselfe

ASKE me, why I do not sing
  To the tension of the string,
As I did, not long ago,
When my numbers full did flow?
Griefe (ay me!) hath struck my Lute,
And my tongue at one time mute.

To Larr

NO more shall I, since I am driven hence,
  Devote to thee my graines of Frankinsence:
No more shall I from mantle-trees hang downe,
To honour thee, my little Parsly crown:

No more shall I (I feare me) to thee bring
My chives of Garlick for an offering:
No more shall I, from henceforth, heare a quire
Of merry Crickets by my Country fire.
Go where I will, thou luckie *Larr* stay here,
Warme by a glit'ring chimnie all the yeare.　　10

The departure of the good Dæmon

WHAT can I do in Poetry,
　Now the good Spirit's gone from me?
Why nothing now, but lonely sit,
And over-read what I have writ.

Clemency

FOR punishment in warre, it will suffice,
　If the chiefe Author of the faction dyes;
Let but few smart, but strike a feare through all:
Where the fault springs, there let the judgement fall.

His age, dedicated to his peculiar friend, M. John Wickes, under the name of Posthumus

1. AH *Posthumus*! Our yeares hence flye,
　And leave no sound; nor piety,
　　　　Or prayers, or vow
　Can keepe the wrinkle from the brow:
　　　　But we must on,
　As Fate do's lead or draw us; none,
　None, *Posthumus*, co'd ere decline
　The doome of cruell *Proserpine*.

2. The pleasing wife, the house, the ground
　Must all be left, no one plant found　　　　10
　　　　To follow thee,
　Save only the *Curst-Cipresse* tree:
　　　　A merry mind
　Looks forward, scornes what's left behind:
　Let's live, my *Wickes*, then, while we may,
　And here enjoy our Holiday.

3. W'ave seen the past-best Times, and these
   Will nere return, we see the Seas,
          And Moons to wain;
   But they fill up their Ebbs again: 20
          But vanisht man,
   Like to a Lilly-lost, nere can,
   Nere can repullulate, or bring
   His dayes to see a second Spring.

4. But on we must, and thither tend,
   Where *Anchus* and rich *Tullus* blend
          Their sacred seed:
   Thus has *Infernall Jove* decreed;
          We must be made,
   Ere long, a song, ere long, a shade.   30
   Why then, since life to us is short,
   Lets make it full up, by our sport.

5. Crown we our Heads with Roses then,
   And 'noint with *Tirian Balme*; for when
          We two are dead,
   The world with us is buried.
          Then live we free,
   As is the Air, and let us be
   Our own fair wind, and mark each one
   Day with the white and Luckie stone.   40

6. We are not poore; although we have
   No roofs of Cedar, nor our brave
          Baiæ, nor keep
   Account of such a flock of sheep;
          Nor Bullocks fed
   To lard the shambles: Barbels bred
   To kisse our hands, nor do we wish
   For *Pollio's* Lampries in our dish.

7. If we can meet, and so conferre,
   Both by a shining Salt-seller;   50
          And have our Roofe,
   Although not archt, yet weather proofe,
          And seeling free,
   From that cheape *Candle baudery*:
   We'le eate our Beane with that full mirth,
   As we were Lords of all the earth.

8. Well then, on what Seas we are tost,
   Our comfort is, we can't be lost.
         Let the winds drive
   Our Barke; yet she will keepe alive   60
         Amidst the deepes;
   'Tis constancy (my *Wickes*) which keepes
   The Pinnace up; which though she erres
   I'th'Seas, she saves her passengers.

9. Say, we must part (sweet mercy blesse
   Us both i'th'Sea, Camp, Wildernesse)
         Can we so farre
   Stray, to become lesse circular,
         Then we are now?
   No, no, that selfe same heart, that vow,   70
   Which made us one, shall ne'r undoe;
   Or ravell so, to make us two.

10. Live in thy peace; as for my selfe,
    When I am bruised on the Shelfe
          Of Time, and show
    My locks behung with frost and snow:
          When with the reume,
    The cough, the ptisick, I consume
    Unto an almost nothing; then,
    The Ages fled, Ile call agen: 80

11. And with a teare compare these last
    Lame, and bad times, with those are past,
          While *Baucis* by,
    My old leane wife, shall kisse it dry:
          And so we'l sit
    By'th'fire, foretelling snow and slit,
    And weather by our aches, grown
    Now old enough to be our own

12. True Calenders, as Pusses eare
    Washt or's to tell what change is neare: 90
          Then to asswage
    The gripings of the chine by age;

I'le call my young
Iülus to sing such a song
I made upon my *Julia's* brest;
And of her blush at such a feast.

13. Then shall he read that flowre of mine
    Enclos'd within a christall shrine:
              A Primrose next;
    A piece, then of a higher text: 100
              For to beget
    In me a more transcendant heate,
    Then that insinuating fire,
    Which crept into each aged Sire.

14. When the faire *Hellen*, from her eyes,
    Shot forth her loving Sorceries:
              At which I'le reare
    Mine aged limbs above my chaire:
              And hearing it,
    Flutter and crow, as in a fit   110
    Of fresh concupiscence, and cry,
    No lust theres like to Poetry.

15. Thus frantick crazie man (God wot)
    Ile call to mind things half forgot:
              And oft between,
    Repeat the Times that I have seen!
              Thus ripe with tears,
    And twisting my *Iülus* hairs;
    Doting, Ile weep and say (In Truth)
    Baucis, these were my sins of youth.   120

16. Then next Ile cause my hopefull Lad
    (If a wild Apple can be had)
              To crown the Hearth,
    (*Larr* thus conspiring with our mirth)
              Then to infuse
    Our browner Ale into the cruse:
    Which sweetly spic't, we'l first carouse
    Unto the *Genius* of the house.

17. Then the next health to friends of mine
    (Loving the brave *Burgundian wine*)   130

High sons of Pith,
Whose fortunes I have frolickt with:
Such as co'd well
Bear up the Magick bough, and spel:
And dancing 'bout the Mystick *Thyrse*,
Give up the just applause to verse:

18. To those, and then agen to thee
We'l drink, my *Wickes*, untill we be
Plump as the cherry,
Though not so fresh, yet full as merry   140
As the crickit;
The untam'd Heifer, or the Pricket,
Untill our tongues shall tell our ears,
W'are younger by a score of years.

19. Thus, till we see the fire lesse shine
From th'embers, then the kitlings eyne,
We'l still sit up,
Sphering about the wassail cup,
To all those times,
Which gave me honour for my Rhimes,   150
The cole once spent, we'l then to bed,
Farre more then night bewearied.

A short hymne to Venus

GODDESSE, I do love a Girle
Rubie-lipt, and tooth'd with *Pearl:*
If so be, I may but prove
Luckie in this Maide I love:
I will promise there shall be
Mirtles offer'd up to Thee.

To a Gentlewoman on just dealing

TRUE to your self, and sheets, you'l have me swear,
You shall; if righteous dealing I find there.
Do not you fall through frailty; Ile be sure
To keep my Bond still free from forfeiture.

The hand and tongue

TWO parts of us successively command;
   The tongue in peace; but then in warre the hand.

Upon a delaying Lady

COME come away,
   Or let me go;
Must I here stay,
Because y'are slow;
And will continue so?
Troth Lady, no.

2. I scorne to be
   A slave to state:
   And since I'm free,
   I will not wait,   10
   Henceforth at such a rate,
   For needy Fate.

3. If you desire
   My spark sho'd glow,
   The peeping fire
   You must blow;
   Or I shall quickly grow,
   To Frost or Snow.

To the Lady Mary Villars, *Governesse to the Princesse* Henretta

WHEN I of *Villars* doe but heare the name,
   It calls to mind, that mighty *Buckingham,*
Who was your brave exalted Uncle here,
(Binding the wheele of Fortune to his Sphere)
Who spurn'd at Envie; and co'd bring, with ease,
An end to all his stately purposes.
For his love then, whose sacred Reliques show
Their Resurrection, and their growth in you:
And for my sake, who ever did prefer
You, above all Those *Sweets* of *Westminster:*   10
Permit my Book to have a free accesse
To kisse your hand, most Dainty Governesse.

3.9 who ever] whoever *48*

Upon his Julia

WILL ye heare, what I can say
    Briefly of my *Julia?*
Black and rowling is her eye,
Double chinn'd, and forehead high:
Lips she has, all Rubie red,
Cheeks like Creame Enclarited:
And a nose that is the grace
And *Proscenium* of her face.
So that we may guesse by these,
The other parts will richly please.   10

To Flowers

IN time of life, I grac't ye with my Verse;
    Doe now your flowrie honours to my Herse.
You shall not languish, trust me: Virgins here
Weeping, shall make ye flourish all the yeere.

To my ill Reader

THOU say'st my lines are hard;
    And I the truth will tell;
They are both hard, and marr'd,
    If thou not read'st them well.

The power in the people

LET Kings Command, and doe the best they may,
    The saucie Subjects still will beare the sway.

A Hymne to Venus, *and* Cupid

SEA-BORN Goddesse, let me be,
    By thy sonne thus grac't, and thee;
That when ere I wooe, I find
Virgins coy, but not unkind.
Let me when I kisse a maid,
Taste her lips, so over-laid
With Loves-sirrop; that I may,
In your Temple, when I pray,
Kisse the Altar, and confess
Ther's in love, no bitterness.   10

On Julia's *Picture*

HOW am I ravisht! When I do but see,
The Painters art in thy *Sciography*?
If so, how much more shall I dote thereon,
When once he gives it incarnation?

Her Bed

SEE'ST thou that Cloud as silver cleare,
Plump, soft, & swelling every where?
Tis *Julia's* Bed, and she sleeps there.

Her Legs

FAIN would I kiss my *Julia's* dainty Leg,
Which is as white and hair-less as an egge.

Upon her Almes

SEE how the poore do waiting stand,
For the expansion of thy hand.
A wafer Dol'd by thee, will swell
Thousands to feed by miracle.

Rewards

STILL to our gains our chief respect is had;
Reward it is, that makes us good or bad.

Nothing new

NOTHING is New: we walk where others went.
Ther's no vice now, but has his president.

The Rainbow

LOOK, how the *Rainbow* doth appeare
But in one onely *Hemisphere:*
So likewise after our disseace,
No more is seen the Arch of Peace.
That Cov'nant's here; The under-bow,
That nothing shoots, but war and woe.

The meddow verse or Aniversary to
Mistris Bridget Lowman

COME with the Spring-time, forth Fair Maid, and be
    This year again, the *medows Deity*.
Yet ere ye enter, give us leave to set
Upon your Head this flowry Coronet:
To make this neat distinction from the rest;
You are the Prime, and Princesse of the Feast:
To which, with silver feet lead you the way,
While sweet-breath Nimphs, attend on you this Day.
This is your houre; and best you may command,
Since you are Lady of this Fairie land.   10
Full mirth wait on you; and such mirth as shall
Cherrish the cheek, but make none blush at all.

The parting verse, the feast there
ended

LOTH to depart, but yet at last, each one
    Back must now go to's habitation:
Not knowing thus much, when we once do sever,
Whether or no, that we shall meet here ever.
As for my self, since time a thousand cares
And griefs hath fil'de upon my silver hairs;
'Tis to be doubted whether I next yeer,
Or no, shall give ye a re-meeting here.
If die I must, then my last vow shall be,
You'l with a tear or two, remember me,   10
Your sometime Poet; but if fates do give
Me longer date, and more fresh springs to live:
Oft as your field, shall her old age renew,
Herrick shall make the meddow-verse for you.

Upon Judith. Epig.

JUDITH has cast her old-skin, and got new;
    And walks fresh varnisht to the publick view.
Foule *Judith* was; and foule she will be known,
For all this fair *Transfiguration*.

Long and lazie

THAT was the Proverb. Let my mistresse be
Lasie to others, but be long to me.

Upon Ralph. Epig.

CURSE not the mice, no grist of thine they eat:
But curse thy children, they consume thy wheat.

To the right honourable, Philip, Earle of Pembroke, and Montgomerie

How dull and dead are books, that cannot show
A *Prince* of *Pembroke*, and that *Pembroke*, you!
You, who are High born, and a Lord no lesse
Free by your fate, then Fortunes mightinesse,
Who hug our Poems (Honourd Sir) and then
The paper gild, and Laureat the pen.
Nor suffer you the Poets to sit cold,
But warm their wits, and turn their lines to gold.
Others there be, who righteously will swear
Those smooth-pac't Numbers, amble every where;   10
And these brave Measures go a stately trot;
Love those, like these; regard, reward them not.
But you my Lord, are One, whose hand along
Goes with your mouth, or do's outrun your tongue;
Paying before you praise; and cockring wit,
Give both the Gold and Garland unto it.

An hymne to Juno

STATELY Goddesse, do thou please,
Who art chief at marriages,
But to dresse the Bridall-Bed,
When my Love and I shall wed:
And a *Peacock* proud shall be
Offerd up by us, to thee.

3.2 of] or *48*

Upon Mease. *Epig.*

MEASE brags of Pullets which he eats: but *Mease*
Ne'r yet set tooth in stump, or rump of these.

Upon Sapho, *sweetly playing, and sweetly singing*

WHEN thou do'st play, and sweetly sing,
Whether it be the voice or string,
Or both of them, that do agree
Thus to en-trance and ravish me:
This, this I know, I'm oft struck mute;
And dye away upon thy Lute.

Upon Paske *a Draper*

PASKE, though his debt be due upon the day
Demands no money by a craving way;
For why sayes he, all debts and their arreares,
Have reference to the shoulders, not the eares.

Chop-Cherry

THOU gav'st me leave to kisse;
Thou gav'st me leave to wooe;
Thou mad'st me thinke by this,
And that, thou lov'dst me too.

2. But I shall ne'r forget,
How for to make thee merry;
Thou mad'st me chop, but yet,
Another snapt the Cherry.

To the most learned, wise, and Arch-Anti-quary, M. John Selden

I WHO have favour'd many, come to be
Grac't (now at last) or glorifi'd by thee.
Loe, I, the Lyrick Prophet, who have set
On many a head the Delphick Coronet,

Come unto thee for Laurell, having spent,
My wreaths on those, who little gave or lent.
Give me the *Daphne*, that the world may know it,
Whom they neglected, thou hast crown'd a Poet.
A City here of *Heroes* I have made,
Upon the rock, whose firm foundation laid,   10
Shall never shrink, where making thine abode,
Live thou a *Selden*, that's a Demi-god.

Upon himself

THOU shalt not All die; for while Love's fire shines
Upon his Altar, men shall read thy lines;
And learn'd Musicians shall to honour *Herricks*
Fame, and his Name, both set, and sing his Lyricks.

Upon wrinkles

WRINKLES no more are, or no lesse,
Then beauty turn'd to sowernesse.

Upon Prigg

PRIGG, when he comes to houses, oft doth use
(Rather then fail) to steal from thence old shoes:
Sound or unsound, be they rent or whole,
Prigg bears away the body and the sole.

Upon Moon

MOON is an Usurer, whose gain,
Seldome or never, knows a wain,
Onely Moons conscience, we confesse,
That ebs from pittie lesse and lesse.

Pray and prosper

FIRST offer Incense, then thy field and meads
Shall smile and smell the better by thy beads.
The spangling Dew dreg'd o're the grasse shall be
Turn'd all to Mell, and Manna there for thee.

Butter of *Amber*, *Cream*, and *Wine*, and *Oile*
Shall run, as rivers, all throughout thy soyl.
Wod'st thou to sincere-silver turn thy mold?
Pray once, twice pray; and turn thy ground to gold.

His *Lachrimæ* or *Mirth*, *turn'd*
to mourning

1.   CALL me no more,
          As heretofore,
  The musick of a Feast;
     Since now (alas)
     The mirth, that was
In me, is dead or ceast.

2.   Before I went
       To banishment
Into the loathed West;
    I co'd rehearse   10
    A Lyrick verse,
And speak it with the best.

3.   But time (Ai me)
      Has laid, I see
My Organ fast asleep;
    And turn'd my voice
    Into the noise
Of those that sit and weep.

Upon Shift

SHIFT now has cast his clothes: got all things new;
Save but his hat, and that he cannot mew.

Upon Cuts

IF wounds in clothes, *Cuts* calls his rags, 'tis cleere,
His linings are the matter running there.

Gain and Gettings

WHEN others gain much by the present cast,
The coblers getting time, is at the Last.

To the most fair and lovely Mistris, Anne Soame, *now Lady* Abdie

So smell those odours that do rise
From out the wealthy spiceries:
So smels the flowre of *blooming Clove*;
Or *Roses* smother'd in the stove:
So smells the Aire of spiced wine;
Or *Essences* of *Jessimine*:
So smells the Breath about the hives,
When well the work of hony thrives;
And all the *busie Factours* come
Laden with wax and hony home: 10
So smell those neat and woven Bowers,
All over-archt with *Oringe flowers*,
And *Almond blossoms*, that do mix
To make rich these *Aromatikes*:
So smell those bracelets, and those bands
Of *Amber* chaf't between the hands,
When thus enkindled they transpire
A noble perfume from the fire.
The wine of cherries, and to these,
The cooling breath of Respasses;   20
The smell of mornings milk, and cream;
Butter of *Cowslips* mixt with them;
Of rosted warden, or bak'd peare,
These are not to be reckon'd here;
When as the meanest part of her,
Smells like the maiden-Pomander.
Thus sweet she smells, or what can be
More lik'd by her, or lov'd by mee.

Upon his kinswoman Mistris Elizabeth Herrick

Sweet virgin, that I do not set
The pillars up of weeping *Jet*,
Or mournfull *Marble*; let thy shade
Not wrathfull seem, or fright the Maide,
Who hither at her wonted howers
Shall come to strew thy earth with flowers.

No, know (Blest Maide) when there's not one
Remainder left of Brasse or stone,
Thy living Epitaph shall be,
Though lost in them, yet found in me.   10
Dear, in thy *bed of Roses*, then,
Till this world shall dissolve as men,
Sleep, while we hide thee from the light,
Drawing thy curtains round: *Good night.*

A Panegerick to Sir Lewis Pemberton

TILL I shall come again, let this suffice,
    I send my salt, my sacrifice
To Thee, thy Lady, younglings, and as farre
    As to thy *Genius* and thy *Larre*;
To the worn Threshold, Porch, Hall, Parlour, Kitchin,
    The fat-fed smoking Temple, which in
The wholsome savour of thy mighty Chines
    Invites to supper him who dines,
Where laden spits, warp't with large Ribbs of Beefe,
    Not represent, but give reliefe   10
To the lanke-Stranger, and the sowre Swain;
    Where both may feed, and come againe:
For no black-bearded *Vigil* from thy doore
    Beats with a button'd-staffe the poore:
But from thy warm-love-hatching gates each may
    Take friendly morsels, and there stay
To Sun his thin-clad members, if he likes,
    For thou no Porter keep'st who strikes.
No commer to thy Roofe his *Guest-rite* wants;
    Or staying there, is scourg'd with taunts   20
Of some rough Groom, who (yirkt with Corns) sayes, Sir
    Y'ave dipt too long i'th Vinegar;
And with our Broth and bread, and bits; Sir, friend,
    Y'ave farced well, pray make an end;
Two dayes y'ave larded here; a third, yee know,
    Makes guests and fish smell strong; pray go
You to some other chimney, and there take
    Essay of other giblets; make
Merry at anothers hearth; y'are here
    Welcome as thunder to our beere: 30

Manners knowes distance, and a man unrude
    Wo'd soon recoile, and not intrude
His Stomach to a second Meale. No, no,
      Thy house, well fed and taught, can show
No such crab'd vizard: Thou hast learnt thy Train,
    With heart and hand to entertain:
And by the Armes-full (with a Brest unhid)
    As the old Race of mankind did,
When eithers heart, and eithers hand did strive
    To be the nearer Relative: 40
Thou do'st redeeme those times; and what was lost
    Of antient honesty, may boast
It keeps a growth in thee; and so will runne
    A course in thy Fames-pledge, *thy Sonne.*
Thus, like a *Roman Tribune,* thou thy gate
    Early setts ope to feast, and late:
Keeping no *currish Waiter* to affright,
    With blasting eye, the appetite,
Which fain would waste upon thy Cates, but that
    The *Trencher-creature* marketh what   50
Best and more suppling piece he cuts, and by
    Some private pinch tels danger's nie
A hand too desp'rate, or a knife that bites
    Skin deepe into the Porke, or lights
Upon some part of Kid, as if mistooke,
    When checked by the Butlers look.
No, no, thy bread, thy wine, thy jocund Beere
    Is not reserv'd for *Trebius* here,
But all, who at thy table seated are,
    Find equall freedome, equall fare;   60
And Thou, like to that *Hospitable God,*
    Jove, joy'st when guests make their abode
To eate thy Bullocks thighs, thy Veales, thy fat
    Weathers, and never grudged at.
The *Phesant, Partridge, Gotwit, Reeve, Ruffe, Raile,*
    The *Cock,* the *Curlew,* and the *quaile*;
These, and thy choicest viands do extend
    Their taste unto the lower end
Of thy glad table: not a dish more known
    To thee, then unto any one: 70
But as thy meate, so thy *immortall wine*
    Makes the smirk face of each to shine,

And spring fresh *Rose-buds*, while the salt, the wit
    Flowes from the Wine, and graces it:
While Reverence, waiting at the bashfull board,
    Honours my Lady and my Lord.
No scurrile jest; no open Sceane is laid
    Here, for to make the face affraid;
But temp'rate mirth dealt forth, and so discreet-
    ly that it makes the meate more sweet;   80
And adds perfumes unto the Wine, which thou
    Do'st rather poure forth, then allow
By cruse and measure; thus devoting Wine,
    As the *Canary* Isles were thine:
But with that wisdome, and that method, as
    No One that's there his guilty glasse
Drinks of distemper, or ha's cause to cry
    Repentance to his liberty.
No, thou know'st order, Ethicks, and ha's read
    All Oeconomicks, know'st to lead   90
A House-dance neatly, and can'st truly show,
    How farre a Figure ought to go,
Forward, or backward, side-ward, and what pace
    Can give, and what retract a grace;
What Gesture, Courtship; Comliness agrees,
    With those thy primitive decrees,
To give subsistance to thy house, and proofe,
    What *Genii* support thy roofe,
Goodnes and *Greatnes*; not the oaken Piles;
    For these, and marbles have their whiles   100
To last, but not their ever: Vertues Hand
    It is, which builds, 'gainst Fate to stand.
Such is thy house, whose firme foundations trust
    Is more in thee, then in her dust,
Or depth, these last may yeeld, and yearly shrinke,
    When what is strongly built, no chinke
Or yawning rupture can the same devoure,
    But fixt it stands, by her own power,
And well-laid bottome, on the iron and rock,
    Which tryes, and counter-stands the shock,   110
And *Ramme* of time and by vexation growes
    The stronger: *Vertue dies when foes*
Are wanting to her exercise, but great
    And large she spreads by dust, and sweat.

Safe stand thy Walls, and Thee, and so both will,
    Since neithers height was rais'd by th'ill
Of others; since no Stud, no Stone, no Piece,
    Was rear'd up by the Poore-mans fleece:
No Widowes Tenement was rackt to guild
    Or fret thy Seeling, or to build   120
A *Sweating-Closset*, to annoint the silke-
    soft-skin, or bath in *Asses milke*:
No *Orphans* pittance, left him, serv'd to set
    The Pillars up of *lasting Jet*,
For which their cryes might beate against thine eares,
    Or in the dampe Jet read their Teares.
No *Planke* from *Hallowed* Altar, do's appeale
    To yond' *Star-chamber*, or do's seale
A curse to Thee, or Thine; but all things even
    Make for thy peace, and pace to heaven.   130
Go on directly so, as just men may
    A thousand times, more sweare, then say,
This is that *Princely Pemberton*, who can
    Teach man to keepe a God in man:
And when wise Poets shall search out to see
    Good men, *They find them all in Thee.*

To his Valentine, *on S.* Valentines *day*

OFT have I heard both Youths and Virgins say,
    Birds chuse their Mates, and couple too, this day:
But by their flight I never can divine,
When I shall couple with my Valentine.

Upon Doll. *Epig.*

DOLL she so soone began the wanton trade;
    She ne'r remembers that she was a maide.

Upon Skrew. *Epig.*

SKREW lives by shifts; yet sweares by no small oathes;
    For all his shifts, he cannot shift his clothes.

Upon Linnit. *Epig.*

LINNIT playes rarely on the Lute, we know;
    And sweetly sings, but yet his breath sayes no.

Upon M. Ben. Johnson. Epig.

AFTER the rare Arch-Poet JOHNSON dy'd,
  The Sock grew loathsome, and the Buskins pride,
Together with the Stages glory stood
Each like a poore and pitied widowhood.
The Cirque prophan'd was; and all postures rackt:
For men did strut, and stride, and stare, not act.
Then temper flew from words; and men did squeake,
Looke red, and blow, and bluster, but not speake:
No Holy-Rage, or frantick-fires did stirre,
Or flash about the spacious Theater.   10
No clap of hands, or shout, or praises-proofe
Did crack the Play-house sides, or cleave her roofe.
Artlesse the Sceane was; and that monstrous sin
Of deep and *arrant ignorance* came in;
Such ignorance as theirs was, who once hist
At thy unequal'd Play, the *Alchymist*:
Oh fie upon 'em! Lastly too, all witt
In utter darkenes did, and still will sit
Sleeping the lucklesse Age out, till that she
Her Resurrection ha's again with Thee.   20

Another

THOU had'st the wreath before, now take the Tree;
  That henceforth none be *Laurel crown'd but Thee*.

To his Nephew, to be prosperous in his art of Painting

ON, as thou hast begunne, brave youth, and get
  The Palme from *Urbin*, *Titian*, *Tintarret*,
Brugel and *Coxie*, and the workes out-doe,
Of *Holben*, and That mighty *Ruben* too.
So draw, and paint, as none may do the like,
No, not the glory of the World, *Vandike*.

3.3 *Coxie ed.*: *Coxu 48*

Upon Glasse. *Epig.*

GLASSE, out of deepe, and out of desp'rate want,
Turn'd, from a Papist here, a Predicant.
A Vicarige at last *Tom Glasse* got here,
Just upon five and thirty pounds a yeare.
Adde to that thirty five, but five pounds more,
He'l turn a Papist, rancker then before.

A Vow to Mars

STORE of courage to me grant,
Now I'm turn'd a combatant:
Helpe me so, that I my *shield*,
(Fighting) lose not in the field.
That's the greatest shame of all,
That in warfare can befall.
Do but this; and there shall be
Offer'd up a Wolfe to thee.

To his maid Prew

THESE *Summer-Birds* did with thy Master stay
The times of warmth; but then they flew away;
Leaving their Poet (being now grown old)
Expos'd to all the comming Winters cold.
But thou *kind Prew* did'st with my Fates abide,
As well the Winters, as the Summers Tide:
For which thy Love, live with thy Master here,
Not two, but all the seasons of the yeare.

A Canticle to Apollo

PLAY *Phœbus* on thy Lute;
And we will all sit mute:
By listning to thy Lire,
That sets all eares on fire.

2. Hark, harke, the God do's play!
And as he leads the way
Through heaven, the very Spheres,
As men, turne all to eares.

A just man

A JUST man's like a Rock that turnes the wroth
Of all the raging Waves, into a froth.

Upon a hoarse singer

SING me to death; for till thy voice be cleare,
'Twill never please the pallate of mine eare.

How Pansies *or* Hearts-ease *came first*

FROLLICK Virgins once these were,
    Over-loving, (living here:)
Being here their ends deny'd
Ranne for Sweet-hearts mad, and dy'd.
Love in pitie of their teares,
And their losse in blooming yeares;
For their restlesse here-spent houres,
Gave them *Hearts-ease* turn'd to Flow'rs.

To his peculiar friend Sir Edward Fish, *Knight Baronet*

SINCE for thy full deserts (with all the rest
    Of these chaste spirits, that are here possest
Of Life eternall) Time has made Thee one,
For growth in this my rich Plantation:
Live here: But know 'twas vertue, & not chance,
That gave Thee this so high inheritance.
Keepe it for ever; grounded with the good,
Who hold fast here an endlesse lively-hood.

Larr's *portion, and the* Poets *part*

AT my homely Country-seat,
    I have there a little wheat;
Which I worke to Meale, and make
Therewithall a *Holy-cake*:
Part of which I give to *Larr*,
Part is my peculiar.

Upon Man

MAN is compos'd here of a two-fold part;
    The first of Nature, and the next of Art:
Art presupposes Nature; Nature shee
Prepares the way to mans docility.

Liberty

THOSE ills that mortall men endure,
    So long are capable of cure,
As they of freedome may be sure:
But that deni'd; a griefe, though small,
Shakes the whole Roofe, or ruines all.

Lots to be liked

LEARN this of me, where e'r thy Lot doth fall;
    Short lot, or not, to be content with all.

Griefes

JOVE may afford us thousands of reliefs;
    Since man expos'd is to a world of griefs.

Upon Eeles. Epig.

EELES winds and turnes, and cheats and steales; yet Eeles
    Driving these sharking trades, is out at heels.

The Dreame

BY Dream I saw, one of the three
    Sisters of Fate appear to me.
Close to my Beds side she did stand
Shewing me there a fire brand;
She told me too, as that did spend,
So drew my life unto an end.
Three quarters were consum'd of it;
Onely remain a little bit,
Which will be burnt up by and by,
Then *Julia* weep, for I must dy.   10

6.10 *Julia*] *Juha* 48

153

Upon Raspe *Epig*.

RASPE playes at Nine-holes; and 'tis known he gets
Many a Teaster by his game, and bets:
But of his gettings there's but little sign;
When one hole wasts more then he gets by Nine.

Upon Center *a Spectacle-maker with a flat nose*

CENTER is known weak sighted, and he sells
To others store of helpfull spectacles.
Why weres he none? Because we may suppose,
Where *Leaven* wants, there *Levill* lies the nose.

Clothes do but cheat and cousen us

AWAY with silks, away with Lawn,
Ile have no Sceans, or Curtains drawn:
Give me my Mistresse, as she is,
Drest in her nak't simplicities:
For as my Heart, ene so mine Eye
Is wone with flesh, not *Drapery*.

To Dianeme

SHEW me thy feet; shew me thy legs, thy thighes;
Shew me Those *Fleshie Principalities*;
Shew me that Hill (where smiling Love doth sit)
Having a living Fountain under it.
Shew me thy waste; Then let me there withall,
By the *Assention* of thy Lawn, see All.

Upon Electra

WHEN out of bed my Love doth spring,
'*Tis but as day a kindling*:
But when She's up and fully drest,
'Tis then *broad Day throughout the East*.

To his Booke

HAVE I not blest Thee? Then go forth; nor fear
Or spice, or fish, or fire, or close-stools here.
But with thy fair Fates leading thee, Go on
With thy most white *Predestination.*
Nor thinke these Ages that do hoarcely sing
The *farting Tanner*, and *familiar King*;
The *dancing Frier*, tatter'd in the bush;
Those monstrous lies of little *Robin Rush*:
Tom Chipperfeild, and pritty-*lisping Ned*,
That doted on a Maide of *Gingerbred*:   10
The *flying Pilcher*, and the *frisking Dace*,
With all the rabble of *Tim-Trundells* race,
(Bred from the dung-hils, and adulterous rhimes,)
Shall live, and thou not superlast all times?
No, no, thy Stars have destin'd Thee to see
The whole world die, and turn to dust with thee.
He's greedie of his life, who will not fall,
When as a publick ruine bears down All.

Of Love ✓

I DO not love, nor can it be
Love will in vain spend shafts on me:
I did this God-head once defie;
Since which I freeze, but cannot frie.
Yet out alas! the deaths the same,
Kil'd by a frost or by a flame.

Upon himself

I DISLIKT but even now;
Now I love I know not how.
Was I idle, and that while
Was I fier'd with a smile?
Ile to work, or pray; and then
I shall quite dislike agen.

Another ✓

LOVE he that will; it best likes me,
To have my neck from Loves yoke free.

3.5 to *Witt's Recreations 1650*: too *48*
4.2 yoke free *Witt's Recreations 1650*: yoke-free *48*

Upon Skinns. *Epig.*

S*KINNS* he din'd well to day; how do you think?
His Nails they were his meat, his Reume the drink.

Upon Pievish. Epig.

P*IEVISH* doth boast, that he's the very first
Of English Poets, and 'tis thought the Worst.

Upon Jolly *and* Jilly,
Epig.

J*OLLY* and *Jillie*, bite and scratch all day,
But yet get children (as the neighbours say.)
The reason is, though all the day they fight,
They cling and close, some minutes of the night.

The mad Maids song

1. G OOD morrow to the Day so fair;
   Good morning Sir to you:
   Good morrow to mine own torn hair
   Bedabled with the dew.

2. Good morning to this Prim-rose too;
   Good morrow to each maid;
   That will with flowers the *Tomb* bestrew,
   Wherein my Love is laid.

3. Ah woe is me, woe, woe is me,
   Alack and welladay!   10
   For pitty, Sir, find out that Bee,
   Which bore my Love away.

4. I'le seek him in your *Bonnet* brave;
   Ile seek him in your eyes;
   Nay, now I think th'ave made his grave
   I'th'bed of strawburies.

5. Ile seek him there; I know, ere this,
   The cold, cold Earth doth shake him;
   But I will go, or send a kisse
   By you, Sir, to awake him.   20

6. Pray hurt him not; though he be dead,
    He knowes well who do love him,
  And who with green-turfes reare his head,
    And who do rudely move him.

7. He's soft and tender (Pray take heed)
    With bands of Cow-slips bind him;
  And bring him home, but 'tis decreed,
    That I shall never find him.

To Springs and Fountains

I HEARD ye co'd coole heat; and came
  With hope you would allay the same:
Thrice I have washt, but feel no cold,
Nor find that true, which was foretold.
Me thinks like mine, your pulses beat;
And labour with unequall heat:
Cure, cure your selves, for I discrie,
Ye boil with Love, as well as I.

Upon Julia's *unlacing*
her self

TELL, if thou canst, (and truly) whence doth come
  This *Camphire, Storax, Spiknard, Galbanum*:
These *Musks*, these *Ambers*, and those other smells
(Sweet as the *Vestrie of the Oracles.*)
Ile tell thee; while my *Julia* did unlace
Her silken bodies, but a breathing space:
The passive Aire such odour then assum'd,
As when to *Jove* Great *Juno* goes perfum'd.
Whose pure-Immortall body doth transmit
A scent, that fills both Heaven and Earth with it.   10

To Bacchus, *a Canticle*

WHITHER dost thou whorry me,
  Bacchus, being full of thee?
This way, that way, that way, this,
Here, and there a fresh Love is.
That doth like me, this doth please;
Thus a thousand Mistresses,
I have now; yet I alone,
Having All, injoy not *One*.

The Lawne.

Wo'd I see Lawn, clear as the Heaven, and thin?
It sho'd be onely in my *Julia's* skin:
Which so betrayes her'blood, as we discover
The blush of cherries, when a Lawn's cast over.

The Frankincense.

When my off'ring next I make,
Be thy hand the hallowed Cake:
And thy brest the Altar, whence
Love may smell the *Frankincense*.

Upon Patrick *a footman, Epig.*

Now *Patrick* with his footmanship has done,
His eyes and ears strive which sho'd fastest run.

Upon Bridget. *Epig.*

Of foure teeth onely *Bridget* was possest;
Two she spat out, a cough forc't out the rest.

To Sycamores

I'm sick of Love; O let me lie
Under your shades, to sleep or die!
Either is welcome; so I have
Or here my Bed, or here my Grave.
Why do you sigh, and sob, and keep
Time with the tears, that I do weep?
Say, have ye sence, or do you prove
What *Crucifixions* are in Love?
I know ye do; and that's the why,
You sigh for Love, as well as I.   10

A Pastorall sung to the King: Montano, Silvio, and Mirtillo, Shepheards.

Mon. Bad are the times. *Sil.* And wors then they are we.
Mon. Troth, bad are both; worse fruit, and ill the tree:
The feast of Shepheards fail. *Sil.* None crowns the cup
Of *Wassaile* now, or sets the *quintell* up:
And He, who us'd to leade the Country-round,
Youthfull *Mirtillo*, Here he comes, Grief drownd.
Ambo Lets cheer him up. *Sil.* Behold him weeping ripe.
Mirt. Ah! *Amarillis*, farewell mirth and pipe;
Since thou art gone, no more I mean to play,
To these smooth Lawns, my mirthfull Roundelay.   10
Dear *Amarillis*! *Mon.* Hark! *Sil.* mark: *Mir.* this earth grew
    sweet
Where, *Amarillis*, Thou didst set thy feet.
Ambo. Poor pittied youth! *Mir.* And here the breth of kine
And sheep, grew more sweet, by that breth of Thine.
This flock of wooll, and this rich lock of hair,
This ball of *Cow-slips*, these she gave me here.
Sil. Words sweet as Love it self. *Montano*, Hark.
Mirt. This way she came, and this way too she went;
How each thing smells divinely redolent!
Like to a field of beans, when newly blown;   20
Or like a medow being lately mown.
Mont. A sweet-sad passion.——
Mirt. In dewie-mornings when she came this way,
Sweet Bents wode bow, to give my Love the day:
And when at night, she folded had her sheep,
Daysies wo'd shut, and closing, sigh and weep.
Besides (Ai me!) since she went hence to dwell,
The voices Daughter nea'r spake syllable.
But she is gone. *Sil.* Mirtillo, tell us whether,
Mirt. Where she and I shall never meet together.   30
Mont. Fore-fend it *Pan*, and *Pales* do thou please
To give an end: *Mir.* To what? *Scil.* such griefs as these.
Mirt. Never, O never! Still I may endure
The wound I suffer, never find a cure.
Mont. Love for thy sake will bring her to these hills
And dales again: *Mir.* No I will languish still;
And all the while my part shall be to weepe;

1.3 feast] (?) feasts

And with my sighs, call home my bleating sheep:
And in the Rind of every comely tree
Ile carve thy name, and in that name kisse thee: 40
Mont. Set with the Sunne, thy woes: *Scil.* The day grows old:
And time it is our full-fed flocks to fold.

Chor. The shades grow great; but greater growes our sorrow,
But lets go steepe
Our eyes in sleepe;
And meet to weepe
To morrow.

The Poet loves a Mistresse, but not to marry

1. I DO not love to wed,
   Though I do like to wooe;
   And for a maidenhead
   Ile beg, and buy it too.

2. Ile praise, and Ile approve
   Those maids that never vary;
   And fervently Ile love;
   But yet I would not marry.

3. Ile hug, Ile kisse, Ile play,
   And Cock-like Hens Ile tread: 10
   And sport it any way;
   But in the Bridall Bed:

4. For why? that man is poore,
   Who hath but one of many;
   But crown'd he is with store,
   That single may have any.

5. Why then, say, what is he
   (To freedome so unknown)
   Who having two or three,
   Will be content with one?   20

Upon Flimsey. *Epig.*

WHY walkes *Nick Flimsey* like a Male-content?
Is it because his money all is spent?
No, but because the Ding-thrift now is poore,
And knowes not where i'th world to borrow more.

Upon Shewbread. *Epig.*

LAST night thou didst invite me home to eate;
  And shew'st me there much Plate, but little meat;
Prithee, when next thou do'st invite, barre State,
And give me meate, or give me else thy Plate.

The Willow Garland

A WILLOW Garland thou did'st send
   Perfum'd (last day) to me:
Which did but only this portend,
   I was forsooke by thee.

Since so it is; Ile tell thee what,
   To morrow thou shalt see
Me weare the Willow; after that,
   To dye upon the Tree.

As Beasts unto the Altars go
   With Garlands drest, so I   10
Will, with my Willow-wreath also,
   Come forth and sweetly dye.

A Hymne to Sir Clipseby Crew

'TWAS not Lov's Dart;
   Or any blow
Of want, or foe,
   Did wound my heart
With an eternall smart:

   But only you,
   My sometimes known
   Companion,
   (My dearest *Crew*,)
That me unkindly slew.   10

   May your fault dye,
   And have no name
   In Bookes of fame;
   Or let it lye
Forgotten now, as I.

We parted are,
And now no more,
As heretofore,
By jocund Larr,
Shall be familiar.   20

But though we Sever
My *Crew* shall see,
That I will be
Here faithlesse never;
But love my *Clipseby* ever.

Upon Roots. *Epig.*

Roots had no money; yet he went o'th score
For a wrought Purse; can any tell wherefore?
Say, What sho'd *Roots* do with a Purse in print,
That h'ad nor Gold or Silver to put in't? ·

Upon Craw

CRAW cracks in sirrop; and do's stinking say,
Who can hold that (my friends) that will away?

Observation

WHO to the North, or South, doth set
His Bed, Male children shall beget.

Empires

EMPIRES of Kings, are now, and ever were,
(As *Salust* saith) co-incident to feare.

Felicity, quick of flight

EVERY time seemes short to be,
That's measur'd by felicity:
But one halfe houre, that's made up here
With griefe; seemes longer then a yeare.

Putrefaction

PUTREFACTION is the end
Of all that Nature doth entend.

Passion

WERE there not a Matter known,
There wo'd be no Passion.

Jack *and* Jill

SINCE *Jack* and *Jill* both wicked be;
It seems a wonder unto me,
That they no better do agree.

Upon Parson Beanes

OLD Parson *Beanes* hunts six dayes of the week,
And on the seaventh, he has his Notes to seek.
Six dayes he hollows so much breath away,
That on the seaventh, he can nor preach, or pray.

The crowd and company

IN holy meetings, there a man may be
One of the crowd, not of the companie.

Short and long both likes

THIS Lady's short, that Mistresse she is tall;
But long or short, I'm well content with all.

Pollicie in Princes

THAT Princes may possesse a surer seat,
'Tis fit they make no One with them too great.

Upon Rook, Epig.

ROOK he sells feathers, yet he still doth crie
Fie on this pride, this Female vanitie.
Thus, though the Rooke do's raile against the sin,
He loves the gain that vanity brings in.

Upon the Nipples of Julia's *Breast*

H AVE ye beheld (with much delight)
A red-Rose peeping through a white?
Or else a Cherrie (double grac't)
Within a Lillies Center plac't?
Or ever mark't the pretty beam,
A Strawberry shewes halfe drown'd in Creame?
Or seen rich Rubies blushing through
A pure smooth Pearle, and Orient too?
So like to this, nay all the rest,
Is each neate Niplet of her breast.   10

To Daisies, *not to shut so soone*

1. S HUT not so soon; the dull-ey'd night
Ha's not as yet begunne
To make a seisure on the light,
Or to seale up the Sun.

2. No Marigolds yet closed are;
No shadowes great appeare;
Nor doth the early Shepheards Starre
Shine like a spangle here.

3. Stay but till my *Julia* close
Her life-begetting eye;   10
And let the whole world then dispose
It selfe to live or dye.

To the little Spinners

Y EE pretty Huswives, wo'd ye know
The worke that I wo'd put ye to?
This, this it sho'd be, for to spin,
A Lawn for me, so fine and thin,
As it might serve me for my skin.
For cruell Love ha's me so whipt,
That of my skin, I all am stript;
And shall dispaire, that any art
Can ease the rawnesse, or the smart;
Unlesse you skin again each part.   10

1.4 Lillies *ed.*: Lillie? *48*

Which mercy if you will but do,
I call all Maids to witnesse too
What here I promise, that no Broom
Shall now, or ever after come
To wrong a *Spinner* or her Loome.

Oberons *Palace*

AFTER the Feast (my *Shapcot*) see,
The Fairie Court I give to thee:
Where we'le present our *Oberon* led
Halfe tipsie to the Fairie Bed,
Where *Mab* he finds; who there doth lie
Not without mickle majesty.
Which, done; and thence remov'd the light,
We'l wish both Them and Thee, good night.

Full as a Bee with Thyme, and Red,
As Cherry harvest, now high fed   10
For Lust and action; on he'l go,
To lye with *Mab*, though all say no.
Lust ha's no eares; He's sharpe as thorn;
And fretfull, carries Hay in's horne,
And lightning in his eyes; and flings
Among the Elves, (if mov'd) the stings
Of peltish wasps; well know his Guard
Kings though th'are hated, will be fear'd.
Wine lead him on. Thus to a Grove
(Sometimes devoted unto Love)   20
Tinseld with *Twilight*, He, and They
Lead by the shine of Snails; a way
Beat with their num'rous feet, which by
Many a neat perplexity,
Many a turn, and man' a crosse-
Track they redeem a bank of mosse
Spungie and swelling, and farre more
Soft then the finest Lemster Ore.
Mildly disparkling, like those fiers,
Which break from the Injeweld tyres   30
Of curious Brides; or like those mites
Of Candi'd dew in Moony nights.

1.17 well know *ed.*: we'l know *48*   wellknowne *MSS.*

Upon this *Convex*, all the flowers,
(Nature begets by th'Sun, and showers,)
Are to a wilde digestion brought,
As if Loves *Sampler* here was wrought:
Or *Citherea's Ceston*, which
All with temptation doth bewitch.
Sweet Aires move here; and more divine
Made by the breath of great-ey'd kine,   40
Who as they lowe empearl with milk
The four-leav'd grasse, or mosse like silk.
The breath of *Munkies* met to mix
With *Musk-flies*, are th'*Aromaticks*,
Which cense this Arch; and here and there,
And farther off, and every where,
Throughout that *Brave Mosaick* yard
Those Picks or Diamonds in the Card:
With peeps of Harts, of Club and Spade
Are here most neatly inter-laid.   50
Many a Counter, many a Die,
Half rotten, and without an eye,
Lies here abouts; and for to pave
The excellency of this Cave,
Squirrils and childrens teeth late shed,
Are neatly here enchequered
With brownest *Toadstones*, and the Gum
That shines upon the blewer Plum.
The nails faln off by Whit-flawes: Art's
Wise hand enchasing here those warts,   60
Which we to others (from our selves)
Sell, and brought hither by the Elves.
The tempting Mole, stoln from the neck
Of the shie Virgin, seems to deck
The holy Entrance; where within
The roome is hung with the blew skin
Of shifted Snake: enfreez'd throughout
With eyes of Peacocks Trains, & Trout-
flies curious wings; and these among
Those silver-pence, that cut the tongue   70
Of the red infant, neatly hung.

l. 40 great-ey'd kine] great ey'd-kine *48* (cf. 230, l. 33)
l. 42 mosse like *MSS*.: mosse-like *48*
l. 56 enchequered *MSS*.: enchequered. *48*

The glow-wormes eyes; the shining scales
Of silv'rie fish; wheat-strawes, the snailes
Soft Candle-light; the Kitling's eyne;
Corrupted wood; serve here for shine.
No glaring light of bold-fac't Day,
Or other over radiant Ray
Ransacks this roome; but what weak beams
Can make reflected from these jems,
And multiply; Such is the light,   80
But ever doubtfull Day, or night.
By this quaint Taper-light he winds
His Errours up; and now he finds
His Moon-tann'd *Mab*, as somewhat sick,
And (Love knowes) tender as a chick.
Upon six plump *Dandillions*, high-
Rear'd, lyes her Elvish-majestie:
Whose woollie-bubbles seem'd to drowne
Hir *Mab-ship* in obedient Downe.
For either sheet, was spread the Caule   90
That doth the Infants face enthrall,
When it is born: (by some enstyl'd
The luckie *Omen* of the child)
And next to these two blankets ore-
Cast of the finest *Gossamore*.
And then a Rug of carded wooll,
Which, *Spunge-like* drinking in the dull-
Light of the Moon, seem'd to comply,
Cloud-like, the *daintie Deitie*.
Thus soft she lies: and over-head   100
A *Spinners* circle is bespread,
With Cob-web-curtains: from the roof
So neatly sunck, as that no proof
Of any tackling can declare
What gives it hanging in the Aire.
The Fringe about this, are those *Threds*
Broke at the Losse of *Maiden-heads*:
And all behung with these pure Pearls,
Dropt from the eyes of *ravisht Girles*
Or *writhing Brides*; when, (panting) they   110
Give unto Love the straiter way.
For Musick now; He has the cries
Of fained-lost-Virginities;

The which the *Elves* make to excite
A more unconquer'd appetite.
The Kings undrest; and now upon
The Gnats-watch-word the *Elves* are gone.
And now the bed, and *Mab* possest
Of this great-little-kingly-Guest.
We'll nobly think, what's to be done,   120
He'll do no doubt; *This flax is spun.*

To his peculiar friend Master Thomas Shapcott, Lawyer

I'VE paid Thee, what I promis'd; that's not All;
Besides I give Thee here a Verse that shall
(When hence thy Circum-mortall-part is gon)
Arch-like, hold up, *Thy Name's Inscription.*
Brave men can't die; whose Candid Actions are
Writ in the Poets Endlesse-Kalendar:
Whose *velome*, and whose *volumne* is the Skie,
And the pure Starres the praising Poetrie.
                                                  Farewell.

To Julia *in the Temple*

BESIDES us two, i'th'Temple here's not one
To make up now a Congregation.
Let's to the *Altar of perfumes* then go,
And say short Prayers; and when we have done so,
Then we shall see, how in a little space,
Saints will come in to fill each Pew and Place.

To Oenone

1. WHAT Conscience, say, is it in thee
        When I a Heart had one,
     To Take away that Heart from me,
        And to retain thy own?

2. For shame or pitty now encline
        To play a loving part;
     Either to send me kindly thine,
        Or give me back my heart.

3. Covet not both; but if thou dost
    Resolve to part with neither;   10
Why! yet to shew that thou art just,
    Take me and mine together.

His weaknesse in woes

I CANNOT suffer; And in this, my part
Of Patience wants. *Grief breaks the stoutest Heart.*

Fame makes us forward

TO Print our Poems, the propulsive cause
    Is Fame, (the breath of popular applause.)

To Groves

YEE silent shades, whose each tree here
    Some Relique of a Saint doth weare:
Who for some sweet-hearts sake, did prove
The fire, and martyrdome of love.
Here is the Legend of those Saints
That di'd for love; and their complaints:
Their wounded hearts; and names we find
Encarv'd upon the Leaves and Rind.
Give way, give way to me, who come
Scorch't with the selfe-same martyrdome: 10
And have deserv'd as much (Love knowes)
As to be canoniz'd 'mongst those,
Whose deeds, and deaths here written are
Within your *Greenie-Kalendar*:
By all those Virgins Fillets hung
Upon your Boughs, and Requiems sung
For Saints and Soules departed hence,
(Here honour'd still with Frankincense)
By all those teares that have been shed,
As a *Drink-offering*, to the dead: 20
By all those True-love-knots, that be
With Motto's carv'd on every tree,
By sweet S. *Phillis*; pitie me:
By deare S. *Iphis*; and the rest,
Of all those other Saints now blest;

Me, me, forsaken, here admit
Among your Mirtles to be writ:
That my poore name may have the glory
To live remembred in your story.

An Epitaph upon a Virgin

H ERE a solemne Fast we keepe,
 While all beauty lyes asleep
Husht be all things; (no noyse here)
But the toning of a teare:
Or a sigh of such as bring
Cowslips for her covering.

To the right gratious Prince, Lodwick, Duke of Richmond and Lenox

O F all those three-brave-brothers, faln i'th'Warre,
 (Not without glory) Noble Sir, you are,
Despite of all concussions left the Stem
To shoot forth Generations like to them.
Which may be done, if (Sir) you can beget
Men in their substance, not in counterfeit.
Such Essences as those Three Brothers; known
Eternall by their own production.
Of whom, from Fame's white Trumpet, This Ile Tell,
Worthy their everlasting Chronicle,   10
Never since first Bellona us'd a Shield,
Such Three brave Brothers fell in Mars his Field.
These were those Three Horatii Rome did boast,
Rom's were these Three Horatii we have lost.
One Cordelion had that Age long since;
This, Three; which Three, you make up Foure Brave Prince.

To Jealousie

O JEALOUSIE, that art
 The Canker of the heart:
And mak'st all hell
Where thou do'st dwell;
For pitie be
No Furie, or no Fire-brand to me.

2.9 Fame's] Fam's 48

2. Farre from me Ile remove
   All thoughts of irksome Love:
      And turn to snow,
      Or Christall grow;   10
      To keep still free
(O! Soul-tormenting Jealousie,) from Thee.

To live Freely

LET's live in hast; use pleasures while we may:
  Co'd life return, 'twod never lose a day.

Upon Spunge. Epig.

SPUNGE makes his boasts that he's the onely man
  Can hold of Beere and Ale an Ocean;
Is this his Glory? then his Triumph's Poore;
I know the *Tunne* of *Hidleberge* holds more.

His Almes.

HERE, here I live,
  And somewhat give,
Of what I have,
To those, who crave.
Little or much,
My Almnes is such:
But if my deal
Of Oyl and Meal
Shall fuller grow,
More Ile bestow: 10
Mean time be it
E'en but a bit,
Or else a crum,
The scrip hath some.

Upon himself

COME, leave this loathed Country-life, and then
  Grow up to be a Roman *Citizen*.
Those mites of Time, which yet remain unspent,
Waste thou in that most Civill Government.

171

Get their comportment, and the gliding tongue
Of those mild Men, thou art to live among:
Then being seated in that smoother *Sphere*,
Decree thy everlasting *Topick* there.
And to the Farm-house nere return at all;
Though Granges do not love thee, Cities shall.   10

To enjoy the Time

WHILE Fate permits us, let's be merry;
    Passe all we must the fatall Ferry:
And this our life too whirles away,
With the Rotation of the Day.

Upon Love ✓

1. LOVE, I have broke
        Thy yoke;
   The neck is free:
   But when I'm next
        Love vext,
   Then shackell me.

2. 'Tis better yet
        To fret
   The feet or hands;
   Then to enthrall,
        Or gall
   The neck with bands.   10

To the right *Honourable* Mildmay, *Earle* of Westmorland

YOU are a Lord, an Earle, nay more, a Man,
    Who writes sweet Numbers well as any can:
If so, why then are not These Verses hurld,
Like *Sybels* Leaves, throughout the ample world?
What is a Jewell if it be not set
Forth by a Ring, or some rich Carkanet?
But being so; then the beholders cry,
See, see a Jemme (as rare as *Bælus* eye.)
Then publick praise do's runne upon the Stone,
For a most rich, a rare, a precious One.   10

1.1 Fate *ed.*: Fates *48*

Expose your jewels then unto the view,
That we may praise Them, or themselves prize You.
Vertue conceal'd (with *Horace* you'l confesse)
Differs not much from drowzie slothfullnesse.

The Plunder

I AM of all bereft;
Save but some few Beanes left,
Whereof (at last) to make
For me, and mine a Cake:
Which eaten, they and I
Will say our grace, and die.

Littlenesse no cause of Leannesse

ONE feeds on Lard, and yet is leane;
And I but feasting with a Beane,
Grow fat and smooth: The reason is,
Jove prospers my meat, more then his.

Upon one who said she was alwayes young

YOU say y'are young; but when your Teeth are told
To be but three, Black-ey'd, wee'l thinke y'are old.

Upon Huncks. Epig.

HUNCKS ha's no money (he do's sweare, or say)
About him, when the Taverns shot's to pay.
If he ha's none in's pockets, trust me, *Huncks*
Ha's none at home, in Coffers, Desks, or Trunks.

The Jimmall Ring, or True-love-knot

THOU sent'st to me a True-love-knot; but I
Return'd a Ring of Jimmals, to imply
Thy Love had one knot, mine a triple tye.

The parting Verse, or charge to his supposed Wife when he travelled

Go hence, and with this parting kisse,
　Which joyns two souls, remember this;
Though thou beest young, kind, soft, and faire,
And may'st draw thousands with a haire:
Yet let these glib temptations be
Furies to others, Friends to me.
Looke upon all; and though on fire
Thou set'st their hearts, let chaste desire
Steere Thee to me; and thinke (me gone)
In having all, that thou hast none.　　　　　　10
Nor so immured wo'd I have
Thee live, as dead and in thy grave;
But walke abroad, yet wisely well
Stand for my comming, Sentinell.
And think (as thou do'st walke the street)
Me, or my shadow thou do'st meet.
I know a thousand greedy eyes
Will on thy Feature tirannize,
In my short absence; yet behold
Them like some Picture, or some Mould　　　20
Fashion'd like Thee; which though 'tave eares
And eyes, it neither sees or heares.
Gifts will be sent, and Letters, which
Are the expressions of that itch,
And salt, which frets thy Suters; fly
Both, lest thou lose thy liberty:
For that once lost, thou't fall to one,
Then prostrate to a million.
But if they wooe thee, do thou say,
(As that chaste Queen of *Ithaca*　　　　　　30
Did to her suitors) this web done
(Undone as oft as done) I'm wonne;
I will not urge Thee, for I know,
Though thou art young, thou canst say no,
And no again, and so deny,
Those thy Lust-burning *Incubi*.

Let them enstile Thee Fairest faire,
The Pearle of Princes, yet despaire
That so thou art, because thou must
Believe, Love speaks it not, but Lust;　　　40
And this their Flatt'rie do's commend
Thee chiefly for their pleasures end.
I am not jealous of thy Faith,
Or will be; for the Axiome saith,
He that doth suspect, do's haste
A gentle mind to be unchaste.
No, live thee to thy selfe, and keep
Thy thoughts as cold, as is thy sleep:
And let thy dreames be only fed
With this, that I am in thy bed.　　　50
And thou then turning in that Sphere,
Waking shalt find me sleeping there.
But yet if boundlesse Lust must skaile
Thy Fortress, and will needs prevaile;
And wildly force a passage in,
Banish consent, and 'tis no sinne
Of Thine; so *Lucrece* fell, and the
Chaste *Syracusian Cyane.*
So *Medullina* fell, yet none
Of these had imputation　　　60
For the least trespasse; 'cause the mind
Here was not with the act combin'd.
The body sins not, 'tis the Will
That makes the Action, good, or ill.
And if thy fall sho'd this way come,
Triumph in such a Martirdome.
I will not over-long enlarge
To thee, this my religious charge.
Take this compression, so by this
Means I shall know what other kisse　　　70
Is mixt with mine; and truly know,
Returning, if't be mine or no:
Keepe it till then; and now my Spouse,
For my wisht safety pay thy vowes,
And prayers to *Venus*; if it please
The *Great-blew-ruler* of the Seas;

Not many full-fac't-moons shall waine,
Lean-horn'd, before I come again
As one triumphant; when I find
In thee, all faith of Woman-kind.   80
Nor wo'd I have thee thinke, that Thou
Had'st power thy selfe to keep this vow;
But having scapt temptations shelfe,
Know vertue taught thee, not thy selfe.

To his *Kinsman,* Sir Tho. Soame

SEEING Thee *Soame,* I see a Goodly man,
And in that Good, a great *Patrician.*
Next to which Two; among the City-Powers,
And Thrones, thy selfe one of Those Senatours:
Not wearing Purple only for the show;
(As many Conscripts of the Citie do)
But for True Service, worthy of that Gowne,
The *Golden* chain too, and the *Civick* Crown.

To Blossoms

1. FAIRE pledges of a fruitfull Tree,
    Why do yee fall so fast?
      Your date is not so past;
    But you may stay yet here a while,
      To blush and gently smile;
        And go at last.

2. What, were yee borne to be
    An houre or half's delight;
      And so to bid goodnight?
    'Twas pitie Nature brought yee forth   10
      Meerly to shew your worth,
        And lose you quite.

3. But you are lovely Leaves, where we
    May read how soon things have
      Their end, though ne'r so brave:
    And after they have shown their pride,
      Like you a while: They glide
        Into the Grave.

Mans dying-place uncertain

MAN knowes where first he ships himselfe; but he
Never can tell, where shall his Landing be.

Nothing Free-cost

NOTHING comes Free-cost here; *Jove* will not let
His gifts go from him; if not bought with sweat.

Few fortunate

MANY we are, and yet but few possesse
Those Fields of everlasting happinesse.

To Perenna

HOW long, *Perenna*, wilt thou see
Me languish for the love of Thee?
Consent and play a friendly part
To save; when thou may'st kill a heart.

To the Ladyes

TRUST me Ladies, I will do
Nothing to distemper you;
If I any fret or vex,
Men they shall be, *not your sex.*

The old Wives Prayer

HOLY-ROOD come forth and shield
Us i'th'Citie, and the Field:
Safely guard us, now and aye,
From the blast that burns by day;
And those sounds that us affright
In the dead of dampish night.
Drive all hurtfull Feinds us fro,
By the Time the Cocks first crow.

Upon a cheap Laundresse. Epig.

FEACIE (some say) doth wash her clothes i'th'Lie
 That sharply trickles from her either eye.
The *Laundresses*, They envie her good-luck,
Who can with so small charges *drive the buck*.
What needs she fire and ashes to consume,
Who can scoure Linnens with her own salt *reeume*?

Upon his departure hence

THUS I
 Passe by,
And die:
As One,
Unknown,
And gon:
I'm made
A shade,
And laid
I'th grave,   10
There have
My Cave.
Where tell
I dwell,
Farewell.

The Wassaile

1. GIVE way, give way ye Gates, and win
  An easie blessing to your Bin,
And Basket, by our entring in.

2. May both with manchet stand repleat;
Your Larders too so hung with meat,
That though a thousand, thousand eat;

3. Yet, ere twelve *Moones* shall whirl about
Their silv'rie Spheres, ther's none may doubt,
But more's sent in, then was serv'd out.

178

4. Next, may your Dairies Prosper so,   10
   As that your pans no Ebbe may know;
   But if they do, the more to flow.

5. Like to a solemne sober Stream
   Bankt all with Lillies, and the Cream
   Of sweetest *Cow-slips* filling Them.

6. Then, may your Plants be prest with Fruit,
   Nor Bee, or Hive you have be mute;
   But sweetly sounding like a Lute.

7. Next may your Duck and teeming Hen
   Both to the Cocks-tread say *Amen*;   20
   And for their two egs render ten.

8. Last, may your Harrows, Shares and Ploughes,
   Your Stacks, your Stocks, your sweetest Mowes,
   All prosper by your Virgin-vowes.

9. Alas! we blesse, but see none here,
   That brings us either Ale or Beere;
   In a drie-house all things are neere.

10. Let's leave a longer time to wait,
   Where Rust and Cobwebs bind the gate;
   And all live here with *needy Fate.*   30

11. Where Chimneys do for ever weepe,
   For want of warmth, and Stomachs keepe
   With noise, the servants eyes from sleep.

12. It is in vain to sing, or stay
   Our free-feet here; but we'l away:
   Yet to the Lares this we'l say,

13. The time will come, when you'l be sad,
   And reckon this for fortune bad,
   T'ave lost the good ye might have had.

Upon a Lady faire, but fruitlesse

TWICE has *Pudica* been a Bride, and led
By holy *Himen* to the Nuptiall Bed.
Two Youths sha's known, thrice two, and twice 3. yeares;
Yet not a Lillie from the Bed appeares;
Nor will; for why, *Pudica*, this may know,
Trees never beare, unlesse they first do blow.

How Springs came first

THESE Springs were Maidens once that lov'd,
But lost to that they most approv'd:
My Story tells, by Love they were
Turn'd to these Springs, which wee see here:
The pretty whimpering that they make,
When of the Banks their leave they take;
Tels ye but this, they are the same,
In nothing chang'd but in their name.

To Rosemary and Baies

MY wooing's ended: now my wedding's neere;
When Gloves are giving, *Guilded be you there.*

Upon Skurffe

SKURFFE by his Nine-bones sweares, and well he may,
All know a Fellon eate the Tenth away.

Upon a Scarre in a Virgins Face

'TIS Heresie in others: In your face
That Scarr's no *Schisme*, but the *sign of grace.*

Upon his eye-sight failing him

I BEGINNE to waine in sight;
Shortly I shall bid goodnight:
Then no gazing more about,
When the Tapers once are out.

To his worthy Friend, M. Tho. Falconbirge

STAND with thy Graces forth, Brave man, and rise
High with thine own *Auspitious Destinies*:
Nor leave the search, and proofe, till Thou canst find
These, or those ends, to which Thou wast design'd.
Thy lucky *Genius*, and thy guiding *Starre*,
Have made Thee prosperous in thy wayes, thus farre:
Nor will they leave Thee, till they both have shown
Thee to the World a *Prime* and *Publique One*.
Then, when Thou see'st thine Age all turn'd to gold,
Remember what thy *Herrick* Thee foretold,   10
When at the holy Threshold of thine house,
He Boded good-luck to thy Selfe and Spouse.
Lastly, be mindfull (when thou art grown great)
That Towrs high rear'd dread most the lightnings threat:
When as the humble Cottages not feare
The cleaving Bolt of Jove *the Thunderer.*

Upon Julia's *haire fill'd with Dew*

DEW sate on *Julia's* haire,
    And spangled too,
Like Leaves that laden are
    With trembling Dew:
Or glitter'd to my sight,
    As when the Beames
Have their reflected light,
    Daunc't by the Streames.

Another on her

HOW can I choose but love, and follow her,
Whose shadow smels like milder *Pomander*!
How can I chuse but kisse her, whence do's come
The *Storax, Spiknard, Myrrhe,* and *Ladanum.*

Losse from the least

GREAT men by small meanes oft are overthrown:
He's Lord of thy life, who contemnes his own.

Rewards and punishments

A LL things are open to these two events,
Or to Rewards, or else to Punishments.

Shame, no Statist

S HAME is a bad attendant to a State:
He rents his Crown, That feares the Peoples hate.

To Sir Clipsebie Crew

S INCE to th'Country first I came,
I have lost my former flame:
And, methinks, I not inherit,
As I did, my ravisht spirit.
If I write a Verse, or two,
'Tis with very much ado;
In regard I want that Wine,
Which sho'd conjure up a line.
Yet, though now of Muse bereft,
I have still the manners left   10
For to thanke you (Noble Sir)
For those gifts you do conferre
Upon him, who only can
Be in Prose a *gratefull man.*

Upon himselfe

I CO'D never love indeed;
Never see mine own heart bleed:
Never crucifie my life;
Or for Widow, Maid, or Wife.

2. I co'd never seeke to please
One, or many Mistresses:
Never like their lips, to sweare
Oyle of Roses still smelt there.

3. I co'd never breake my sleepe,
Fold mine Armes, sob, sigh, or weep: 10
Never beg, or humbly wooe
With oathes, and lyes, (as others do.)

1 (*title*) *Rewards ed.*: *Reward 48*
3 (*title*) Clipsebie] Clisebie *48* (see 161.3)   )

4. I co'd never walke alone;
   Put a shirt of sackcloth on:
   Never keep a fast, or pray
   For good luck in love (that day.)

5. But have hitherto liv'd free,
   As the aire that circles me:
   And kept credit with my heart,
   Neither broke i'th whole, or part.   20

Fresh Cheese and Cream

W O'D yee have fresh Cheese and Cream?
   Julia's Breast can give you them:
And if more; Each *Nipple* cries,
To your *Cream,* here's *Strawberries.*

An Eclogue, or Pastorall between Endimion Por-ter *and* Lycidas Herrick, *set and sung*

Endym. A H! *Lycidas,* come tell me why
          Thy whilome merry Oate
By thee doth so neglected lye;
          And never purls a Note?

2.   I prithee speake: *Lyc.* I will. *End.* Say on:
Lyc.   'Tis thou, and only thou,
         That art the cause *Endimion*;
End.   For Loves-sake, tell me how.

3. *Lyc.* In this regard, that thou do'st play
             Upon an other Plain: 10
         And for a Rurall Roundelay,
             Strik'st now a Courtly strain.

4.   Thou leav'st our Hills, our Dales, our Bowers,
             Our finer fleeced sheep:
         (Unkind to us) to spend thine houres,
             Where Shepheards sho'd not keep.

5.   I meane the Court: Let *Latmos* be
             My lov'd *Endymions* Court;
End.   But I the Courtly State wo'd see:
Lyc.   Then see it in report.   20

1.4 here's] her's 48

6.   What ha's the Court to do with Swaines,
               Where *Phillis* is not known?
         Nor do's it mind the Rustick straines
               Of us, or *Coridon.*

7.   Breake, if thou lov'st us, this delay;
End.   Dear *Lycidas*, e're long,
         I vow by *Pan*, to come away
               And Pipe unto thy Song.

8.   Then *Jessimine*, with *Florabell*;
               And dainty *Amarillis*,   30
         With handsome-handed *Drosomell*
               Shall pranke thy Hooke with Lillies.

9. *Lyc.*   Then *Tityrus*, and *Coridon*,
               And *Thyrsis*, they shall follow
         With all the rest; while thou alone
               Shalt lead, like young *Apollo.*

10.   And till thou com'st, thy *Lycidas*,
               In every *Geniall* Cup,
         Shall write in Spice, *Endimion* 'twas
               That kept his Piping up.   40

And my most luckie Swain, when I shall live to see
Endimions Moon to fill up full, remember me:
Mean time, let *Lycidas* have leave to Pipe to thee.

To a Bed of Tulips

1.   **B**RIGHT Tulips, we do know,
          You had your comming hither;
         And Fading-time do's show,
         That Ye must quickly wither.

2.   Your *Sister-hoods* may stay,
         And smile here for your houre;
         But dye ye must away:
         Even as the meanest Flower.

3.   Come Virgins then, and see
         Your frailties; and bemone ye;   10
         For lost like these, 'twill be,
         As Time had never known ye.

A Caution

THAT Love last long; let it thy first care be
  To find a Wife, that is most fit for Thee.
Be She too wealthy, or too poore; be sure,
Love in extreames, can never long endure.

To the Water Nymphs, drinking at the Fountain

1. REACH, with your whiter hands, to me,
     Some Christall of the Spring;
   And I, about the Cup shall see
     Fresh Lillies flourishing.

2. Or else sweet Nimphs do you but this;
     To'th'Glasse your lips encline;
   And I shall see by that one kisse,
     The Water turn'd to Wine.

To his Honoured Kinsman, Sir Richard Stone

TO this *white Temple* of my *Heroes,* here
  Beset with stately Figures (every where)
Of such rare *Saint-ships,* who did here consume
Their lives in sweets, and left in death perfume.
Come thou *Brave man*! And bring with Thee a Stone
Unto thine own *Edification.*
High are These Statues here, besides no lesse
Strong then the Heavens for everlastingnesse:
Where build aloft; and being fixt by These,
Set up Thine own *eternall Images.*   10

Upon a Flie

A GOLDEN Flie one shew'd to me,
  Clos'd in a Box of Yvorie:
Where both seem'd proud; the Flie to have
His buriall in an yvory grave:
The yvorie tooke State to hold
A Corps as bright as burnisht gold.
One Fate had both; both equall Grace;
The Buried, and the Burying-place.

Not *Virgils Gnat*, to whom the Spring
All Flowers sent to'is burying.   10
Not *Marshals Bee*, which in a Bead
Of *Amber* quick was buried.
Nor that fine Worme that do's interre
Her selfe i'th'*silken Sepulchre*.
Nor my rare ★*Phil*, that lately was   ★ Sparrow
With Lillies Tomb'd up in a Glasse;
More honour had, then this same *Flie*;
Dead, and clos'd up in *Yvorie*.

Upon Jack *and* Jill. *Epig.*

WHEN *Jill* complaines to *Jack* for want of meate;
    Jack kisses *Jill*, and bids her freely eate:
Jill sayes, of what? sayes *Jack*, on that sweet kisse,
Which full of Nectar and Ambrosia is,
The food of Poets; so I thought sayes *Jill*,
That makes them looke so lanke, so Ghost-like still.
Let Poets feed on aire, or what they will;
Let me feed full, till that I fart, sayes *Jill*.

To Julia

JULIA, when thy *Herrick* dies,
    Close thou up thy Poets eyes:
And his last breath, let it be
Taken in by none but Thee.

To Mistresse Dorothy Parsons

IF thou aske me (Deare) wherefore
    I do write of thee no more:
I must answer (Sweet) thy part
Lesse is here, then in my heart.

Upon Parrat

PARRAT protests 'tis he, and only he
    Can teach a man the *Art of memory*:
Believe him not; for he forgot it quite,
Being drunke, who 'twas that Can'd his Ribs last night.

How he would drinke his Wine

FILL me my Wine in Christall; thus, and thus
  I see't in's *puris naturalibus*:
Unmixt. I love to have it smirke and shine,
'*Tis sin I know, 'tis sin to throtle Wine.*
What Mad-man's he, that when it sparkles so,
Will coole his flames, or quench his fires with snow?

How Marigolds *came yellow*

JEALOUS *Girles* these sometimes were,
  While they liv'd, or lasted here:
Turn'd to *Flowers*, still they be
Yellow, markt for Jealousie.

The broken Christall

TO Fetch me Wine my *Lucia* went,
  Bearing a Christall *continent*:
But making haste, it came to passe,
She brake in two the purer Glasse,
Then smil'd, and sweetly chid her speed;
So with a blush, beshrew'd the deed.

Precepts

GOOD Precepts we must firmly hold,
  By daily *Learning* we wax old.

To the right Honourable Edward *Earle of* Dorset

IF I dare write to You, my Lord, who are,
  Of your own selfe, a *Publick Theater*.
And sitting, see the wiles, wayes, walks of wit,
And give a righteous judgement upon it.
What need I care, though some dislike me sho'd,
If *Dorset* say, what *Herrick* writes, is good?
We know y'are learn'd i'th'Muses, and no lesse
In our *State-sanctions*, deep, or bottomlesse.
Whose smile can make a Poet; and your glance
Dash all bad Poems out of countenance.   10

187

So, that an Author needs no other Bayes
For Coronation, then Your onely Praise.
And no one mischief greater then your frown,
To null his Numbers, and to blast his Crowne.
Few live the life immortall. He ensures
His Fame's long life, who strives to set up Yours.

Upon himself

TH'ART hence removing, (like a Shepherds Tent)
    And walk thou must the way that others went:
Fall thou must first, then rise to life with These,
Markt in thy Book for faithfull Witnesses.

Hope well and Have well: or,
Faire after Foule weather

WHAT though the Heaven be lowring now,
    And look with a contracted brow?
We shall discover, by and by,
A Repurgation of the Skie:
And when those clouds away are driven,
Then will appeare a cheerfull Heaven.

Upon Love

I HELD Love's head while it did ake;
    But so it chanc't to be;
The cruell paine did his forsake,
    And forthwith came to me.

2. Ai me! How shal my griefe be stil'd?
    Or where else shall we find
One like to me, who must be kill'd
    For being too-too-kind?

To his Kinswoman, Mrs. Penelope Wheeler

NEXT is your lot (Faire) to be number'd one,
    Here, in my Book's Canonization:
Late you come in; but you a Saint shall be,
In Chiefe, in this Poetick Liturgie.

Another upon her

FIRST, for your shape, the curious cannot shew
  Any one part that's dissonant in you:
And 'gainst your chast behaviour there's no Plea,
Since you are knowne to be *Penelope*.
Thus faire and cleane you are, although there be
A mighty strife 'twixt Forme and Chastitie.

Kissing and Bussing

KISSING and bussing differ both in this;
  We busse our Wantons, but our Wives we kisse.

Crosse and Pile

FAIRE and foule dayes trip Crosse and Pile; The faire
  Far lesse in number, then our foule dayes are.

To the Lady Crew, upon the death of her Child

WHY, Madam, will ye longer weep,
  When as your Baby's lull'd asleep?
And (pretty Child) feeles now no more
Those paines it lately felt before.
All now is silent; groanes are fled:
Your Child lyes still, yet is not dead:
But rather like a flower hid here
To spring againe another yeare.

His Winding-sheet

COME thou, who art the Wine, and wit
      Of all I've writ:
The Grace, the Glorie, and the best
      Piece of the rest.
Thou art of what I did intend
      The All, and End.

And what was made, was made to meet
  Thee, thee my sheet.
Come then, and be to my chast side
  Both Bed, and Bride.   10
We two (as Reliques left) will have
  One Rest, one Grave.
And, hugging close, we will not feare
  Lust entring here:
Where all Desires are dead, or cold
  As is the mould:
And all Affections are forgot,
  Or Trouble not.
Here, here the Slaves and Pris'ners be
  From Shackles free: 20
And weeping Widowes long opprest
  Doe here find rest.
The wronged Client ends his Lawes
  Here, and his Cause.
Here those long suits of Chancery lie
  Quiet, or die:
And all Star-chamber-Bils doe cease,
  Or hold their peace.
Here needs no Court for our Request,
  Where all are best;   30
All wise; all equall; and all just
  Alike i'th'dust.
Nor need we here to feare the frowne
  Of Court, or Crown.
Where Fortune bears no sway o're things,
  There all are Kings.
In this securer place we'l keep,
  As lull'd asleep;
Or for a little time we'l lye,
  As Robes laid by;   40
To be another day re-worne,
  Turn'd, but not torn:
Or like old Testaments ingrost,
  Lockt up, not lost:
And for a while lye here conceal'd,
  To be reveal'd
Next, at that great Platonick yeere,
  And then meet here.

To Mistresse Mary Willand

ONE more by Thee, Love, and Desert have sent,
T'enspangle this expansive Firmament.
O Flame of Beauty! come, appeare, appeare
A Virgin Taper, ever shining here.

Change gives content

WHAT now we like, anon we disapprove:
The new successor drives away old Love.

Upon Magot a frequenter of Ordinaries

MAGOT frequents those houses of good-cheere,
Talkes most, eates most, of all the Feeders there.
He raves through leane, he rages through the fat;
(What gets the master of the Meal by that?)
He who with talking can devoure so much,
How wo'd he eate, were not his hindrance such?

On himselfe

BORNE I was to meet with Age,
And to walke Life's pilgrimage.
Much I know of Time is spent,
Tell I can't, what's Resident.
Howsoever, cares, adue;
Ile have nought to say to you:
But Ile spend my comming houres,
Drinking wine, & crown'd with flowres.

Fortune favours

FORTUNE did never favour one
Fully, without exception;
Though free she be, ther's something yet
Still wanting to her Favourite.

3.6 not] nor 48
5 (title) Fortune] (?) Fortunes

To Phillis *to love, and live with him*

LIVE, live with me, and thou shalt see
 The pleasures Ile prepare for thee:
What sweets the Country can afford
Shall blesse thy Bed, and blesse thy Board.
The soft sweet Mosse shall be thy bed,
With crawling Woodbine over-spread:
By which the silver-shedding streames
Shall gently melt thee into dreames.
Thy clothing next, shall be a Gowne
Made of the Fleeces purest Downe.   10
The tongues of Kids shall be thy meate;
Their Milke thy drinke; and thou shalt eate
The Paste of Filberts for thy bread
With Cream of Cowslips buttered:
Thy Feasting-Tables shall be Hills
With *Daisies* spread, and *Daffadils*;
Where thou shalt sit, and *Red-brest* by,
For meat, shall give thee melody.
Ile give thee Chaines and Carkanets
Of *Primroses* and *Violets*.   20
A Bag and Bottle thou shalt have;
That richly wrought, and This as brave;
So that as either shall expresse
The Wearer's no meane Shepheardesse.
At Sheering-times, and yearely Wakes,
When *Themilis* his pastime makes,
There thou shalt be; and be the wit,
Nay more, the Feast, and grace of it.
On Holy-dayes, when Virgins meet
To dance the Heyes with nimble feet;   30
Thou shalt come forth, and then appeare
The *Queen of Roses* for that yeere.
And having danc't ('bove all the best)
Carry the Garland from the rest.
In Wicker-baskets Maids shal bring
To thee, (my dearest Shephardling)
The blushing Apple, bashfull Peare,
And shame-fac't Plum, (all simp'ring there).   40

1.36 Shephardling] Sheparling *48*

Walk in the Groves, and thou shalt find
The name of *Phillis* in the Rind 40
Of every straight, and smooth-skin tree;
Where kissing that, Ile twice kisse thee.
To thee a Sheep-hook I will send,
Be-pranckt with Ribbands, to this end,
This, this alluring Hook might be
Lesse for to catch a sheep, then me.
Thou shalt have Possets, Wassails fine,
Not made of Ale, but spiced Wine;
To make thy Maids and selfe free mirth,
All sitting neer the glitt'ring Hearth. 50
Thou sha't have Ribbands, Roses, Rings,
Gloves, Garters, Stockings, Shooes, and Strings
Of winning Colours, that shall move
Others to Lust, but me to Love.
These (nay) and more, thine own shal be,
If thou wilt love, and live with me.

To his Kinswoman, Mistresse
Susanna Herrick

WHEN I consider (Dearest) thou dost stay
But here awhile, to languish and decay;
Like to these Garden-glories, which here be
The Flowrie-sweet resemblances of Thee:
With griefe of heart, methinks, I thus doe cry,
Wo'd thou hast ne'r been born, or might'st not die.

Upon Mistresse Susanna Southwell
her cheeks

RARE are thy cheeks *Susanna*, which do show
Ripe Cherries smiling, while that others blow.

Upon her Eyes

CLEERE are her eyes,
Like purest Skies.
Discovering from thence
A Babie there
That turns each Sphere,
Like an Intelligence.

Upon her feet

H ER pretty feet
Like snailes did creep
A little out, and then,
As if they started at Bo-peep,
Did soon draw in agen.

To his honoured friend, Sir John Mynts

F OR civill, cleane, and circumcised wit,
And for the comely carriage of it;
Thou art The Man, the onely Man best known,
Markt for the *True-wit* of a Million:
From whom we'l reckon. Wit came in, but since
The *Calculation* of thy Birth, *Brave Mince.*

Upon his gray haires

F LY me not, though I be gray,
Lady, this I know you'l say;
Better look the Roses red,
When with white commingled.
Black your haires are; mine are white;
This begets the more delight,
When things meet most opposite:
As in Pictures we descry,
Venus standing *Vulcan* by.

Accusation

I F Accusation onely can draw blood,
None shall be guiltlesse, be he ne'r so good.

Pride allowable in Poets

A s thou deserv'st, be proud; then gladly let
The Muse give thee the Delphick Coronet.

1.4 started *some copies of 48*: played *other copies*

A Vow to Minerva

G ODDESSE, I begin an Art;
Come thou in, with thy best part,
For to make the Texture lye
Each way smooth and civilly:
And a broad-fac't Owle shall be
Offer'd up with Vows to Thee.

On Jone

J ONE wo'd go tel her haires; and well she might,
Having but seven in all; three black, foure white.

Upon Letcher. *Epig.*

L ETCHER was Carted first about the streets,
For false Position in his neighbours sheets:
Next, hang'd for Theeving: Now the people say,
His Carting was the *Prologue* to this Play.

Upon Dundrige

D UNDRIGE his Issue hath; but is not styl'd
For all his Issue, Father of one Child.

To Electra

'T IS Ev'ning, my Sweet,
And dark; let us meet;
Long time w'ave here been a toying:
And never, as yet,
That season co'd get,
Wherein t'ave had an enjoying.

2.   For pitty or shame,
Then let not Love's flame,
Be ever and ever a spending;
Since now to the Port
The path is but short;
And yet our way has no ending.

10

195

3. Time flyes away fast;
    Our houres doe waste:
The while we never remember,
    How soone our life, here,
    Growes old with the yeere,
That dyes with the next *December*.

Discord not disadvantageous

FORTUNE no higher Project can devise,
Then to sow Discord 'mongst the Enemies.

Ill Government

PREPOSTEROUS is that Government, (and rude)
When Kings obey the wilder Multitude.

To Marygolds

GIVE way, and be ye ravisht by the Sun,
(And hang the head when as the Act is done)
Spread as He spreads; wax lesse as He do's wane;
And as He shuts, close up to Maids again.

To Dianeme

GIVE me one kisse,
    And no more;
If so be, this
    Makes you poore;
To enrich you,
    Ile restore
For that one, two
    Thousand score.

To Julia, *the* Flaminica Dialis, *or* Queen-Priest

THOU know'st, my *Julia*, that it is thy turne
This Mornings Incense to prepare, and burne.
The Chaplet, and *Inarculum here be,
With the white Vestures, all attending Thee.

* A twig of a Pomgranat, which the queen-priest did use to weare on her head at sacrificing.

This day, the *Queen-Priest*, thou art made t'appease
Love for our very-many Trespasses.
One chiefe transgression is among the rest,
Because with Flowers her Temple was not drest:
The next, because her Altars did not shine
With daily Fyers: The last, neglect of Wine: 10
For which, her wrath is gone forth to consume
Us all, unlesse preserv'd by thy Perfume.
Take then thy Censer; Put in Fire, and thus,
O *Pious-Priestresse!* make a Peace for us.
For our neglect, Love did our Death decree,
That we escape.   *Redemption comes by Thee.*

Anacreontike

BORN I was to be old,
  And for to die here:
After that, in the mould
  Long for to lye here.
But before that day comes,
  Still I be Bousing;
For I know, in the Tombs
  There's no Carousing.

Meat without mirth

EATEN I have; and though I had good cheere,
  I did not sup, because no friends were there.
Where Mirth and Friends are absent when we Dine
Or Sup, there wants the Incense and the Wine.

Large Bounds doe but bury us

ALL things o'r-rul'd are here by Chance;
  The greatest mans Inheritance,
Where ere the luckie Lot doth fall,
Serves but for place of Buriall.

Upon Ursley

URSLE*Y*, she thinks those Velvet Patches grace
  The Candid Temples of her comely face:
But he will say, who e'r those Circlets seeth,
They be but signs of *Ursleys* hollow teeth.

3.2 Inheritance,] Inheritance. *48*

An Ode to Sir Clipsebie Crew

1. HERE we securely live, and eate
  The Creame of meat;
 And keep eternal fires,
By which we sit, and doe Divine
  As Wine
 And Rage inspires.

2. If full we charme; then call upon
  Anacreon
 To grace the frantick Thyrse:
And having drunk, we raise a shout   10
  Throughout
 To praise his Verse.

3. Then cause we *Horace* to be read,
  Which sung, or seyd,
 A Goblet, to the brim,
Of Lyrick Wine, both swell'd and crown'd,
  A Round
 We quaffe to him.

4. Thus, thus, we live, and spend the houres
  In Wine and Flowers: 20
 And make the frollick yeere,
The Month, the Week, the instant Day
  To stay
 The longer here.

5. Come then, brave Knight, and see the Cell
  Wherein I dwell;
 And my Enchantments too;
Which Love and noble freedome is;
  And this
 Shall fetter you.   30

6. Take Horse, and come; or be so kind,
  To send your mind
 (Though but in Numbers few)
And I shall think I have the heart,
  Or part
 Of *Clipseby Crew.*

To his worthy Kinsman, Mr.
Stephen Soame

NOR is my Number full, till I inscribe
Thee sprightly *Soame*, one of my righteous Tribe:
A Tribe of one Lip, Leven, and of One
Civil Behaviour, and Religion.
A Stock of Saints; where ev'ry one doth weare
A stole of white, (and Canonized here)
Among which Holies, be Thou ever known,
Brave Kinsman, markt out with the whiter stone:
Which seals Thy Glorie; since I doe prefer
Thee here in my eternall Calender.   10

To his Tomb-maker

GO I must; when I am gone,
Write but this upon my Stone;
Chaste I liv'd, without a wife,
That's the Story of my life.
Strewings need none, every flower
Is in this word, Batchelour.

Great Spirits supervive

OUR mortall parts may wrapt in Seare-cloths lye:
Great Spirits never with their bodies dye.

None free from fault

OUT of the world he must, who once comes in:
No man exempted is from Death, or sinne.

Upon himselfe being buried

LET me sleep this night away,
Till the Dawning of the day:
Then at th'opening of mine eyes,
I, and all the world shall rise.

Pitie to the prostrate

TIS worse then barbarous cruelty to show
No part of pitie on a conquer'd foe.

1.3 Lip, *ed.*: Lip; 48
199

Way in a crowd

ONCE on a Lord-Mayors day, in Cheapside, when
  Skulls co'd not well passe through that scum of men.
For quick dispatch, *Sculls* made no longer stay,
Then but to breath, and every one gave way:
For as he breath'd, the People swore from thence
A Fart flew out, or a *Sir-reverence*.

His content in the Country

HERE, here I live with what my Board,
  Can with the smallest cost afford.
Though ne'r so mean the Viands be,
They well content my *Prew* and me.
Or Pea, or Bean, or Wort, or Beet,
What ever comes, content makes sweet:
Here we rejoyce, because no Rent
We pay for our poore Tenement:
Wherein we rest, and never feare
The Landlord, or the Usurer.   10
The Quarter-day do's ne'r affright
Our Peacefull slumbers in the night.
We eate our own, and batten more,
Because we feed on no mans score:
But pitie those, whose flanks grow great,
Swel'd with the Lard of others meat.
We blesse our Fortunes, when we see
Our own beloved privacie:
And like our living, where w'are known
To very few, or else to none.   20

The credit of the Conquerer

HE who commends the vanquisht, speaks the Power,
  And glorifies the worthy Conquerer.

On himselfe

SOME parts may perish; dye thou canst not all:
  The most of Thee shall scape the funerall.

Upon one-ey'd Broomsted. *Epig.*

BROOMSTED a lamenesse got by cold and Beere;
And to the *Bath* went, to be cured there:
His feet were helpt, and left his Crutch behind:
But home return'd, as he went forth, halfe blind.

The Fairies

IF ye will with *Mab* find grace,
Set each Platter in his place:
Rake the Fier up, and get
Water in, ere Sun be set.
Wash your Pailes, and clense your Dairies;
Sluts are loathsome to the Fairies:
Sweep your house: Who doth not so,
Mab will pinch her by the toe.

To his honoured friend, *M.* John Weare, Councellour

DID I or love, or could I others draw
To the indulgence of the rugged Law:
The first foundation of that zeale sho'd be
By Reading all her *Paragraphs* in Thee.
Who dost so fitly with the Lawes unite,
As if You Two, were one *Hermophrodite*:
Nor courts thou Her because she's well attended
With wealth, but for those ends she was entended:
Which were, (and still her offices are known)
Law is to give to ev'ry one his owne.   10
To shore the Feeble up, against the strong;
To shield the Stranger, and the Poore from wrong:
This was the Founders grave and good intent,
To keepe the out-cast in his Tenement:
To free the Orphan from that Wolfe-like-man,
Who is his *Butcher* more then *Guardian.*
To drye the Widowes teares; and stop her Swoones,
By pouring Balme and Oyle into her wounds.
This was the old way; and 'tis yet thy course,
To keep those pious Principles in force.   20
Modest I will be; but one word Ile say
(Like to a sound that's vanishing away)

Sooner the in-side of thy hand shall grow
Hisped, and hairie, ere thy Palm shall know
A *Postern-bribe* tooke, or a *Forked-Fee*
To fetter Justice, when She might be free.
Eggs Ile not shave: But yet brave man, if I
Was destin'd forth to golden Soveraignty:
A Prince I'de be, that I might Thee preferre
To be my Counsell both, and Chanceller.   30

The Watch

MAN is a Watch, wound up at first, but never
Wound up again: Once down, He's down for ever.
The Watch once downe, all motions then do cease;
And Mans Pulse stopt, *All passions sleep in Peace.*

Lines have their Linings, and Bookes their Buckram

AS in our clothes, so likewise he who lookes,
Shall find much farcing Buckram in our Books.

Art above Nature, *to* Julia

WHEN I behold a Forrest spread
With silken trees upon thy head;
And when I see that other Dresse
Of flowers set in comlinesse:
When I behold another grace
In the ascent of curious Lace,
Which like a Pinacle doth shew
The top, and the top-gallant too.
Then, when I see thy Tresses bound
Into an Ovall, square, or round;   10
And knit in knots far more then I
Can tell by tongue; or true-love tie:
Next, when those Lawnie Filmes I see
Play with a wild civility:
And all those airie silks to flow,
Alluring me, and tempting so:
I must confesse, mine eye and heart
Dotes less on Nature, then on Art.

Upon Sibilla

WITH paste of Almonds, *Syb* her hands doth scoure;
  Then gives it to the children to devoure.
In Cream she bathes her thighs (more soft then silk)
Then to the poore she freely gives the milke.

Upon his kinswoman Mistresse Bridget Herrick

SWEET *Bridget* blusht, & therewithall,
  Fresh blossoms from her cheekes did fall.
I thought at first 'twas but a dream,
Till after I had handled them;
And smelt them, then they smelt to me,
As Blossomes of the *Almond* Tree.

Upon Love ✓

I PLAID with Love, as with the fire
      The wanton Satyre did;
  Nor did I know, or co'd descry
      What under there was hid.

2. That Satyre he but burnt his lips;
        (But min's the greater smart)
  For kissing Loves dissembling chips,
        The fire scorcht my heart.

Upon a comely, and curious Maide

I F Men can say that beauty dyes;
  Marbles will sweare that here it lyes.
If Reader then thou canst forbeare,
In publique loss to shed a Teare:
The Dew of griefe upon this stone
Will tell thee *Pitie* thou hast none.

Upon the losse of his Finger

ONE of the five straight branches of my hand
  Is lopt already; and the rest but stand
Expecting when to fall: which soon will be;
First dyes the Leafe, the Bough next, next the Tree.

Upon Irene

ANGRY if *Irene* be
But a Minutes life with me:
Such a fire I espie
Walking in and out her eye,
As at once I freeze, and frie.

Upon Electra's *Teares*

UPON her cheekes she wept, and from those showers
Sprang up a sweet *Nativity* of Flowres.

Upon Tooly

THE Eggs of Pheasants wrie-nos'd *Tooly* sells;
But ne'r so much as licks the speckled shells:
Only, if one prove addled, that he eates
With superstition, (as the Cream of meates.)
The Cock and Hen he feeds; but not a bone
He ever pickt (as yet) of any one.

A Hymne to the Graces

WHEN I love, (as some have told,
Love I shall when I am old)
O ye Graces! Make me fit
For the welcoming of it.
Clean my Roomes, as Temples be,
T'entertain that Deity.
Give me words wherewith to wooe,
Suppling and successefull too:
Winning postures; and withall,
Manners each way musicall: 10
Sweetnesse to allay my sowre
And unsmooth behaviour.
For I know you have the skill
Vines to prune, though not to kill,
And of any wood ye see,
You can make a *Mercury*.

To Silvia

NO more my *Silvia*, do I mean to pray
For those good dayes that ne'r will come away.
I want beliefe; O gentle *Silvia*, be
The patient Saint, and send up vowes for me.

Upon Blanch. *Epig.*

I HAVE seen many Maidens to have haire;
  Both for their comely need, and some to spare:
But *Blanch* has not so much upon her head,
As to bind up her chaps when she is dead.

Upon Umber. *Epig.*

UMBER was painting of a Lyon fierce,
  And working it, by chance from *Umbers* Erse
Flew out a crack, so mighty, that the Fart,
(As *Umber* sweares) did make his Lyon start.

The Poet hath lost his pipe

I CANNOT pipe as I was wont to do,
  Broke is my Reed, hoarse is my singing too:
My wearied Oat Ile hang upon the Tree,
And give it to the *Silvan Deitie.*

True Friendship

WILT thou my true Friend be?
  Then love not mine, but me.

The Apparition of his Mistresse calling him to Elizium

Desunt nonnulla————

COME then, and like two Doves with silv'rie wings,
  Let our soules flie to'th'shades, where ever springs
Sit smiling in the Meads; where Balme and Oile,
Roses and Cassia crown the untill'd soyle.
Where no disease raignes, or infection comes
To blast the Aire, but *Amber-greece* and *Gums.*
This, that, and ev'ry Thicket doth transpire
More sweet, then *Storax* from the hallowed fire:
Where ev'ry tree a wealthy issue beares
Of fragrant Apples, blushing Plums, or Peares: 10
And all the shrubs, with sparkling spangles, shew
Like Morning-Sun-shine tinsilling the dew.
Here in green Meddowes sits eternall May,

Purfling the Margents, while perpetuall Day
So double gilds the Aire, as that no night
Can ever rust th'Enamel of the light.
Here, naked Younglings, handsome Striplings run
Their Goales for Virgins kisses; which when done,
Then unto Dancing forth the learned Round
Commixt they meet, with endlesse Roses crown'd.   20
And here we'l sit on Primrose-banks, and see
Love's *Chorus* led by *Cupid*; and we'l be
Two loving followers too unto the Grove,
Where Poets sing the stories of our love.
There thou shalt hear Divine *Musæus* sing
Of *Hero*, and *Leander*; then Ile bring
Thee to the Stand, where honour'd *Homer* reades
His *Odisees*, and his high *Iliades*.
About whose Throne the crowd of Poets throng
To heare the incantation of his tongue: 30
To *Linus*, then to *Pindar*; and that done,
Ile bring thee *Herrick* to *Anacreon*,
Quaffing his full-crown'd bowles of burning Wine,
And in his Raptures speaking Lines of Thine,
Like to His subject; and as his Frantick-
Looks, shew him truly *Bacchanalian* like,
Besmear'd with Grapes; welcome he shall thee thither,
Where both may rage, both drink and dance together.
Then stately *Virgil*, witty *Ovid*, by
Whom faire *Corinna* sits, and doth comply   40
With Yvorie wrists, his Laureat head, and steeps
His eye in dew of kisses, while he sleeps.
Then soft *Catullus*, sharp-fang'd *Martial*,
And towring *Lucan*, *Horace*, *Juvenal*,
And Snakie *Perseus*, these, and those, whom Rage
(Dropt from the jarres of heaven) fill'd t'engage
All times unto their frenzies; Thou shalt there
Behold them in a spacious Theater.
Among which glories, (crown'd with sacred Bayes,
And flatt'ring Ivie) Two recite their Plaies,   50
Beumont and *Fletcher*, Swans, to whom all eares
Listen, while they (like Syrens in their Spheres)
Sing their *Evadne*; and still more for thee
There yet remaines to know, then thou can'st see

l. 46 from *MSS*.: for *48*

By glim'ring of a fancie: Doe but come,
And there Ile shew thee that capacious roome
In which thy Father *Johnson* now is plac't,
As in a Globe of Radiant fire, and grac't
To be in that Orbe crown'd (that doth include
Those Prophets of the former Magnitude)   60
And be our chiefe; But harke, I heare the Cock,
(The Bell-man of the night) proclaime the clock
Of late struck one; and now I see the prime
Of Day break from the pregnant East, 'tis time
I vanish; more I had to say;
But Night determines here, Away.

Life is the Bodies Light

LIFE is the Bodies light; which once declining,
  Those crimson clouds i'th'cheeks & lips leave shining.
Those counter-changed *Tabbies* in the ayre,
(The Sun once set) all of one colour are.
So, when Death comes, *Fresh tinctures* lose their place,
And dismall Darknesse then doth smutch the face.

Upon Urles. Epig.

URLES had the Gout so, that he co'd not stand;
  Then from his Feet, it shifted to his Hand:
When 'twas in's Feet, his Charity was small;
Now tis in's Hand, he gives no Almes at all.

Upon Franck

FRANCK ne'r wore silk she sweares; but I reply,
  She now weares silk to hide her blood-shot eye.

Love lightly pleased

LET faire or foule my Mistresse be,
  Or low, or tall, she pleaseth me:
Or let her walk, or stand, or sit,
The posture hers, I'm pleas'd with it.
Or let her tongue be still, or stir,
Gracefull is ev'ry thing from her.
Or let her Grant, or else Deny,
My Love will fit each Historie.

l. 61 be our *ed.*: he one *48*. 'one' and 'our' are confused elsewhere in *48*.
'be our' links up grammatically with l. *59*.

The Primrose

A SKE me why I send you here
    This sweet *Infanta* of the yeere?
Aske me why I send to you
This Primrose, thus bepearl'd with dew?
    I will whisper to your eares,
The sweets of Love are mixt with tears.

2.   Ask me why this flower do's show
So yellow-green, and sickly too?
    Ask me why the stalk is weak
And bending, (yet it doth not break?)   10
    I will answer, These discover
What fainting hopes are in a Lover.

The Tythe. To the Bride

I F nine times you your Bride-groome kisse;
    The tenth you know the Parsons is.
Pay then your Tythe; and doing thus,
Prove in your Bride-bed numerous.
If children you have ten, Sir *John*
Won't for his tenth part ask you one.

A Frolick

B RING me my Rose-buds, Drawer come;
    So, while I thus sit crown'd;
Ile drink the aged *Cecubum*,
    Untill the roofe turne round.

Change common to all

A LL things subjected are to Fate;
    Whom this Morne sees most fortunate,
The Ev'ning sees in poore estate.

To Julia

THE Saints-bell calls; and, *Julia*, I must read
The Proper Lessons for the Saints now dead:
To grace which Service, *Julia*, there shall be
One *Holy Collect*, said or sung for Thee.
Dead when thou art, Deare *Julia*, thou shalt have
A *Trentall* sung by Virgins o're thy Grave:
Meane time we two will sing the Dirge of these;
Who dead, deserve our best remembrances.

No luck in Love

I DOE love I know not what;
Sometimes this, & sometimes that:
All conditions I aime at.

2. But, as lucklesse, I have yet
Many shrewd disasters met,
To gaine her whom I wo'd get.

3. Therefore now Ile love no more,
As I've doted heretofore:
He who must be, shall be poore.

In the darke none dainty

NIGHT hides our thefts; all faults then pardon'd be:
All are alike faire, when no spots we see.
Lais and *Lucrece*, in the night time are
Pleasing alike; alike both singular:
Jone, and my *Lady* have at that time one,
One and the selfe-same priz'd complexion.
Then please alike the Pewter and the Plate;
The chosen *Rubie*, and the *Reprobate*.

A charme, or an allay for Love

IF so be a Toad be laid
In a Sheeps-skin newly flaid,
And that ty'd to man 'twil sever
Him and his affections ever.

1.6 *Trentall*] *Tentrall* 48

Upon a free Maid, with a foule breath

Y OU say you'l kiss me, and I thanke you for it:
But stinking breath, I do as hell abhorre it.

Upon Coone. *Epig.*

W HAT is the reason *Coone* so dully smels?
His Nose is over-cool'd with Isicles.

To his Brother in Law Master John Wingfield

F OR being comely, consonant, and free
To most of men, but most of all to me:
For so decreeing, that thy clothes expence
Keepes still within a just circumference:
Then for contriving so to loade thy Board,
As that the Messes ne'r o'r-laid the Lord:
Next for Ordaining, that thy words not swell
To any one unsober *syllable*.
These I co'd praise thee for beyond another,
Wert thou a *Winckfield* onely, not a Brother.   10

The Head-ake

M Y head doth ake,
O *Sappho*! take
Thy fillit,
And bind the paine;
Or bring some bane
To kill it.

2. But lesse that part,
Then my poore heart,
Now is sick:
One kisse from thee   10
Will counsell be,
And Physick.

On himselfe

L IVE by thy Muse thou shalt; when others die
Leaving no Fame to long Posterity:
When Monarchies trans-shifted are, and gone;
Here shall endure thy vast Dominion.

Upon a Maide

HENCE a blessed soule is fled,
Leaving here the body dead:
Which (since here they can't combine)
For the Saint, we'l keep the Shrine.

Upon Spalt

OF Pushes *Spalt* has such a knottie race,
He needs a Tucker for to burle his face.

Of Horne *a Comb-maker*

HORNE sells to others teeth; but has not one
To grace his own Gums, or of Box, or bone.

Upon the troublesome times

O! TIMES most bad,
Without the scope
Of hope
Of better to be had!

2.   Where shall I goe,
Or whither run
To shun
This publique overthrow?

3.   No places are
(This I am sure)
Secure
In this our wasting Warre.

4.   Some storms w'ave past;
Yet we must all
Down fall,
And perish at the last.

Cruelty base in Commanders

NOTHING can be more loathsome, then to see
Power conjoyn'd with Natures *Crueltie*.

10

Upon a sowre-breath Lady. Epig.

FIE, (quoth my Lady) what a stink is here?
When 'twas her breath that was the *Carrionere*.

Upon Lucia

I ASKT my *Lucia* but a kisse;
And she with scorne deny'd me this:
Say then, how ill sho'd I have sped,
Had I then askt her Maidenhead?

Little and loud

LITTLE you are; for Womans sake be proud;
For my sake next, (though little) *be not loud*.

Ship-wrack

HE, who has suffer'd Ship-wrack, feares to saile
Upon the Seas, though with a gentle gale.

Paines without profit

A LONG-LIFES-DAY I've taken paines
For very little, or no gaines:
The Ev'ning's come; here now Ile stop,
And work no more; but shut up Shop.

To his Booke

BE bold my Booke, nor be abasht, or feare
The cutting Thumb-naile, or the Brow severe.
But by the *Muses* sweare, all here is good,
If but well read; or ill read, understood.

His Prayer to Ben. Johnson

WHEN I a Verse shall make,
Know I have praid thee,
For old *Religions* sake,
Saint *Ben* to aide me.

2. Make the way smooth for me,
  When I, thy *Herrick*,
  Honouring thee, on my knee
  Offer my *Lyrick*.

3. Candles Ile give to thee,
  And a new Altar;   10
  And thou Saint *Ben*, shalt be
  Writ in my *Psalter*.

Poverty and Riches

GIVE *Want* her welcome if she comes; we find,
Riches to be but burthens to the mind.

Again

WHO with a little cannot be content,
Endures an everlasting punishment.

The Covetous still Captives

LET'S live with that smal pittance that we have;
Who covets more, is evermore a slave.

Lawes

WHEN Lawes full power have to sway, we see
Little or no part there of Tyrannie.

Of Love ✓

ILE get me hence,
  Because no fence,
Or Fort that I can make here;
  But Love by charmes,
  Or else by Armes
Will storme, or starving take here.

Upon Cock

COCK calls his Wife his Hen: when *Cock* goes too't,
Cock treads his Hen, but treads her under-foot.

To his Muse

Go wooe young *Charles* no more to looke,
    Then but to read this in my Booke:
How *Herrick* beggs, if that he can-
Not like the Muse; to love the man,
Who by the Shepheards, sung (long since)
The Starre-led-birth of Charles the *Prince*.

The bad season makes the Poet sad

Dull to my selfe, and almost dead to these
    My many fresh and fragrant Mistresses:
Lost to all Musick now; since every thing
Puts on the semblance here of sorrowing.
Sick is the Land to'th'heart; and doth endure
More dangerous faintings by her desp'rate cure.
But if that golden Age wo'd come again,
And *Charles* here Rule, as he before did Raign;
If smooth and unperplext the Seasons were,
As when the *Sweet Maria* lived here: 10
I sho'd delight to have my Curles halfe drown'd
In *Tyrian Dewes*, and Head with Roses crown'd.
And once more yet (ere I am laid out dead)
Knock at a Starre with my exalted Head.

To Vulcan

Thy sooty *Godhead*, I desire
    Still to be ready with thy fire:
That sho'd my Booke despised be,
Acceptance it might find of thee.

Like Pattern, like People

This is the height of Justice, that to doe
    Thy selfe, which thou put'st other men unto.
As great men lead; the meaner follow on,
Or to the good, or evill action.

Purposes

No wrath of Men, or rage of Seas
  Can shake a just mans purposes:
No threats of Tyrants, or the Grim
Visage of them can alter him;
But what he doth at first entend,
That he holds firmly to the end.

To the Maids to walke abroad

Come sit we under yonder Tree,
  Where merry as the Maids we'l be.
And as on *Primroses* we sit,
We'l venter (if we can) at wit:
If not, at *Draw-gloves* we will play;
So spend some minutes of the day:
Or else spin out the thread of sands,
Playing at *Questions* and *Commands*:
Or tell what strange Tricks Love can do,
By quickly making one of two.   10
Thus we will sit and talke; but tell
No cruell truths of *Philomell*,
Or *Phillis*, whom hard Fate forc't on,
To kill her selfe for *Demophon*.
But Fables we'l relate; how *Jove*
Put on all shapes to get a Love:
As now a *Satyr*, then a *Swan*;
A *Bull* but then; and now a man.
Next we will act, how young men wooe;
And sigh, and kiss, as Lovers do: 20
And talke of Brides; & who shall make
That wedding-smock, this Bridal-Cake;
That Dress, this Sprig, that Leaf, this Vine;
That smooth and silken Columbine.
This done, we'l draw lots, who shall buy
And guild the Baies and Rosemary:

What Posies for our Wedding Rings;
What Gloves we'l give, and Ribanings:
And smiling at our selves, decree,
Who then the joyning *Priest* shall be.   30
What short sweet Prayers shall be said;
And how the Posset shall be made
With Cream of Lillies (not of Kine)
And *Maiden's-blush*, for spiced wine.
Thus, having talkt, we'l next commend
A kiss to each; and *so we'l end*.

His own Epitaph

As wearied *Pilgrims*, once possest
  Of long'd-for lodging, go to rest:
So I, now having rid my way;
Fix here my Button'd Staffe and stay.
Youth (I confess) hath me mis-led;
But Age hath brought me right to Bed.

A Nuptiall Verse to Mistresse Elizabeth Lee, now Lady Tracie

Spring with the Larke, most comely Bride, and meet
  Your eager Bridegroome with *auspitious* feet.
The Morn's farre spent; and the immortall Sunne
Corrols his cheeke, to see those Rites not done.
Fie, *Lovely maid*! Indeed you are too slow,
When to the Temple Love sho'd runne, not go.
Dispatch your dressing then; and quickly wed:
Then feast, and coy't a little; then to bed.
This day is Loves day; and this busie night
Is yours, in which you challeng'd are to fight   10
With such an arm'd, but such an easie Foe,
As will if you yeeld, lye down conquer'd too.
The Field is pitcht; but such must be your warres,
As that your kisses must out-vie the Starres.
Fall down together vanquisht both, and lye
Drown'd in the bloud of Rubies there, not die.

The Night-piece, to Julia

H ER Eyes the Glow-worme lend thee,
The Shooting Starres attend thee;
And the Elves also,
Whose little eyes glow,
Like the sparks of fire, befriend thee.

2. No *Will-o'th'-Wispe* mis-light thee;
Nor Snake, or Slow-worme bite thee:
But on, on thy way
Not making a stay,
Since Ghost ther's none to affright thee.   10

3. Let not the darke thee cumber;
What though the Moon do's slumber?
The Starres of the night
Will lend thee their light,
Like Tapers cleare without number.

4. Then *Julia* let me wooe thee,
Thus, thus to come unto me:
And when I shall meet
Thy silv'ry feet,
My soule Ile poure into thee.   20

To Sir Clipseby Crew

G IVE me wine, and give me meate,
To create in me a heate,
That my Pulses high may beate.

2. Cold and hunger never yet
Co'd a noble Verse beget;
But your Boules with Sack repleat.

3. Give me these (my Knight) and try
In a Minutes space how I
Can runne mad, and Prophesie.

4. Then if any Peece proves new,   10
And rare, Ile say (my dearest *Crew*)
It was full enspir'd by you.

Good Luck not lasting

IF well the Dice runne, lets applaud the cast:
The happy fortune will not always last.

A Kisse

WHAT is a Kisse? Why this, as some approve;
The sure sweet-Sement, Glue, and Lime of Love.

Glorie

I MAKE no haste to have my Numbers read.
Seldome comes Glorie till a man be dead.

Poets

WANTONS we are; and though our words be such,
Our Lives do differ from our Lines by much.

No despight to the dead

REPROACH we may the living; not the dead:
'Tis cowardice to bite the buried.

To his Verses

WHAT will ye (my poor Orphans) do
When I must leave the World (and you)
Who'l give ye then a sheltring shed,
Or credit ye, when I am dead?
Who'l let ye by their fire sit?
Although ye have a stock of wit,
Already coin'd to pay for it.
I cannot tell; unlesse there be
Some Race of old humanitie
Left (of the large heart, and long hand)   10
Alive, as Noble *Westmorland*;
Or gallant *Newark*; which brave two
May fost'ring fathers be to you.
If not; expect to be no less
Ill us'd, then Babes left fatherless.

His charge to Julia at his death

Dearest of thousands, now the time drawes neere,
That with my Lines, my Life must full-stop here.
Cut off thy haires; and let thy Teares be shed
Over my Turfe, when I am buried.
Then for *effusions*, let none wanting be,
Or other Rites that doe belong to me;
As Love shall helpe thee, when thou do'st go hence
Unto thy everlasting residence.

Upon Love ✓

In a Dreame, Love bad me go
To the Gallies there to Rowe;
In the Vision I askt, why?
Love as briefly did reply;
'Twas better there to toyle, then prove
The turmoiles they endure that love.
I awoke, and then I knew
What Love said was too too true:
Henceforth therefore I will be
As from Love, from trouble free.   10
None pities him that's in the snare,
And warn'd before, wo'd not beware.

The Coblers Catch

Come sit we by the fires side;
And roundly drinke we here;
Till that we see our cheekes Ale-dy'd
And noses tann'd with Beere.

Upon Bran. *Epig.*

What made that mirth last night? the neighbours say,
That *Bran* the Baker did his Breech bewray:
I rather thinke (though they may speake the worst)
'Twas to his Batch, but Leaven laid there first.

Upon Snare, *an Usurer*

SNARE, ten i'th'hundred calls his wife; and why?
Shee brings in much, by carnall usury.
He by extortion brings in three times more:
Say, who's the worst, th'exactor, or the whore?

Upon Grudgings

GRUDGINGS turnes bread to stones, when to the Poore
He gives an almes, and chides them from his doore.

Connubii Flores, *or the well-wishes at Weddings*

Chorus Sacerdotum

1. FROM the Temple to your home
      May a thousand blessings come!
   And a sweet concurring stream
   Of all joyes, to joyn with them.

Chorus Juvenum

2.   Happy day
             Make no long stay
                   Here
               In thy Sphere;
       But give thy place to night,
                  That she,   10
                  As Thee,
                   May be
       Partaker of this sight.
       And since it was thy care
       To see the Younglings wed;
       'Tis fit that Night, the Paire,
       Sho'd see safe brought to Bed.

Chorus Senum

3. Go to your banquet then, but use delight,
   So as to rise still with an appetite.
   Love is a thing most nice; and must be fed   20
   To such a height; but never surfeited.
   What is beyond the mean is ever ill:
   'Tis best to feed Love; but not over-fill:
   Go then discreetly to the Bed of pleasure;
   And this remember, *Vertue keepes the measure.*

Chorus Virginum

4. Luckie signes we have discri'd
   To encourage on the Bride;
   And to these we have espi'd,
   Not a kissing *Cupid* flyes
   Here about, but has his eyes,   30
   To imply your Love is wise.

Chorus Pastorum

5. Here we present a fleece
        To make a peece
            Of cloth;
   Nor Faire, must you be loth
   Your Finger to apply
            To huswiferie.
            Then, then begin
        To spin:
   And (Sweetling) marke you, what a Web will come   40
   Into your Chests, drawn by your painfull Thumb.

Chorus Matronarum

6.   Set you to your Wheele, and wax
        Rich, by the Ductile Wool and Flax.
   Yarne is an Income; and the Huswives thread
   The Larder fils with meat; the Bin with bread.

Chorus Senum

7.   Let wealth come in by comely thrift,
        And not by any sordid shift:
            'Tis haste
            Makes waste;
            Extreames have still their fault;   50
   The softest Fire makes the sweetest Mault.
   Who gripes too hard the dry and slip'rie sand,
   Holds none at all, or little in his hand.

Chorus Virginum

8. Goddesse of Pleasure, Youth and Peace,
   Give them the blessing of encrease:
   And thou *Lucina*, that do'st heare
   The vowes of those, that children beare:
   When as her Aprill houre drawes neare,
   Be thou then propitious there.

Chorus Juvenum

9. Farre hence be all speech, that may anger move: 60
Sweet words must nourish soft and gentle Love.

Chorus omnium

10. Live in the Love of Doves, and having told
The Ravens yeares, go hence more Ripe then old.

To his lovely Mistresses

ONE night i'th'yeare, my dearest Beauties, come
And bring those *dew-drink-offerings* to my Tomb.
When thence ye see my reverend Ghost to rise,
And there to lick th'effused sacrifice:
Though palenes be the Livery that I weare,
Looke ye not wan, or colourlesse for feare.
Trust me I will not hurt ye; or once shew
The least grim looke, or cast a frown on you:
Nor shall the Tapers when I'm there, burn blew.
This I may do (perhaps) as I glide by, 10
Cast on my Girles a glance, and loving eye:
Or fold mine armes, and sigh, because I've lost
The world so soon, and in it, you the most.
Then these, no feares more on your Fancies fall,
Though then I smile, and speake no words at all.

Upon Love ✓

A CHRISTALL Violl *Cupid* brought,
Which had a juice in it:
Of which who drank, he said no thought
Of Love he sho'd admit.

2. I greedy of the prize, did drinke,
And emptied soon the glasse;
Which burnt me so, that I do thinke
The fire of hell it was.

3. Give me my earthen Cups again,
The Christall I contemne; 10
Which, though enchas'd with Pearls, contain
A deadly draught in them.

4. And thou O *Cupid*! come not to
    My Threshold, since I see,
For all I have, or else can do,
    Thou still wilt cozen me.

Upon Gander. *Epig.*

SINCE *Gander* did his prettie Youngling wed;
  Gander (they say) doth each night pisse a Bed:
What is the cause? Why *Gander* will reply,
No Goose layes good eggs that is trodden drye.

Upon Lungs. *Epig.*

LUNGS (as some say) ne'r sets him down to eate,
  But that his breath do's Fly-blow all the meate.

The Beggar to Mab, *the* Fairie Queen

PLEASE your Grace, from out your Store,
  Give an Almes to one that's poore,
That your mickle, may have more.
Black I'm grown for want of meat;
Give me then an Ant to eate;
Or the cleft eare of a Mouse
Over-sowr'd in drinke of Souce:
Or *sweet Lady* reach to me
The *Abdomen* of a Bee;
Or commend a *Crickets-hip*,   10
Or his *Huckson*, to my Scrip.
Give for bread, a little bit
Of a Pease, that 'gins to chit,
And my full thanks take for it.
Floure of Fuz-balls, that's too good
For a man in needy-hood:
But the Meal of Mill-dust can
Well content a craving man.
Any Orts the Elves refuse
Well will serve the Beggars use.   20
But if this may seem too much
For an Almes; then give me such

Little bits, that nestle there
In the Pris'ners *Panier*.
So a blessing light upon
You, and mighty *Oberon*:
That your plenty last till when,
I return your Almes agen.

An end decreed

L ET'S be jocund while we may;
   All things have an ending day:
And when once the Work is done;
Fates revolve no Flax th'ave spun.

Upon a child

H ERE a pretty Baby lies
   Sung asleep with Lullabies:
Pray be silent, and not stirre
Th'easie earth that covers her.

Painting sometimes permitted

I F Nature do deny
  Colours, let Art supply.

Farwell Frost, or welcome the Spring

F LED are the Frosts, and now the Fields appeare
  Re-cloth'd in fresh and verdant Diaper.
Thaw'd are the snowes, and now the lusty Spring
Gives to each Mead a neat enameling.
The Palms put forth their Gemmes, and every Tree
Now swaggers in her Leavy gallantry.
The while the *Daulian Minstrell* sweetly sings,
With warbling Notes, her *Tyrrean* sufferings.
What gentle Winds perspire? As if here
Never had been the *Northern Plunderer*   10
To strip the Trees, and Fields, to their distresse,
Leaving them to a pittied nakednesse.

And look how when a frantick Storme doth tear
A stubborn Oake, or Holme (long growing there)
But lul'd to calmnesse, then succeeds a breeze
That scarcely stirs the nodding leaves of Trees:
So when this War (which tempest-like doth spoil
Our salt, our Corn, our Honie, Wine, and Oile)
Falls to a temper, and doth mildly cast
His inconsiderate Frenzie off (at last)   20
The gentle Dove may, when these turmoils cease,
Bring in her Bill, once more, *the Branch of Peace.*

The Hag

THE Hag is astride,
   This night for to ride;
The Devill and shee together:
   Through thick, and through thin,
   Now out, and then in,
Though ne'r so foule be the weather.

2.   A Thorn or a Burr
   She takes for a Spurre:
With a lash of a Bramble she rides now,
   Through Brakes and through Bryars,   10
   O're Ditches, and Mires,
She followes the Spirit that guides now.

3.   No Beast, for his food,
   Dares now range the wood;
But husht in his laire he lies lurking:
   While mischeifs, by these,
   On Land and on Seas,
At noone of Night are a working.

4.   The storme will arise,
   And trouble the skies;   20
This night, and more for the wonder,
   The ghost from the Tomb
   Affrighted shall come,
Cal'd out by the clap of the Thunder.

Upon an old man a Residenciarie

TREAD, Sirs, as lightly as ye can
   Upon the grave of this old man.
Twice fortie (bating but one year,
And thrice three weekes) he lived here.
Whom gentle fate translated hence
To a more happy Residence.
Yet, Reader, let me tell thee this
(Which from his ghost a promise is)
If here ye will some few teares shed,
He'l never haunt ye now he's dead.   10

Upon Teares

TEARES, though th'are here below the sinners brine,
   Above they are the Angels spiced wine.

Physitians

PHYSITIANS fight not against men; but these
   Combate for men, by conquering the disease.

The Primitiæ to Parents

OUR *Houshold-gods* our Parents be;
   And manners good requires, that we
The first Fruits give to them, who gave
Us hands to get what here we have.

Upon Cob. Epig.

COB clouts his shooes, and as the story tells,
   His thumb-nailes-par'd, afford him sperrables.

Upon Lucie. Epig.

SOUND Teeth has *Lucie*, pure as Pearl, and small,
   With mellow Lips, and luscious there withall.

Upon Skoles. Epig.

SKOLES stinks so deadly, that his Breeches loath
   His dampish Buttocks furthermore to cloath:
Cloy'd they are up with Arse; but hope, one blast
Will whirle about, and blow them thence at last.

To Silvia

I AM holy, while I stand
   Circum-crost by thy pure hand:
But when that is gone; Again,
I, as others, am *Prophane.*

To his Closet-Gods

WHEN I goe Hence ye *Closet-Gods,* I feare
   Never againe to have ingression here:
Where I have had, what ever thing co'd be
Pleasant, and precious to my Muse and me.
Besides rare sweets, I had a Book which none
Co'd reade the Intext but my selfe alone.
About the Cover of this Book there went
A curious-comely clean *Compartiement:*
And, in the midst, to grace it more, was set
A blushing-pretty-peeping Rubelet: 10
But now 'tis clos'd; and being shut, & seal'd,
Be it, O be it, never more reveal'd!
Keep here still, *Closet-Gods,* 'fore whom I've set
Oblations oft, of sweetest Marmelet.

A Bacchanàlian Verse

FILL me a mighty Bowle
      Up to the brink:
      That I may drink
Unto my *Johnsons* soule.

2. Crowne it agen agen;
      And thrice repeat
      That happy heat;
To drink to Thee my *Ben.*

3. Well I can quaffe, I see,
      To th'number five,   10
      Or nine; but thrive
In frenzie ne'r like thee.

2.8 *Compartiement*] *Compartlement 48*
3.2 brink] brim *48*

Long lookt for comes at last

THOUGH long it be, yeeres may repay the debt;
None loseth that, which he in time may get.

To Youth

DRINK Wine, and live here blithefull, while ye may:
The morrowes life too late is, Live to day.

Never too late to dye

NO man comes late unto that place from whence
Never man yet had a regredience.

A Hymne to the Muses

O! YOU the Virgins nine!
  That doe our soules encline
To noble Discipline!
Nod to this vow of mine:
Come then, and now enspire
My violl and my lyre
With your eternall fire:
And make me one entire
Composer in your Quire.
Then I'le your Altars strew   10
With Roses sweet and new;
And ever live a true
Acknowledger of you.

On himselfe

ILE sing no more, nor will I longer write
Of that sweet Lady, or that gallant Knight:
Ile sing no more of Frosts, Snowes, Dews and Showers;
No more of Groves, Meades, Springs, and wreaths of Flowers:
Ile write no more, nor will I tell or sing
Of *Cupid*, and his wittie coozning:
Ile sing no more of death, or shall the grave
No more my Dirges, and my Trentalls have.

Upon Jone *and* Jane

JONE is a wench that's painted;
  Jone is a Girle that's tainted;
    Yet *Jone* she goes
    Like one of those
Whom purity had Sainted.

Jane is a Girle that's prittie;
Jane is a wench that's wittie;
    Yet, who wo'd think,
    Her breath do's stinke,
As so it doth? that's pittie.   10

To Momus

WHO read'st this Book that I have writ,
  And can'st not mend, but carpe at it:
By all the muses! thou shalt be
Anathema to it, and me.

Ambition

IN wayes to greatnesse, think on this,
  That slippery all Ambition is.

The Country life, to the honoured M. End. Porter, *Groome of the Bed-Chamber to His Maj.*

SWEET Country life, to such unknown,
  Whose lives are others, not their own!
But serving Courts, and Cities, be
Less happy, less enjoying thee.
Thou never Plow'st the Oceans foame
To seek, and bring rough Pepper home:
Nor to the Eastern Ind dost rove
To bring from thence the scorched Clove.
Nor, with the losse of thy lov'd rest,
Bring'st home the Ingot from the West.   10
No, thy Ambition's Master-piece
Flies no thought higher then a fleece:

Or how to pay thy Hinds, and cleere
All scores; and so to end the yeere:
But walk'st about thine own dear bounds,
Not envying others larger grounds:
For well thou know'st, *'tis not th'extent*
Of Land makes life, but sweet content.
When now the Cock (the Plow-mans Horne)
Calls forth the lilly-wristed Morne;   20
Then to thy corn-fields thou dost goe,
Which though well soyl'd, yet thou dost know,
That the best compost for the Lands
Is the wise Masters Feet, and Hands.
There at the Plough thou find'st thy Teame,
With a Hind whistling there to them:
And cheer'st them up, by singing how
The Kingdoms portion *is the Plow.*
This done, then to th'enameld Meads
Thou go'st; and as thy foot there treads,   30
Thou seest a present God-like Power
Imprinted in each Herbe and Flower:
And smell'st the breath of great-ey'd Kine,
Sweet as the blossomes of the Vine.
Here thou behold'st thy large sleek Neat
Unto the Dew-laps up in meat:
And, as thou look'st, the wanton Steere,
The Heifer, Cow, and Oxe draw neere
To make a pleasing pastime there.
These seen, thou go'st to view thy flocks   40
Of sheep, (safe from the Wolfe and Fox)
And find'st their bellies there as full
Of short sweet grasse, as backs with wool.
And leav'st them (as they feed and fill)
A Shepherd piping on a hill.
For Sports, for Pagentrie, and Playes,
Thou hast thy Eves, and Holydayes:
On which the young men and maids meet,
To exercise their dancing feet:
Tripping the comely country round,   50
With Daffadils and Daisies crown'd.
Thy Wakes, thy Quintels, here thou hast,
Thy May-poles too with Garlands grac't:
Thy Morris-dance; thy Whitsun-ale;

⌐ Thy Sheering-feast, which never faile.
⌐Thy Harvest home; thy Wassaile bowle,
ˋThat's tost up after Fox i'th'Hole.
ˋThy Mummeries; thy Twelfe-tide Kings
ˋAnd Queenes; thy Christmas revellings:
Thy Nut-browne mirth; thy Russet wit;   60
And no man payes too deare for it.
To these, thou hast thy times to goe
And trace the Hare i'th'trecherous Snow:
Thy witty wiles to draw, and get
The Larke into the Trammell net:
Thou hast thy Cockrood, and thy Glade
To take the precious Phesant made:
Thy Lime-twigs, Snares, and Pit-falls then
To catch the pilfring Birds, not Men.
O happy life! if that their good   70
The Husbandmen but understood!
Who all the day themselves doe please,
And Younglings, with such sports as these.
And, lying down, have nought t'affright
Sweet sleep, that makes more short the night.
                    Cætera desunt————

To *Electra*

I DARE not ask a kisse;
  I dare not beg a smile;
Lest having that, or this,
  I might grow proud the while.

2. No, no, the utmost share
  Of my desire, shall be
Onely to kisse that Aire,
  That lately kissed thee.

To his worthy friend, *M*. Arthur Bartly

WHEN after many Lusters thou shalt be
  Wrapt up in Seare-cloth with thine Ancestrie:
When of thy ragg'd *Escutcheons* shall be seene
So little left, as if they ne'r had been:
Thou shalt thy Name have, and thy Fames best trust,
Here with the Generation of my Just.

231

What kind of Mistresse he would have

BE the Mistresse of my choice,
    Cleane in manners, cleere in voice:
Be she witty, more then wise;
Pure enough, though not Precise:
Be she shewing in her dresse,
Like a civill Wilderness;
That the curious may detect
Order in a sweet neglect:
Be she rowling in her eye,
Tempting all the passers by: 10
And each Ringlet of her haire,
An Enchantment, or a Snare,
For to catch the Lookers on;
But her self held fast by none.
Let her *Lucrece* all day be,
Thais in the night, to me.
Be she such, as neither will
Famish me, nor over-fill.

Upon Zelot

IS *Zelot* pure? he is: ye see he weares
    The signe of *Circumcision* in his eares.

The Rosemarie branch

GROW for two ends, it matters not at all,
    Be't for my *Bridall*, or my *Buriall*.

Upon Madam Ursly, *Epig.*

FOR ropes of pearle, first Madam *Ursly* showes
    A chaine of Cornes, pickt from her eares and toes:
Then, next, to match *Tradescant's* curious shels,
Nailes from her fingers mew'd, she shewes: what els?
Why then (forsooth) a Carcanet is shown
Of teeth, as deaf as nuts, and all her own.

Upon Crab, *Epigr.*

CRAB faces gownes with sundry Furres; 'tis known,
    He keeps the Fox-furre for to face his own.

A Paranæticall, or Advisive Verse, to his friend, M. John Wicks

Is this a life, to break thy sleep?
   To rise as soon as day doth peep?
To tire thy patient Oxe or Asse
By noone, and let thy good dayes passe,
Not knowing This, that *Jove* decrees
Some mirth, t'adulce mans miseries?
No; 'tis a life, to have thine oyle,
Without extortion, from thy soyle:
Thy faithfull fields to yeeld thee Graine,
Although with some, yet little paine: 10
To have thy mind, and nuptiall bed,
With feares, and cares uncumbered:
A Pleasing Wife, that by thy side
Lies softly panting like a Bride.
This is to live, and to endeere
Those minutes, Time has lent us here.
Then, while Fates suffer, live thou free,
(As is that ayre that circles thee)
And crown thy temples too, and let
Thy servant, not thy own self, sweat,   20
To strut thy barnes with sheafs of Wheat.
Time steals away like to a stream,
And we glide hence away with them.
No sound recalls the houres once fled,
Or Roses, being withered:
Nor us (my Friend) when we are lost,
Like to a Deaw, or melted Frost.
Then live we mirthfull, while we should,
And turn the iron Age to Gold.
Let's feast, and frolick, sing, and play,   30
And thus lesse last, then live our Day.
Whose life with care is overcast,
That man's not said to live, but last:
Nor is't a life, seven yeares to tell,
But for to live that half seven well:
And that wee'l do; as men, who know,
Some few sands spent, we hence must go,
Both to be blended in the Urn,
From whence there's never a return.

Once seen, and no more

THOUSANDS each day passe by, which wee,
Once past and gone, no more shall see.

Love

THIS Axiom I have often heard,
Kings ought to be more lov'd, then fear'd.

To M. Denham, *on his Prospective Poem*

OR lookt I back unto the Times hence flown,
To praise those Muses, and dislike our own?
Or did I walk those *Pean*-Gardens through,
To kick the Flow'rs, and scorn their odours too?
I might (and justly) be reputed (here)
One nicely mad, or peevishly severe.
But by *Apollo!* as I worship wit,
(Where I have cause to burn perfumes to it:)
So, I confesse, 'tis somwhat to do well
In our high art, although we can't excell,   10
Like thee; or dare the Buskins to unloose
Of thy brave, bold, and sweet *Maronian* Muse.
But since I'm cal'd (rare *Denham*) to be gone,
Take from thy *Herrick* this conclusion:
'Tis dignity in others, if they be
Crown'd Poets; yet live Princes under thee:
The while their wreaths and Purple Robes do shine,
Lesse by their own jemms, then those beams of thine.

A Hymne, *to the* Lares

IT was, and still my care is,
To worship ye, the *Lares*,
With crowns of greenest Parsley,
And Garlick chives not scarcely:
For favours here to warme me,
And not by fire to harme me.
For gladding so my hearth here,
With inoffensive mirth here;

That while the Wassaile Bowle here
With *North-down* Ale doth troule here,   10
No sillable doth fall here,
To marre the mirth at all here.
For which, ô *Chimney-keepers!*
(I dare not call ye Sweepers)
So long as I am able
To keep a countrey-table,
Great be my fare, or small cheere,
I'le eat and drink up all here.

Deniall in women no disheartning to men

WOMEN, although they ne're so goodly make it,
Their fashion is, but to say no, to take it.

Adversity

LOVE *is maintain'd by wealth; when all is spent,*
Adversity then breeds the discontent.

To Fortune

TUMBLE me down, and I will sit
Upon my ruines (smiling yet:)
Teare me to tatters; yet I'le be
Patient in my necessitie.
Laugh at my scraps of cloaths, and shun
Me, as a fear'd infection:
Yet scarre-crow-like I'le walk, as one,
Neglecting thy derision.

To Anthea

COME *Anthea*, know thou this,
Love at no time idle is:
Let's be doing, though we play
But at push-pin (half the day:)
Chains of sweet bents let us make,
Captive one, or both, to take:
In which bondage we will lie,
Soules transfusing thus, and die.

Cruelties

NERO commanded; but withdrew his eyes
From the beholding Death, and cruelties.

Perseverance

HAST thou begun an act? ne're then give o're:
No man despaires to do what's done before.

Upon his Verses

WHAT off-spring other men have got,
The how, where, when, I question not.
These are the Children I have left;
Adopted some; none got by theft.
But all are toucht (like lawfull plate)
And no Verse illegitimate.

Distance betters Dignities

KINGS must not oft be seen by publike eyes;
State at a distance adds to dignities.

Health

HEALTH is no other (as the learned hold)
But a just measure both of Heat and Cold.

To Dianeme. A Ceremonie in Glocester

I'LE to thee a Simnell bring,
'Gainst thou go'st a *mothering*,
So that, when she blesseth thee,
Half that blessing thou'lt give me.

To the King

GIVE way, give way, now, now my *Charles* shines here,
A Publike Light (in this immensive Sphere.)
Some starres were fixt before; but these are dim,
Compar'd (in this my ample Orbe) to Him.
Draw in your feeble fiers, while that He
Appeares but in His Meaner Majestie.

Where, if such glory flashes from His Name,
Which is His Shade, who can abide His Flame!
Princes, and such like Publike Lights as these,
Must not be lookt on, but at distances: 10
For, if we gaze on These brave Lamps too neer,
Our eyes they'l blind, or if not blind, they'l bleer.

The Funerall Rites of the Rose

THE Rose was sick, and smiling di'd;
   And (being to be sanctifi'd)
About the Bed, there sighing stood
The sweet, and flowrie Sisterhood.
Some hung the head, while some did bring
(To wash her) water from the Spring.
Some laid her forth, while other wept,
But all a solemne Fast there kept.
The holy Sisters some among
The sacred *Dirge* and *Trentall* sung.   10
But ah! what sweets smelt every where,
As Heaven had spent all perfumes there.
At last, when prayers for the dead,
And Rites were all accomplished;
They, weeping, spread a Lawnie Loome,
And clos'd her up, as in a Tombe.

The Rainbow: or curious Covenant

MINE eyes, like clouds, were drizling raine,
   And as they thus did entertaine
The gentle Beams from *Julia's* sight
To mine eyes level'd opposite:
O Thing admir'd! there did appeare
A curious Rainbow smiling there;
Which was the Covenant, that she
No more wo'd drown mine eyes, or me.

The last stroke strike sure

THOUGH by well-warding many blowes w'ave past,
   That stroke most fear'd is, which is struck the last.

3 *(title) strike*] *(?) strikes*

Fortune

FORTUNE's a blind profuser of her own,
Too much she gives to some, enough to none.

Stool-ball

1 AT Stool-ball, *Lucia*, let us play,
For Sugar-cakes and Wine;
Or for a Tansie let us pay,
The losse or thine, or mine.

2 If thou, my Deere, a winner be
At trundling of the Ball,
The wager thou shalt have, and me,
And my misfortunes all.

3 But if (my Sweetest) I shall get,
Then I desire but this;   10
That likewise I may pay the Bet,
And have for all a kisse.

To Sappho

LET us now take time, and play,
Love, and live here while we may;
Drink rich wine; and make good cheere,
While we have our being here:
For, once dead, and laid i'th grave,
No return from thence we have.

On Poet Prat, *Epigr.*

PRAT He writes Satyres; but herein's the fault,
In no one Satyre there's a mite of salt.

Upon Tuck, *Epigr.*

AT Post and Paire, or Slam, *Tom Tuck* would play
This Christmas, but his want wherwith, sayes Nay.

Biting of Beggars

WHO, railing, drives the Lazar from his door,
Instead of almes, sets dogs upon the poor.

The May-pole

THE May-pole is up,
Now give me the cup;
I'le drink to the Garlands a-round it:
But first unto those
Whose hands did compose
The glory of flowers that crown'd it.

A health to my Girles,
Whose husbands may Earles
Or Lords be, (granting my wishes)
And when that ye wed   10
To the Bridall Bed,
Then multiply all, like to Fishes.

Men mind no state in sicknesse

THAT flow of Gallants which approach
To kisse thy hand from out the coach;
That fleet of Lackeyes, which do run
Before thy swift Postilion;
Those strong-hoof'd Mules, which we behold,
Rein'd in with Purple, Pearl, and gold,
And shod with silver, prove to be
The drawers of the *axeltree*.
Thy Wife, thy Children, and the state
Of *Persian* Loomes, and *antique* Plate: 10
All these, and more, shall then afford
No joy to thee their sickly Lord.

Adversity

ADVERSITY hurts none, but onely such
Whom whitest Fortune dandled has too much.

Want

NEED is no vice at all; though here it be,
With men, a loathed inconveniencie.

Griefe

SORROWES divided amongst many, lesse
Discruciate a man in deep distresse.

239

Love palpable

I PREST my *Julia's* lips, and in the kisse
Her Soule and Love were palpable in this.

No action hard to affection

NOTHING hard, or harsh can prove
Unto those that truly love.

Meane things overcome mighty

BY the weak'st means things mighty are o'rethrown,
He's Lord of thy life, who contemnes his own.

Upon Trigg, *Epig.*

TRIGG having turn'd his sute, he struts in state,
And tells the world, he's now regenerate.

Upon Smeaton

HOW co'd *Luke Smeaton* weare a shoe, or boot,
Who two and thirty cornes had on a foot.

The Bracelet of Pearle: *to* Silvia

I BRAKE thy Bracelet 'gainst my will;
        And, wretched, I did see
Thee discomposed then, and still
        Art discontent with me.

One jemme was lost; and I will get
        A richer pearle for thee,
Then ever, dearest *Silvia*, yet
        Was drunk to *Antonie*.

Or, for revenge, I'le tell thee what
        Thou for the breach shalt do;   10
First, crack the strings, and after that,
        Cleave thou my heart in two.

How Roses came red

'TIS said, as *Cupid* danc't among
    The *Gods*, he down the Nectar flung;
Which, on the white *Rose* being shed,
Made it for ever after red.

Kings

MEN are not born Kings, but are men renown'd;
    Chose first, confirm'd next, & at last are crown'd.

First work, and then wages

PREPOST'ROUS is that order, when we run
    To ask our wages, e're our work be done.

Teares, and Laughter

KNEW'ST thou, one moneth wo'd take thy life away,
    Thou'dst weep; but laugh, sho'd it not last a day.

Glory

GLORY no other thing is (*Tullie* sayes)
    Then a mans frequent Fame, spoke out with praise.

Possessions

THOSE possessions short-liv'd are,
    Into the which we come by warre.

Laxare fibulam

TO loose the button, is no lesse,
    Then to cast off all bashfulnesse.

His returne to London

FROM the dull confines of the drooping West,
To see the day spring from the pregnant East,
Ravisht in spirit, I come, nay more, I flie
To thee, blest place of my Nativitie!
Thus, thus with hallowed foot I touch the ground,
With thousand blessings by thy Fortune crown'd.
O fruitfull Genius! that bestowest here
An everlasting plenty, yeere by yeere.
O *Place!* O *People!* Manners! fram'd to please
All *Nations, Customes, Kindreds, Languages!*   10
I am a free-born *Roman*; suffer then,
That I amongst you live a Citizen.
London my home is: though by hard fate sent
Into a long and irksome banishment;
Yet since cal'd back; henceforward let me be,
O native countrey, repossest by thee!
For, rather then I'le to the West return,
I'le beg of thee first here to have mine Urn.
Weak I am grown, and must in short time fall;
Give thou my sacred Reliques Buriall.   20

Not every day fit for Verse

'TIS not ev'ry day, that I
Fitted am to prophesie:
No, but when the Spirit fils
The fantastick Pannicles:
Full of fier; then I write
As the Godhead doth indite.
Thus inrag'd, my lines are hurl'd,
Like the *Sybells*, through the world.
Look how next the holy fier
Either slakes, or doth retire;   10
So the Fancie cooles, till when
That brave Spirit comes agen.

Poverty the greatest pack

TO mortall men great loads allotted be,
But of all packs, no pack like poverty.

A Beucolick, or discourse of Neatherds

1 COME blithefull Neatherds, let us lay
   A wager, who the best shall play,
   Of thee, or I, the Roundelay,
   That fits the businesse of the Day.

Chor. And *Lallage* the Judge shall be,
   To give the prize to thee, or me.

2 Content, begin, and I will bet
   A Heifer smooth, and black as jet,
   In every part alike compleat,
   And wanton as a Kid as yet.   10

Chor. And *Lallage* (with cow-like eyes)
   Shall be Disposeresse of the prize.

1 Against thy Heifer, I will here
   Lay to thy stake a lustie Steere,
   With gilded hornes, and burnisht cleere.
Chor. Why then begin, and let us heare
   The soft, the sweet, the mellow note
   That gently purles from eithers Oat.

2 The stakes are laid: let's now apply
   Each one to make his melody: 20
Lal. The equall Umpire shall be I,
   Who'l hear, and so judge righteously.

Chor. Much time is spent in prate; begin,
   And sooner play, the sooner win.
                [*He playes.*

1 That's sweetly touch't, I must confesse:
   Thou art a man of worthinesse:
   But hark how I can now expresse
   My love unto my Neatherdesse.
                [*He sings.*

Chor. A suger'd note! and sound as sweet
   As Kine, when they at milking meet.   30

1 Now for to win thy Heifer faire,
   I'le strike thee such a nimble Ayre,
   That thou shalt say (thy selfe) 'tis rare;
   And title me without compare.

Chor. Lay by a while your Pipes, and rest,
   Since both have here deserved best.

2 To get thy Steerling, once again,
I'le play thee such another strain;
That thou shalt swear, my Pipe do's raigne
Over thine Oat, as Soveraigne.   40

                              [*He sings.*

Chor. And *Lallage* shall tell by this,
Whose now the prize and wager is.

1 Give me the prize: 2. The day is mine:
1 Not so; my Pipe has silenc't thine:
And hadst thou wager'd twenty Kine,
They were mine own. *Lal.* In love combine.

Chor. And lay we down our Pipes together,
As wearie, not o'recome by either.

True safety

'TIS not the Walls, or purple, that defends
A Prince from Foes; but 'tis his Fort of Friends.

A Prognostick

As many Lawes and Lawyers do expresse
Nought but a Kingdoms ill-affectednesse:
Ev'n so, those streets and houses do but show
Store of diseases, where Physitians flow.

Upon Julia's sweat

WO'D ye oyle of Blossomes get?
Take it from my *Julia's* sweat:
Oyl of Lillies, and of Spike,
From her moysture take the like:
Let her breath, or let her blow,
All rich spices thence will flow.

Proof to no purpose

YOU see this gentle streame, that glides,
Shov'd on, by quick succeeding Tides:
Trie if this sober streame you can
Follow to th'wilder Ocean:

And see, if there it keeps unspent
In that congesting element.
Next, from that world of waters, then
By poares and cavernes back agen
Induc't that inadultrate same
Streame to the Spring from whence it came.   10
This with a wonder when ye do,
As easie, and els easier too:
Then may ye recollect the graines
Of my particular Remaines;
After a thousand Lusters hurld,
By ruffling winds, about the world.

Fame

'TIS still observ'd, that Fame ne're sings
     The order, but the Sum of things.

By use comes easinesse

OFT bend the Bow, and thou with ease shalt do,
     What others can't with all their strength put to.

To the Genius of his house

COMMAND the Roofe great *Genius*, and from thence
     Into this house powre downe thy influence,
That through each room a golden pipe may run
Of living water by thy *Benizon*.
Fulfill the Larders, and with strengthning bread
Be evermore these Bynns replenished.
Next, like a Bishop consecrate my ground,
That luckie Fairies here may dance their Round:
And after that, lay downe some silver pence,
The Masters charge and care to recompence.   10
Charme then the chambers; make the beds for ease,
More then for peevish pining sicknesses.
Fix the foundation fast, and let the Roofe
Grow old with time, but yet keep weather-proofe.

His Grange, or private wealth

THOUGH Clock,
To tell how night drawes hence, I've none,
    A Cock,
I have, to sing how day drawes on.
    I have
A maid (my *Prew*) by good luck sent,
    To save
That little, Fates me gave or lent.
    A Hen
I keep, which creeking day by day,   10
    Tells when
She goes her long white egg to lay.
    A goose
I have, which, with a jealous eare,
    Lets loose
Her tongue, to tell what danger's neare.
    A Lamb
I keep (tame) with my morsells fed,
    Whose Dam
An Orphan left him (lately dead.)   20
    A Cat
I keep, that playes about my House,
    Grown fat,
With eating many a miching Mouse.
    To these
A * *Trasy* I do keep, whereby   * His Spaniel.
    I please
The more my rurall privacie:
    Which are
But toyes, to give my heart some ease: 30
    Where care
None is, slight things do lightly please.

Good precepts, or counsell

IN all thy need, be thou possest
  Still with a well-prepared brest:
Nor let the shackles make thee sad;
Thou canst but have, what others had.

And this for comfort thou must know,
Times that are ill wo'nt still be so.
Clouds will not ever powre down raine;
A sullen day will cleere againe.
First, peales of Thunder we must heare,
Then Lutes and Harpes shall stroke the eare.   10

Money makes the mirth

WHEN all Birds els do of their musick faile,
Money's the still-sweet-singing *Nightingale.*

Up tailes all

BEGIN with a kisse,
Go on too with this:
And thus, thus, thus let us smother
Our lips for a while,
But let's not beguile
Our hope of one for the other.

This play, be assur'd,
Long enough has endur'd,
Since more and more is exacted;
For love he doth call   10
For his Uptailes all;
And that's the part to be acted.

Upon Franck

FRANCK wo'd go scoure her teeth; and setting to't,
Twice two fell out, all rotten at the root.

Upon Lucia *dabled in the deaw*

MY *Lucia* in the deaw did go,
And prettily bedabled so,
Her cloaths held up, she shew'd withall
Her decent legs, cleane, long and small.
I follow'd after to descrie
Part of the nak't sincerity;
But still the envious Scene between
Deni'd the Mask I wo'd have seen.

Charon *and* Phylomel, *a Dialogue sung*

Ph. CHARON! O gentle *Charon*! let me wooe thee,
    By tears and pitie now to come unto mee.
Ch. What voice so sweet and charming do I heare?
    Say what thou art. *Ph.* I prithee first draw neare.
Ch. A sound I heare, but nothing yet can see,
    Speak where thou art. *Ph.* O *Charon* pittie me!
    I am a bird, and though no name I tell,
    My warbling note will say I'm *Phylomel.*
Ch. What's that to me, I waft nor fish or fowles,
    Nor Beasts (fond thing) but only humane soules.   10
Ph. Alas for me! *Ch.* Shame on thy witching note,
    That made me thus hoist saile, and bring my Boat:
    But Ile returne; what mischief brought thee hither?
Ph. A deale of Love, and much, much Griefe together.
Ch. What's thy request? *Ph.* that since she's now beneath
    Who fed my life, I'le follow her in death.
Ch. And is that all? I'm gone. *Ph.* By love I pray thee,
Ch. Talk not of love, all pray, but few soules pay me.
Ph. Ile give thee vows & tears. *Ch.* can tears pay skores
    For mending sails, for patching Boat and Oares?   20
Ph. I'le beg a penny, or Ile sing so long,
    Till thou shalt say, I've paid thee with a song.
Ch. Why then begin, and all the while we make
    Our slothfull passage o're the Stygian Lake,
    Thou & I'le sing to make these dull Shades merry,
    Who els with tears wo'd doubtles drown my ferry.

Upon Paul. *Epigr.*

PAULS hands do give, what give they bread or meat,
    Or money? no, but onely deaw and sweat.
As stones and salt gloves use to give, even so
Pauls hands do give, nought else for ought we know.

2.3 gloves] *Possibly a misprint for* shores, *which would make better sense*

Upon Sibb. *Epigr.*

SIBB when she saw her face how hard it was,
For anger spat on thee her Looking-glasse:
But weep not *Christall*; for the shame was meant
Not unto thee, but That thou didst present.

A Ternarie of littles, upon a pipkin of Jellie sent to a Lady

1 A LITTLE Saint best fits a little Shrine,
  A little prop best fits a little Vine,
   As my small Cruse best fits my little Wine.

2 A little Seed best fits a little Soyle,
  A little Trade best fits a little Toyle:
  As my small Jarre best fits my little Oyle.

3 A little Bin best fits a little Bread,
  A little Garland fits a little Head:
  As my small stuffe best fits my little Shed.

4 A little Hearth best fits a little Fire,
  A little Chappell fits a little Quire,
  As my small Bell best fits my little Spire.

5 A little streame best fits a little Boat;
  A little lead best fits a little Float;
  As my small Pipe best fits my little note.

6 A little meat best fits a little bellie,
  As sweetly Lady, give me leave to tell ye,
  This little Pipkin fits this little Jellie.

Upon the Roses in Julias *bosome*

THRICE happie Roses, so much grac't, to have
Within the Bosome of my Love your grave.
Die when ye will, your sepulchre is knowne,
Your Grave her Bosome is, the Lawne the Stone.

Maids nay's are nothing

MAIDS nay's are nothing, they are shie
But to desire what they denie.

The smell of the Sacrifice

THE Gods require the thighes
    Of Beeves for sacrifice;
Which rosted, we the steam
Must sacrifice to them:
Who though they do not eat,
Yet love the smell of meat.

Lovers how they come and part

A GYGES Ring they beare about them still,
    To be, and not seen when and where they will.
They tread on clouds, and though they sometimes fall,
They fall like dew, but make no noise at all.
So silently they one to th'other come,
As colours steale into the Peare or Plum,
And Aire-like, leave no pression to be seen
Where e're they met, or parting place has been.

To women, to hide their teeth, if they be rotten or rusty

CLOSE keep your lips, if that you meane
    To be accounted inside cleane:
For if you cleave them, we shall see
There in your teeth much Leprosie.

In praise of women

O JUPITER, sho'd I speake ill
    Of woman-kind, first die I will;
Since that I know, 'mong all the rest
Of creatures, woman is the best.

The Apron of Flowers

TO gather Flowers *Sappha* went,
    And homeward she did bring
Within her Lawnie Continent,
    The treasure of the Spring.

She smiling blusht, and blushing smil'd,
    And sweetly blushing thus,
She lookt as she'd been got with child
    By young *Favonius*.

Her Apron gave (as she did passe)
    An Odor more divine,   10
More pleasing too, then ever was
    The lap of *Proserpine*.

The Candor of Julias *teeth*

WHITE as *Zenobias* teeth, the which the Girles
Of Rome did weare for their most precious Pearles.

Upon her weeping

SHE wept upon her cheeks, and weeping so,
She seem'd to quench loves fires that there did glow.

Another upon her weeping ✓

SHE by the River sate, and sitting there,
She wept, and made it deeper by a teare.

Delay

BREAK off Delay, since we but read of one
That ever prosper'd by *Cunctation*.

To Sir John Berkley, *Governour of Exeter*

STAND forth brave man, since Fate has made thee here
The *Hector* over *Aged Exeter*;
Who for a long sad time has weeping stood,
Like a *poore Lady* lost in Widdowhood:
But feares not now to see her safety sold
(As other Townes and Cities were) for gold,
By those ignoble *Births*, which shame the stem
That gave Progermination unto them:

Whose restlesse *Ghosts* shall heare their children sing,
Our Sires betraid their Countrey and their King. 10
True, if this Citie seven times rounded was
With rock, and seven times circumflankt with brasse,
Yet if thou wert not, *Berkley*, loyall proofe,
The Senators down tumbling with the Roofe,
Would into prais'd (but pitied) ruines fall,
Leaving no shew, where stood the *Capitoll*.
But thou art just and itchlesse, and dost please
Thy *Genius* with two strength'ning *Buttresses*,
Faith, and *Affection:* which will never slip
To weaken this thy great *Dictator-ship.* 20

To Electra. *Love looks for Love*

LOVE love begets, then never be
Unsoft to him who's smooth to thee.
Tygers and Beares (I've heard some say)
For profer'd love will love repay:
None are so harsh, but if they find
Softnesse in others, will be kind;
Affection will affection move,
Then you must like, because I love.

Regression spoiles Resolution

HAST thou attempted greatnesse? then go on,
Back-turning slackens Resolution.

Contention

DISCREET and prudent we that Discord call,
That either profits, or not hurts at all.

Consultation

CONSULT ere thou begin'st, that done, go on
With all wise speed for execution.

Love dislikes nothing

WHATSOEVER thing I see,
Rich or poore although it be;
'Tis a Mistresse unto mee.

Be my Girle, or faire or browne,
Do's she smile, or do's she frowne:
Still I write a Sweet-heart downe.

Be she rough, or smooth of skin;
When I touch, I then begin
For to let Affection in.

Be she bald, or do's she weare   10
Locks incurl'd of other haire;
I shall find enchantment there.

Be she whole, or be she rent,
So my fancie be content,
She's to me most excellent.

Be she fat, or be she leane,
Be she sluttish, be she cleane,
I'm a man for ev'ry Sceane.

Our own sinnes unseen

OTHER mens sins wee ever beare in mind;
None sees the fardell of his faults behind.

No Paines, no Gaines

IF little labour, little are our gaines:
Mans fortunes are according to his paines.

Upon Slouch

SLOUCH he packs up, and goes to sev'rall Faires,
And weekly Markets for to sell his wares:
Meane time that he from place to place do's rome,
His wife her owne ware sells as fast at home.

Vertue best united

B Y so much, vertue is the lesse,
By how much, neere to singlenesse.

The eye

A WANTON and lascivious eye
Betrayes the Hearts Adulterie.

To Prince Charles *upon his coming to Exeter*

W HAT Fate decreed, Time now ha's made us see
A Renovation of the West by Thee.
That Preternaturall Fever, which did threat
Death to our Countrey, now hath lost his heat:
And calmes succeeding, we perceive no more
Th'unequall Pulse to beat, as heretofore.
Something there yet remaines for Thee to do;
Then reach those ends that thou wast destin'd to.
Go on with *Sylla's* Fortune; let thy Fate
Make Thee like Him, this, that way fortunate,   10
Apollos Image side with Thee to blesse
Thy Warre (discreetly made) with white successe.
Meane time thy Prophets Watch by Watch shall pray;
While young *Charles* fights, and fighting wins the day.
That done, our smooth-pac't Poems all shall be
Sung in the high *Doxologie* of Thee.
Then maids shall strew Thee, and thy Curles from them
Receive (with Songs) a flowrie Diadem.

A Song

B URNE, or drowne me, choose ye whether,
So I may but die together:
Thus to slay me by degrees,
Is the height of Cruelties.
What needs twenty stabs, when one
Strikes me dead as any stone?
O shew mercy then, and be
Kind at once to murder mee.

Princes and Favourites

PRINCES and Fav'rites are most deere, while they
By giving and receiving hold the play:
But the Relation then of both growes poor,
When These can aske, and Kings can give no more.

Examples, or like Prince, like People

EXAMPLES lead us, and wee likely see,
Such as the Prince is, will his People be.

Potentates

LOVE and the *Graces* evermore do wait
Upon the man that is a Potentate.

The Wake

COME *Anthea* let us two
Go to Feast, as others do.
Tarts and Custards, Creams and Cakes,
Are the Junketts still at Wakes:
Unto which the Tribes resort,
Where the businesse is the sport:
Morris-dancers thou shalt see,
Marian too in Pagentrie:
And a Mimick to devise
Many grinning properties.   10
Players there will be, and those
Base in action as in clothes:
Yet with strutting they will please
The incurious Villages.
Neer the dying of the day,
There will be a *Cudgell*-Play,
Where a *Coxcomb* will be broke,
Ere a good *word* can be spoke:
But the anger ends all here,
Drencht in Ale, or drown'd in Beere.   20
Happy Rusticks, best content
With the cheapest Merriment:
And possesse no other feare,
Then to want the Wake next Yeare.

The Peter-*penny*

FRESH strowings allow
  To my Sepulcher now,
To make my lodging the sweeter;
  A staffe or a wand
  Put then in my hand,
With a pennie to pay S. *Peter*.

  Who has not a Crosse,
  Must sit with the losse,
And no whit further must venture;
  Since the Porter he
  Will paid have his fee,
Or els not one there must enter.

  Who at a dead lift,
  Can't send for a gift
A Pig to the Priest for a Roster,
  Shall heare his Clarke say,
  By yea and by nay,
No pennie, no Pater Noster.

To *Doctor* Alablaster

NOR art thou lesse esteem'd, that I have plac'd
  (Amongst mine honour'd) Thee (almost) the last:
In great Processions many lead the way
To him, who is the triumph of the day,
As these have done to Thee, who art the one,
One onely glory of a million,
In whom the spirit of the Gods do's dwell,
Firing thy soule, by which thou dost foretell
When this or that vast *Dinastie* must fall
Downe to a *Fillit* more *Imperiall*.
When this or that *Horne* shall be broke, and when
Others shall spring up in their place agen:
When times and seasons and all yeares must lie
Drown'd in the Sea of wild Eternitie:
When the *Black Dooms-day Bookes* (as yet unseal'd)
Shall by the mighty *Angell* be reveal'd:

And when the Trumpet which thou late hast found
Shall call to Judgment; tell us when the sound
Of this or that great Aprill day shall be,
And next the Gospell wee will credit thee.   20
Meane time like Earth-wormes we will craule below,
And wonder at Those Things that thou dost know.

Upon his Kinswoman Mrs. M. S.

HERE lies a Virgin, and as sweet
    As ere was wrapt in winding sheet.
Her name if next you wo'd have knowne,
The Marble speaks it *Mary Stone*:
Who dying in her blooming yeares,
This Stone, for names sake, melts to teares.
If fragrant Virgins you'l but keep
A Fast, while Jets and Marbles weep,
And praying, strew some Roses on her,
You'l do my *Neice* abundant honour.   10

Felicitie knowes no Fence

OF both our Fortunes good and bad we find
    Prosperitie more searching of the mind:
Felicitie flies o're the Wall and Fence,
While misery keeps in with patience.

Death ends all woe

TIME is the Bound of things, where e're we go,
    Fate gives a meeting. Death's the end of woe.

A Conjuration, to Electra

BY those soft Tods of wooll
    With which the aire is full:
By all those Tinctures there,
That paint the *Hemisphere*:
By Dewes and drisling Raine,
That swell the Golden Graine:
By all those sweets that be
I'th flowrie Nunnerie:

By silent Nights, and the
Three Formes of *Heccate*:   10
By all Aspects that blesse
The sober *Sorceresse*,
While juice she straines, and pith
To make her Philters with:
By Time, that hastens on
Things to perfection:
And by your self, the best
Conjurement of the rest:
O my *Electra*! be
In love with none, but me.   20

Courage cool'd

I CANNOT love, as I have lov'd before:
For, I'm grown old; &, with mine age, grown poore:
Love must be fed by wealth: this blood of mine
Must needs wax cold, if wanting bread and wine.

The Spell

H OLY Water come and bring;
Cast in Salt, for seasoning:
Set the Brush for sprinkling:
Sacred Spittle bring ye hither;
Meale and it now mix together;
And a little Oyle to either:
Give the Tapers here their light,
Ring the *Saints-Bell*, to affright
Far from hence the evill Sp'rite.

His wish to privacie

G IVE me a Cell
To dwell,
Where no foot hath
A path:
There will I spend,
And end
My wearied yeares
In teares.

258

A good Husband

A MASTER of a house (as I have read)
  Must be the first man up, and last in bed:
With the Sun rising he must walk his grounds;
See this, View that, and all the other bounds:
Shut every gate; mend every hedge that's torne,
Either with old, or plant therein new thorne:
Tread ore his gleab, but with such care, that where
He sets his foot, he leaves rich *compost* there.

A Hymne to Bacchus

I SING thy praise *Iacchus*,
  Who with thy *Thyrse* dost thwack us:
And yet thou so dost back us
With boldness that we feare
No *Brutus* entring here;
Nor *Cato* the severe.
What though the *Lictors* threat us,
We know they dare not beate us;
So long as thou dost heat us.
When we thy *Orgies* sing,   10
Each Cobler is a King;
Nor dreads he any thing:
And though he doe not rave,
Yet he'l the courage have
To call my *Lord Maior* knave;
Besides too, in a brave,
Although he has no riches,
But walks with dangling breeches,
And skirts that want their stiches,
And shewes his naked flitches;   20
Yet he'le be thought or seen,
So good as *George-a-Green*;
And calls his Blouze, his Queene;
And speaks in language keene:
O *Bacchus*! let us be
From cares and troubles free;
And thou shalt heare how we
Will chant new *Hymnes* to thee.

Upon Pusse *and her Prentice. Epig.*

PUSSE and her Prentice both at Draw-gloves play;
That done, they kisse, and so draw out the day:
At night they draw to Supper; then well fed,
They draw their clothes off both, so draw to bed.

Blame the reward of Princes

AMONG disasters that discention brings,
This not the least is, which belongs to Kings.
If Wars goe well; each for a part layes claime:
If ill, then Kings, not Souldiers beare the blame.

Clemency in Kings

KINGS must not only cherish up the good,
But must be niggards of the meanest bloud.

Anger

WRONGS if neglected, vanish in short time;
But heard with anger, we confesse the crime.

A Psalme or Hymne to the Graces

GLORY be to the Graces!
That doe in publike places,
Drive thence what ere encumbers,
The listning to my numbers.

Honour be to the Graces!
Who doe with sweet embraces,
Shew they are well contented
With what I have invented.

Worship be to the Graces!
Who do from sowre faces,
And lungs that wo'd infect me,
For evermore protect me.

10

An Hymne to the Muses

HONOUR to you who sit!
  Neere to the well of wit;
And drink your fill of it.

Glory and worship be!
To you sweet Maids (thrice three)
Who still inspire me.

And teach me how to sing
Unto the *Lyrick* string
My measures ravishing.

Then while I sing your praise,   10
My *Priest-hood* crown with bayes
Green, to the end of dayes.

Upon Julia's *Clothes*

WHEN as in silks my *Julia* goes,
  Then, then (me thinks) how sweetly flowes
That liquefaction of her clothes.

Next, when I cast mine eyes and see
That brave Vibration each way free;
O how that glittering taketh me!

Moderation

IN things a moderation keepe,
  Kings ought to sheare, not skin their sheepe.

To Anthea

LETS call for *Hymen* if agreed thou art;
  Delays in love but crucifie the heart.
Loves thornie Tapers yet neglected lye:
Speak thou the word, they'l kindle by and by.
The nimble howers wooe us on to wed,
And *Genius* waits to have us both to bed.
Behold, for us the *Naked Graces* stay
With maunds of roses for to strew the way:

Besides, the most religious Prophet stands
Ready to joyne, as well our hearts as hands.   10
Juno yet smiles; but if she chance to chide,
Ill luck 'twill bode to th'Bridegroome and the Bride.
Tell me *Anthea*, dost thou fondly dread
The loss of that we call a Maydenhead?
Come, Ile instruct thee. Know, the vestall fier
Is not by mariage quencht, but flames the higher.

Upon Prew *his Maid*

IN this little Urne is laid
  Prewdence Baldwin (once my maid)
From whose happy spark here let
Spring the purple Violet.

The Invitation

TO sup with thee thou didst me home invite;
  And mad'st a promise that mine appetite
Sho'd meet and tire, on such lautitious meat,
The like not *Heliogabalus* did eat:
And richer Wine wo'dst give to me (thy guest)
Then Roman *Sylla* powr'd out at his feast.
I came; (tis true) and lookt for Fowle of price,
The bastard *Phenix*; bird of *Paradice*;
And for no less then Aromatick Wine
Of *Maydens-blush*, commixt with *Jessimine*.   10
Cleane was the herth, the mantle larded jet;
Which wanting *Lar*, and smoke, hung weeping wet;
At last, i'th'noone of winter, did appeare
A ragd-soust-neats-foot with sick vineger:
And in a burnisht Flagonet stood by
Beere small as Comfort, dead as Charity.
At which amaz'd, and pondring on the food,
How cold it was, and how it child my blood;
I curst the master; and I damn'd the souce;
And swore I'de got the ague of the house.   20
Well, when to eat thou dost me next desire,
I'le bring a Fever; since thou keep'st no fire.

Ceremonies for Christmasse.

COME, bring with a noise,
  My merrie merrie boyes,
The Christmas Log to the firing;
  While my good Dame, she
  Bids ye all be free;
And drink to your hearts desiring.

  With the last yeeres brand
  Light the new block, And
For good successe in his spending,
  On your Psaltries play,
  That sweet luck may
Come while the Log is a teending.

  Drink now the strong Beere,
  Cut the white loafe here,
The while the meat is a shredding
  For the rare Mince-Pie;
  And the Plums stand by
To fill the Paste that's a kneading.

10

Christmasse-Eve, another Ceremonie

COME guard this night the Christmas-Pie,
  That the Thiefe, though ne'r so slie,
With his Flesh-hooks, don't come nie
    To catch it

From him, who all alone sits there,
Having his eyes still in his eare,
And a deale of nightly feare
    To watch it.

Another to the Maids

WASH your hands, or else the fire
  Will not teend to your desire;
Unwasht hands, ye Maidens, know,
Dead the Fire, though ye blow.

1. 15–16 *The semicolon is at the end of* 15 *in* 48
2.4 it *ed.:* it. 48

Another

WASSAILE the Trees, that they may beare
 You many a Plum, and many a Peare:
For more or lesse fruits they will bring,
As you doe give them Wassailing.

Power and Peace

'TIS never, or but seldome knowne,
 Power and Peace to keep one Throne.

To his deare Valentine, Mistresse Margaret Falconbrige

NOW is your turne (my Dearest) to be set
 A Jem in this eternall Coronet:
'Twas rich before; but since your Name is downe,
It sparkles now like *Ariadne's* Crowne.
Blaze by this Sphere for ever: Or this doe,
Let Me and It shine evermore by you.

To Oenone

SWEET *Oenone*, doe but say
 Love thou dost, though Love sayes Nay.
Speak me faire; for Lovers be
Gently kill'd by Flatterie.

Verses

WHO will not honour Noble Numbers, when
 Verses out-live the bravest deeds of men?

Happinesse

THAT Happines do's still the longest thrive,
 Where Joyes and Griefs have Turns Alternative.

Things of choice, long a comming

WE pray 'gainst Warre, yet we enjoy no Peace;
 Desire deferr'd is, that it may encrease.

264

Poetry perpetuates the Poet

HERE I my selfe might likewise die,
    And utterly forgotten lye,
But that eternall Poetrie
Repullulation gives me here
Unto the thirtieth thousand yeere,
When all now dead shall re-appeare.

Upon Bice

BICE laughs, when no man speaks; and doth protest
    It is his own breech there that breaks the jest.

Upon Trencherman

TOM shifts the Trenchers; yet he never can
    Endure that luke-warme name of Serving-man:
Serve or not serve, let *Tom* doe what he can,
He is a serving, who's a Trencher-man.

Kisses

GIVE me the food that satisfies a Guest:
    Kisses are but dry banquets to a Feast.

Orpheus

ORPHEUS he went (as Poets tell)
    To fetch *Euridice* from Hell;
And had her; but it was upon
This short but strict condition:
Backward he should not looke while he
Led her through Hells obscuritie:
But ah! it hapned as he made
His passage through that dreadfull shade:
Revolve he did his loving eye;
(For gentle feare, or jelousie)   10
And looking back, that look did sever
Him and *Euridice* for ever.

Upon Comely *a good speaker but an ill singer*, Epig.

COMELY Acts well; and when he speaks his part,
He doth it with the sweetest tones of Art:
But when he sings a *Psalme*, ther's none can be
More curst for singing out of tune then he.

Any way for wealth

E'ENE all Religious courses to be rich
Hath been reherst, by *Joell Micheldit ch*:
But now perceiving that it still do's please
The sterner Fates, to cross his purposes;
He tacks about, and now he doth profess
Rich he will be by all unrighteousness:
Thus if our ship fails of her Anchor hold,
We'l love the Divell, so he lands the˙gold.

Upon an old Woman

OLD widdow *Prouse* to do her neighbours evill
Wo'd give (some say) her soule unto the Devill.
Well, when sh'as kild, that Pig, Goose, Cock or Hen,
What wo'd she give to get that soule agen?

Upon Pearch. *Epig.*

THOU writes in Prose, how sweet all Virgins be;
But ther's not one, doth praise the smell of thee.

To Sapho

SAPHO, I will chuse to go
Where the Northern winds do blow
Endlesse Ice, and endlesse Snow:
Rather then I once wo'd see,
But a Winters face in thee,
To benumme my hopes and me.

To his faithfull friend, Master John Crofts, *Cup-bearer to the King*

FOR all thy many courtesies to me,
Nothing I have (my *Crofts*) to send to Thee
For the requitall; save this only one
Halfe of my just remuneration.
For since I've travail'd all this Realm throughout
To seeke, and find some few *Immortals* out
To *circumspangle* this my spacious Sphere,
(As Lamps for everlasting shining here:)
And having fixt Thee in mine *Orbe* a Starre
(Amongst the rest) both bright and singular;   10
The present Age will tell the world thou art
If not to th'whole, yet satisfy'd in part.
As for the rest, being too great a summe
Here to be paid; Ile pay't i'th'world to come.

The Bride-Cake

THIS day my *Julia* thou must make
For Mistresse Bride, the wedding Cake:
Knead but the Dow and it will be
To paste of Almonds turn'd by thee:
Or kisse it thou, but once, or twice,
And for the Bride-Cake ther'l be Spice.

To be merry

LETS now take our time;
While w'are in our Prime;
And old, old Age is a farre off:
For the evill evill dayes
Will come on apace;
Before we can be aware of.

Buriall

MAN may want Land to live in; but for all,
Nature finds out some place for buriall.

Lenitie

'TIS the Chyrurgions praise, and height of Art,
Not to cut off, but cure the vicious part.

Penitence

WHO after his transgression doth repent,
Is halfe, or altogether innocent.

Griefe

CONSIDER sorrowes, how they are aright:
Griefe, if't be great, 'tis short; if long, 'tis light.

The Maiden-blush

SO look the mornings when the Sun
Paints them with fresh Vermilion:
So Cherries blush, and Kathern Peares,
And Apricocks, in youthfull yeares:
So Corrolls looke more lovely Red,
And Rubies lately polished:
So purest Diaper doth shine,
Stain'd by the Beames of Clarret wine:
As *Julia* looks when she doth dress
Her either cheeke with bashfullness.   10

The Meane

IMPARITIE *doth ever discord bring:*
The Mean the Musique makes in every thing.

Haste hurtfull

HASTE *is unhappy: What we Rashly do*
Is both unluckie; I, and foolish too.
Where War with rashnesse is attempted, there
The Soldiers leave the Field with equall feare.

Purgatory

READERS wee entreat ye pray
   For the soule of *Lucia*;
That in little time she be
From her *Purgatory* free:
In th'*intrim* she desires
That your teares may coole her fires.

The Cloud

SEEST thou that Cloud that rides in State
   Part *Ruby-like*, part *Candidate*?
It is no other then the Bed
Where *Venus* sleeps (halfe smothered.)

Upon Loach

SEEAL'D up with Night-gum, *Loach* each morning lyes,
   Till his Wife licking, so unglews his eyes.
No question then, but such a lick is sweet,
When a warm tongue do's with such Ambers meet.

The Amber Bead

I SAW a Flie within a Beade
  Of Amber cleanly buried:
The Urne was little, but the room
More rich then *Cleopatra's* Tombe.

To my dearest Sister M. Mercie Herrick

WHEN ere I go, or what so ere befalls
   Me in mine Age, or forraign Funerals,
This Blessing I will leave thee, ere I go,
Prosper thy Basket, and therein thy Dow.
Feed on the paste of Filberts, or else knead
And Bake the floure of Amber for thy bread.
Balm may thy Trees drop, and thy Springs runne oyle
And everlasting Harvest crown thy Soile!
These I but wish for; but thy selfe shall see,
The Blessing fall in mellow times on Thee.   10

269

The Transfiguration

IMMORTALL clothing I put on,
So soone as *Julia* I am gon
To mine eternall Mansion.

Thou, thou art here, to humane sight
Cloth'd all with incorrupted light;
But yet how more admir'dly bright

Wilt thou appear, when thou art set
In thy refulgent Thronelet,
That shin'st thus in thy counterfeit?

Suffer that thou canst not shift

DO's Fortune rend thee? Beare with thy hard Fate:
Vertuous instructions ne'r are delicate.
Say, do's she frown? still countermand her threats:
Vertue best loves those children that she beates.

To the Passenger

IF I lye unburied Sir,
These my Reliques, (pray) interre:
'Tis religions part to see
Stones, or turfes to cover me.
One word more I had to say;
But it skills not; go your way;
He that wants a buriall roome
For a Stone, ha's Heaven his Tombe.

Upon Nodes

WHERE ever *Nodes* do's in the Summer come,
He prayes his Harvest may be well brought home.
What store of Corn has carefull *Nodes*, thinke you,
Whose Field his foot is, and whose Barn his shooe?

TO THE KING,
Upon his taking of *Leicester*

THIS Day is Yours *Great CHARLES* ! and in this War
 Your Fate, and Ours, alike Victorious are.
In her white Stole; now Victory do's rest
Enspher'd with Palm on Your Triumphant Crest.
Fortune is now Your Captive; other Kings
Hold but her hands; You hold both hands and wings.

To Julia, *in her Dawn, or Day-breake*

BY the next kindling of the day
 My *Julia* thou shalt see,
Ere *Ave-Mary* thou canst say
 Ile come and visit thee.

Yet ere thou counsel'st with thy Glasse,
 Appeare thou to mine eyes
As smooth, and nak't, as she that was
 The prime of *Paradice.*

If blush thou must, then blush thou through
 A Lawn, that thou mayst looke   10
As purest Pearles, or Pebles do
 When peeping through a Brooke.

As Lillies shrin'd in Christall, so
 Do thou to me appeare;
Or Damask Roses, when they grow
 To sweet acquaintance there.

Counsell

'TWAS *Cesars* saying: *Kings no lesse Conquerors are*
 By their wise Counsell, then they be by Warre.

Bad Princes pill their People

LIKE those infernall Deities which eate
  The best of all the sacrificed meate;
And leave their servants, but the smoak & sweat:
So many *Kings*, and *Primates* too there are,
Who claim the Fat, and Fleshie for their share,
And leave their Subjects but the starved ware.

Most Words, lesse Workes

IN desp'rate cases, all, or most are known
  Commanders, *few for execution.*

To Dianeme

I CO'D but see thee yesterday
    Stung by a fretfull Bee;
And I the Javelin suckt away,
    And heal'd the wound in thee.

A thousand thorns, and Bryars & Stings,
    I have in my poore Brest;
Yet ne'r can see that salve which brings
    My Passions any rest.

As Love shall helpe me, I admire
    How thou canst sit and smile,   10
To see me bleed, and not desire
    To stench the blood the while.

If thou compos'd of gentle mould
    Art so unkind to me;
What dismall Stories will be told
    Of those that cruell be?

Upon Tap

TAP (better known then trusted) as we heare
  Sold his old Mothers Spectacles for Beere:
And not unlikely; rather too then fail,
He'l sell her Eyes, and Nose, for Beere and Ale.

His Losse

ALL has been plundered from me, but my wit;
  Fortune her selfe can lay no claim to it.

Draw, and Drinke

MILK stil your Fountains, and your Springs, for why?
The more th'are drawn, the lesse they wil grow dry.

Upon Punchin. *Epig.*

GIVE me a reason why men call
Punchin a dry *plant-animall.*
Because as Plants by water grow,
Punchin by Beere and Ale, spreads so.

To Oenone

THOU sayest Loves Dart
Hath prickt thy heart;
And thou do'st languish too:
If one poore prick,
Can make thee sick,
Say, what wo'd many do?

Upon Blinks. *Epig.*

TOM *Blinks* his Nose is full of wheales, and these
Tom calls not pimples, but *Pimpleides:*
Sometimes (in mirth) he sayes each whelk's a sparke
(When drunke with Beere) to light him home, i'th'dark.

Upon Adam Peapes. *Epig.*

PEAPES he do's strut, and pick his Teeth, as if
His jawes had tir'd on some large Chine of Beefe.
But nothing so; The Dinner *Adam* had,
Was cheese full ripe with Teares, with Bread as sad.

To Electra

SHALL I go to Love and tell,
Thou art all turn'd isicle?
Shall I say her Altars be
Disadorn'd, and scorn'd by thee?
O beware! in time submit;
Love has yet no wrathfull fit:
If her patience turns to ire,
Love is then consuming fire.

To Mistresse Amie Potter

A I me! I love, give him your hand to kisse
Who both your wooer, and your Poet is.
Nature has pre-compos'd us both to Love;
Your part's to grant; my Scean must be to move.
Deare, can you like, and liking love your Poet?
If you say (I) Blush-guiltinesse will shew it.
Mine eyes must wooe you; (though I sigh the while)
True Love is tonguelesse as a Crocodile.
And you may find in Love these differing Parts;
Wooers have Tongues of Ice, but burning hearts.   10

Upon a Maide

H ERE she lyes (in Bed of Spice)
Faire as *Eve* in Paradice:
For her beauty it was such
Poets co'd not praise too much.
Virgins Come, and in a Ring
Her supreamest *Requiem* sing;
Then depart, but see ye tread
Lightly, lightly ore the dead.

Upon Love

L OVE is a Circle, and an Endlesse Sphere;
From good to good, revolving here, & there.

Beauty

B EAUTIE'S no other but a lovely Grace
Of lively colours, flowing from the face.

Upon Love

S OME salve to every sore, we may apply;
Only for my wound there's no remedy.
Yet if my *Julia* kisse me, there will be
A soveraign balme found out to cure me.

Upon Hanch *a Schoolmaster. Epig.*

H*ANCH*, since he (lately) did interre his wife,
He weepes and sighs (as weary of his life.)
Say, is't for reall griefe he mourns? not so;
Teares have their springs from joy, as well as woe.

Upon Peason. *Epig.*

L ONG Locks of late our Zelot *Peason* weares,
Not for to hide his high and mighty eares;
No, but because he wo'd not have it seen,
That Stubble stands, where once large eares have been.

To his Booke

M AKE haste away, and let one be
A friendly Patron unto thee:
Lest rapt from hence, I see thee lye
Torn for the use of Pasterie:
Or see thy injur'd Leaves serve well,
To make loose Gownes for Mackarell:
Or see the Grocers in a trice,
Make hoods of thee to serve out Spice.

Readinesse

T HE readinesse of doing, doth expresse
No other, but the doers willingnesse.

Writing

W HEN words we want, Love teacheth to endite;
And what we blush to speake, she bids us write.

Society

T WO things do make society to stand;
The first *Commerce* is, & the next *Command.*

Upon a Maid

GONE she is a long, long way,
    But she has decreed a day
Back to come, (and make no stay.)
So we keepe till her returne
Here, her ashes, or her Urne.

Satisfaction for sufferings

FOR all our workes, a recompence is sure:
    'Tis sweet to thinke on what was hard t'endure.

The delaying Bride

WHY so slowly do you move
    To the centre of your love?
On your niceness though we wait,
Yet the houres say 'tis late:
Coynesse takes us to a measure;
But o'racted deads the pleasure.
Go to Bed, and care not when
Cheerfull day shall spring agen.
One *Brave Captain* did command
(By his word) the Sun to stand: 10
One short charme if you but say
Will enforce the Moon to stay,
Till you warn her hence (away)
T'ave your blushes seen by day.

To M. Henry Lawes, *the excellent* Composer of his Lyricks

TOUCH but thy Lire (my *Harrie*) and I heare
    From thee some raptures of the rare *Gotire.*
Then if thy voice commingle with the String
I heare in thee rare *Laniere* to sing;
Or curious *Wilson*: Tell me, canst thou be
Less then *Apollo*, that usurp'st such Three?
Three, unto whom the whole world give applause;
Yet their Three praises, praise but One; that's *Lawes.*

Age unfit for Love

MAIDENS tell me I am old;
Let me in my Glasse behold
Whether smooth or not I be,
Or if haire remaines to me.
Well, or be't or be't not so,
This for certainty I know;
Ill it fits old men to play,
When that Death bids come away.

The Bed-man, or Grave-maker

THOU hast made many Houses for the Dead;
When my Lot calls me to be buried,
For Love or Pittie, prethee let there be
I'th'Church-yard, made, one Tenement for me.

To Anthea

ANTHEA I am going hence
With some small stock of innocence:
But yet those blessed gates I see
Withstanding entrance unto me.
To pray for me doe thou begin,
The Porter then will let me in.

Need

WHO begs to die for feare of humane need,
Wisheth his body, not his soule, good speed.

To Julia

I AM zeallesse, prethee pray
For my well-fare (*Julia*)
For I thinke the gods require
Male perfumes, but Female fire.

On Julias *lips*

SWEET are my *Julia's* lips and cleane,
As if or'e washt in Hippocrene.

T

Twilight

TWILIGHT, no other thing is, Poets say,
Then the last part of night, and first of day.

To his Friend, Master J. Jincks

LOVE, love me now, because I place
Thee here among my righteous race:
The bastard Slips may droop and die
Wanting both Root, and Earth; but thy
Immortall selfe, shall boldly trust
To live for ever, with my Just.

On himselfe

IF that my Fate has now fulfill'd my yeere,
And so soone stopt my longer living here;
What was't (ye Gods!) a dying man to save,
But while he met with his Paternall grave;
Though while we living 'bout the world do roame,
We love to rest in peacefull Urnes at home,
Where we may snug, and close together lye
By the dead bones of our deare Ancestrie.

Kings and Tyrants

'TWIXT Kings & Tyrants there's this difference known;
Kings seek their Subjects good: Tyrants their owne.

Crosses

OUR Crosses are no other then the rods,
And our Diseases, Vultures of the Gods:
Each griefe we feele, that likewise is a Kite
Sent forth by them, our flesh to eate, or bite.

Upon Love

LOVE brought me to a silent Grove,
And shew'd me there a Tree,
Where some had hang'd themselves for love,
And gave a Twist to me.

The Halter was of silk, and gold,
    That he reacht forth unto me:
No otherwise, then if he would
    By dainty things undo me.

He bade me then that Neck-lace use; ·
    And told me too, he maketh   10
A glorious end by such a Noose,
    His Death for Love that taketh.

'Twas but a dream; but had I been
    There really alone;
My desp'rate feares, in love, had seen *feare*
    Mine Execution.

No difference i'th' dark

NIGHT makes no difference 'twixt the Priest and Clark;
  Jone as my Lady is as good i'th'dark.

The Body

THE Body is the Soules poore house, or home,
  Whose Ribs the Laths are, & whose Flesh the Loame.

To Sapho

THOU saist thou lov'st me *Sapho*; I say no;
  But would to Love I could beleeve 'twas so!
Pardon my feares (sweet *Sapho*,) I desire
That thou be righteous found; and I the Lyer.

Out of Time, out of Tune

WE blame, nay we despise her paines
  That wets her Garden when it raines:
But when the drought has dri'd the knot;
Then let her use the watring pot.
We pray for showers (at our need)
To drench, but not to drown our seed.

To his Booke

TAKE mine advise, and go not neere
  Those faces (sower as Vineger.)
For these, and Nobler numbers can
Ne'r please the *supercillious* man.

To his Honour'd friend, Sir Thomas Heale

STAND by the *Magick* of my powerfull Rhymes
'Gainst all the indignation of the Times.
Age shall not wrong thee; or one jot abate
Of thy both Great, and everlasting fate.
While others perish, here's thy life decreed
Because begot of my *Immortall* seed.

The Sacrifice, by way of Discourse betwixt himselfe and Julia

Herr. COME and let's in solemn wise
        Both addresse to sacrifice:
Old Religion first commands
That we wash our hearts, and hands.
Is the beast exempt from staine,
Altar cleane, no fire prophane?
Are the Garlands, Is the Nard
Jul. Ready here? All well prepar'd,
With the Wine that must be shed
(Twixt the hornes) upon the head   10
Of the holy Beast we bring
For our Trespasse-offering.
Herr. All is well; now next to these
Put we on pure Surplices;
And with Chaplets crown'd, we'l rost
With perfumes the Holocaust:
And (while we the gods invoke)
Reade acceptance by the smoake.

To Apollo

THOU mighty Lord and master of the Lyre,
    Unshorn *Apollo*, come, and re-inspire
My fingers so, the Lyrick-strings to move,
That I may play, and sing a Hymne to Love.

On Love ✓

LOVE is a kind of warre; Hence those who feare,
    No cowards must his royall Ensignes beare.

Another ✓

WHERE love begins, there dead thy first desire:
A sparke neglected makes a mighty fire.

An Hymne to Cupid

THOU, thou that bear'st the sway
  With whom the Sea-Nimphs play;
And *Venus*, every way:
When I embrace thy knee;
And make short pray'rs to thee:
In love, then prosper me.
This day I goe to wooe;
Instruct me how to doe
This worke thou put'st me too.
From shame my face keepe free,   10
From scorne I begge of thee,
Love to deliver me:
So shall I sing thy praise;
And to thee Altars raise,
Unto the end of daies.

To Electra

LET not thy Tomb-stone er'e be laid by me:
  Nor let my Herse, be wept upon by thee:
But let that instant when thou dy'st be known,.
The minute of mine *expiration*.
One knell be rung for both; and let one grave
To hold us two, an endlesse honour have.

How his soule came ensnared

MY soule would one day goe and seeke
  For Roses, and in *Julia's* cheeke,
A richess of those sweets she found,
(As in an other *Rosamond*.)
But gathering Roses as she was;
(Not knowing what would come to passe)
It chanst a ringlet of her haire,
Caught my poore soule, as in a snare:
Which ever since has been in thrall,
Yet freedome, shee enjoyes withall.   10

Factions

THE factions of the great ones call,
  To side with them, the Commons all.

Kisses Loathsome

I ABHOR the slimie kisse,
  (Which to me most loathsome is.)
Those lips please me which are plac't
Close, but not too strictly lac't:
Yeilding I wo'd have them; yet
Not a wimbling Tongue admit:
What sho'd poking-sticks make there,
When the ruffe is set elsewhere?

Upon Reape

REAPES eyes so rawe are, that (it seemes) the flyes
  Mistake the flesh, and flye-blow both his eyes;
So that an Angler, for a daies expence,
May baite his hooke, with maggots taken thence.

Upon Teage

TEAGE has told lyes so long, that when *Teage* tells
  Truth, yet *Teages* truths are untruths, (nothing else.)

Upon Julia's haire, bundled up in a golden net

TELL me, what needs those rich deceits,
  These golden Toyles, and Trammel-nets,
To take thine haires when they are knowne
Already tame, and all thine owne?
'Tis I am wild, and more then haires
Deserve these Mashes and those snares.
Set free thy Tresses, let them flow
As aires doe breathe, or winds doe blow:
And let such curious Net-works be
Lesse set for them, then spred for me.   10

Upon Truggin

TRUGGIN a Footman was; but now, growne lame,
Truggin now lives but to belye his name.

The showre of Blossomes

LOVE in a showre of Blossomes came
Down, and halfe drown'd me with the same:
The Blooms that fell were white and red;
But with such sweets commingled,
As whether (this) I cannot tell
My sight was pleas'd more, or my smell:
But true it was, as I rowl'd there,
Without a thought of hurt, or feare;
Love turn'd himselfe into a Bee,
And with his Javelin wounded me: 10
From which mishap this use I make,
Where most sweets are, there lyes a Snake.
Kisses and Favours are sweet things;
But Those have thorns, and These have stings.

Upon Spenke

SPENKE has a strong breath, yet short Prayers saith:
Not out of want of breath, but want of faith.

A defence for Women

NAUGHT are all Women: I say no,
Since for one Bad, one Good I know:
For *Clytemnestra* most unkind,
Loving *Alcestis* there we find:
For one *Medea* that was bad,
A good *Penelope* was had:
For wanton *Lais*, then we have
Chaste *Lucrece*, or a wife as grave:
And thus through Woman-kind we see
A Good and Bad. *Sirs credit me.*   10

283

Upon Lulls

LULLS swears he is all heart; but you'l suppose
By his *Probossis* that he is all nose.

Slavery

'TIS liberty to serve one Lord; but he
Who many serves, serves base servility.

Charmes

BRING the holy crust of Bread,
Lay it underneath the head;
'Tis a certain Charm to keep
Hags away, while Children sleep.

Another

LET the superstitious wife
Neer the childs heart lay a knife:
Point be up, and Haft be downe;
(While she gossips in the towne)
This 'mongst other mystick charms
Keeps the sleeping child from harms.

Another to bring in the Witch

TO house the Hag, you must doe this;
Commix with Meale a little Pisse
Of him bewitcht: then forthwith make
A little Wafer or a Cake;
And this rawly bak't will bring
The old Hag in. No surer thing.

Another Charme for Stables

HANG up Hooks, and Sheers to scare
Hence the Hag, that rides the Mare,
Till they be all over wet,
With the mire, and the sweat:
This observ'd, the Manes shall be
Of your horses, all knot-free.

Ceremonies for Candlemasse Eve

DOWN with the Rosemary and Bayes,
  Down with the Misleto;
In stead of Holly, now up-raise
  The greener Box (for show.)

The Holly hitherto did sway;
  Let Box now domineere;
Untill the dancing Easter-day,
  Or Easters Eve appeare.

Then youthfull Box which now hath grace,
  Your houses to renew;   10
Grown old, surrender must his place,
  Unto the crisped Yew.

When Yew is out, then Birch comes in,
  And many Flowers beside;
Both of a fresh, and fragrant kinne
  To honour Whitsontide.

Green Rushes then, and sweetest Bents,
  With cooler Oken boughs;
Come in for comely ornaments,
  To re-adorn the house.   20
Thus times do shift; each thing his turne do's hold;
New things succeed, as former things grow old.

The Ceremonies for Candlemasse day

KINDLE the Christmas Brand, and then
  Till Sunne-set, let it burne;
Which quencht, then lay it up agen,
  Till Christmas next returne.

Part must be kept wherewith to teend
  The Christmas Log next yeare;
And where 'tis safely kept, the Fiend,
  Can do no mischiefe (there.)

Upon Candlemasse day

END now the White-loafe, & the Pye,
  And let all sports with Christmas dye.

Surfeits

BAD are all surfeits: but Physitians call
That surfeit tooke by bread, the worst of all.

Upon Nis

NIS, he makes Verses; but the Lines he writes,
Serve but for matter to make Paper-kites.

To Biancha, *to blesse him*

WO'D I wooe, and wo'd I winne,
Wo'd I well my worke begin?
Wo'd I evermore be crown'd
With the end that I propound?
Wo'd I frustrate, or prevent
All Aspects malevolent?
Thwart all Wizzards, and with these
Dead all black contingencies:
Place my words, and all works else
In most happy Parallels?   10
All will prosper, if so be
I be kist, or blest by thee.

Julia's *Churching, or Purification*

PUT on thy *Holy Fillitings*, and so
To th'Temple with the sober *Midwife* go.
Attended thus (in a most solemn wise)
By those who serve the Child-bed misteries.
Burn first thine incense; next, when as thou see'st
The candid Stole thrown ore the *Pious Priest*;
With reverend Curtsies come, and to him bring
Thy free (and not decurted) offering.
All Rites well ended, with faire Auspice come
(As to the breaking of a Bride-Cake) home: 10
Where ceremonious *Hymen* shall for thee
Provide a second *Epithalamie*.
She who keeps chastly to her husbands side
Is not for one, but every night his Bride:
And stealing still with love, and feare to Bed,
Brings him not one, but many a Maiden-head.

To his Book

BEFORE the Press scarce one co'd see
  A little-peeping-part of thee:
But since th'art Printed, thou dost call
To shew thy nakedness to all.
My care for thee is now the less;
(Having resign'd thy shamefac'tness:)
Go with thy Faults and Fates; yet stay
And take this sentence, then away;
Whom one belov'd will not suffice,
She'l runne to all adulteries.   10

Teares

TEARES most prevaile; with teares too thou mayst move
  Rocks to relent, and coyest maids to love.

To his friend to avoid contention of words

WORDS beget Anger; Anger brings forth blowes:
  Blowes make of dearest friends immortall Foes.
For which prevention (Sociate) let there be
Betwixt us two no more *Logomachie.*
Farre better 'twere for either to be mute,
Then for to murder friendship, by dispute.

Truth

TRUTH is best found out by the time, and eyes;
  Falsehood winnes credit by uncertainties.

Upon Prickles. *Epig.*

PRICKLES is waspish, and puts forth his sting,
  For Bread, Drinke, Butter, Cheese; for every thing
That *Prickles* buyes, puts *Prickles* out of frame;
How well his nature's fitted to his name!

The Eyes before the Eares

WE credit most our sight; one eye doth please
  Our trust farre more then ten eare-witnesses.

6.2 then ten] ten then *48*

Want

WANT is a softer Wax, that takes thereon,
This, that, and every base impression.

To a Friend

LOOKE in my Book, and herein see,
Life endlesse sign'd to thee and me.
We o're the tombes, and Fates shall flye;
While other generations dye.

Upon M. William Lawes, *the rare Musitian*

SHO'D I not put on Blacks, when each one here
Comes with his Cypresse, and devotes a teare?
Sho'd I not grieve (my *Lawes*) when every Lute,
Violl, and Voice, is (by thy losse) struck mute?
Thy loss brave man! whose Numbers have been hurl'd,
And no less prais'd, then spread throughout the world.
Some have Thee call'd *Amphion*; some of us,
Nam'd thee *Terpander*, or sweet *Orpheus*:
Some this, some that, but all in this agree,
Musique had both her birth, and death with Thee.   10

A song upon Silvia

FROM me my *Silvia* ranne away,
And running therewithall;
A *Primrose* Banke did cross her way,
And gave my Love a fall.

But trust me now I dare not say,
What I by chance did see;
But such the Drap'ry did betray
That fully ravisht me.

The Hony-combe

IF thou hast found an honie-combe,
Eate thou not all, but taste on some:
For if thou eat'st it to excess;
That sweetness turnes to Loathsomness.
Taste it to Temper; then 'twill be
Marrow, and Manna unto thee.

Upon Ben. Johnson

HERE lyes *Johnson* with the rest
Of the Poets; but the Best.
Reader, wo'dst thou more have known?
Aske his Story, not this Stone.
That will speake what this can't tell
Of his glory. *So farewell.*

An Ode for him

AH *Ben*!
Say how, or when
Shall we thy Guests
Meet at those *Lyrick* Feasts,
Made at the *Sun*,
The *Dog*, the triple *Tunne?*
Where we such clusters had,
As made us nobly wild, not mad;
And yet each Verse of thine
Out-did the meate, out-did the frolick wine.   10

My *Ben*
Or come agen:
Or send to us,
Thy wits great over-plus;
But teach us yet
Wisely to husband it;
Lest we that Tallent spend:
And having once brought to an end
That precious stock; the store
Of such a wit the world sho'd have no more.   20

Upon a Virgin

SPEND Harmless shade thy nightly Houres,
Selecting here, both Herbs, and Flowers;
Of which make Garlands here, and there,
To dress thy silent sepulchre.
Nor do thou feare the want of these,
In everlasting Properties.
Since we fresh strewings will bring hither,
Farre faster then the first can wither.

Blame

IN Battailes what disasters fall,
The King he beares the blame of all.

A request to the Graces

PONDER my words, if so that any be
Known guilty here of incivility:
Let what is graceless, discompos'd, and rude,
With sweetness, smoothness, softness, be endu'd.
Teach it to blush, to curtsie, lisp, and shew
Demure, but yet, full of temptation too.
Numbers ne'r tickle, or but lightly please,
Unlesse they have some wanton carriages.
This if ye do, each Piece will here be good,
And gracefull made, by your neate Sisterhood.   10

Upon himselfe

I LATELY fri'd, but now behold
I freeze as fast, and shake for cold.
And in good faith I'd thought it strange
T'ave found in me this sudden change;
But that I understood by dreames,
These only were but Loves extreames;
Who fires with hope the Lovers heart,
And starves with cold the self-same part.

Multitude

WE Trust not to the multitude in Warre,
But to the stout; and those that skilfull are.

Feare

MAN must do well out of a good intent;
Not for the servile feare of punishment.

To M. Kellam

WHAT can my *Kellam* drink his Sack
In Goblets to the brim,
And see his *Robin Herrick* lack,
Yet send no Boules to him?

For love or pitie to his Muse,
   (That she may flow in Verse)
Contemne to recommend a Cruse,
   But send to her a Tearce.

Happinesse to hospitalitie, or a hearty wish to good house-keeping

FIRST, may the hand of bounty bring
  Into the daily offering
Of full provision; such a store,
Till that the Cooke cries, Bring no more.
Upon your hogsheads never fall
A drought of wine, ale, beere (at all)
But, like full clouds, may they from thence
Diffuse their mighty influence.
Next, let the Lord, and Ladie here
Enjoy a Christning yeare by yeare;   10
And this *good blessing* back them still,
T'ave Boyes, and Gyrles too, as they will.
Then from the porch may many a Bride
Unto the Holy Temple ride:
And thence return, (short prayers seyd)
A wife most richly married.
Last, may the Bride and Bridegroome be
Untoucht by cold *sterility*;
But in their springing blood so play,
As that in *Lusters* few they may,   20
By laughing too, and lying downe,
People a *City* or a *Towne*.

Cunctation in Correction

THE *Lictors* bundl'd up their rods: beside,
  Knit them with knots (with much adoe unty'd)
That if (unknitting) men wo'd yet repent,
They might escape the lash of punishment.

Present Government grievous

MEN are suspicious; prone to discontent:
  Subjects still loath the present Government.

Rest Refreshes

LAY by the good a while; a resting field
  Will, after ease, a richer harvest yeild:
Trees this year beare; next, they their wealth with-hold:
Continuall reaping makes a land wax old.

Revenge

MANS disposition is for to requite
  An injurie, before a benefite:
Thanksgiving is a burden, and a paine;
Revenge is pleasing to us, as our gaine.

The first marrs or makes

IN all our high designments, 'twill appeare,
  The first event breeds confidence or feare.

Beginning, difficult

HARD are the two first staires unto a Crowne;
  Which got, the third, bids him a King come downe.

Faith four-square

FAITH is a thing that's four-square; let it fall
  This way or that, it not declines at all.

The present time best pleaseth

PRAISE they that will Times past, I joy to see
  My selfe now live: *this age best pleaseth mee.*

Cloathes, are conspirators

THOUGH from without no foes at all we feare;
  We shall be wounded by the cloathes we weare.

Cruelty

'TIS but a dog-like madnesse in bad Kings,
  For to delight in wounds and murderings.
As some plants prosper best by cuts and blowes;
So Kings by killing doe encrease their foes.

Faire after foule

TEARES *quickly drie: griefes will in time decay:*
A cleare will come after a cloudy day.

Hunger

ASKE me what hunger is, and Ile reply,
'Tis but a fierce desire of hot and drie.

Bad wages for good service

IN this misfortune Kings doe most excell,
To heare the worst from men, when they doe well.

The End

CONQUER we shall, but we must first contend;
'Tis not the Fight that crowns us, but the end.

The Bondman

BIND me but to thee with thine haire,
  And quickly I shall be
Made by that fetter or that snare
  A bondman unto thee.

Or if thou tak'st that bond away,
  Then bore me through the eare;
And by the Law I ought to stay
  For ever with thee here.

Choose for the best

GIVE house-roome to the best; *'Tis never known*
Vertue and pleasure, both to dwell in one.

To Silvia

PARDON my trespasse (*Silvia*) I confesse,
My kisse out-went the bounds of shamfastnesse:
None is discreet at all times; no, *not Jove*
Himselfe, at one time, can be wise, and Love.

Faire shewes deceive

SMOOTH was the Sea, and seem'd to call
Two prettie girles to play withall:
Who padling there, the Sea soone frown'd,
And on a sudden both were drown'd.
What credit can we give to seas,
Who, kissing, kill such Saints as these?

His wish

FAT be my Hinde; unlearned be my wife;
Peacefull my night; my day devoid of strife:
To these a comely off-spring I desire,
Singing about my everlasting fire.

Upon Julia's *washing her self in the river*

HOW fierce was I, when I did see
My *Julia* wash her self in thee!
So *Lillies* thorough Christall look:
So purest pebbles in the brook:
As in the River *Julia* did,
Halfe with a Lawne of water hid,
Into thy streames my self I threw,
And strugling there, I kist thee too;
And more had done (it is confest)
Had not thy waves forbad the rest.   10

2.2 Two] To *48*   3.2 my night] by night *48* ('sit nox cum somno, sit sine
lite dies'. Martial, ii. 90. 10)

A Meane in our Meanes

THOUGH Frankinsense the *Deities* require,
We must not give all to the hallowed fire.
Such be our gifts, and such be our expence,
As for our selves to leave some frankinsence.

Upon Clunn

A ROWLE of Parchment *Clunn* about him beares,
Charg'd with the Armes of all his Ancestors:
And seems halfe ravisht, when he looks upon
That *Bar*, this *Bend*; that *Fess*, this *Cheveron*;
This *Manch*, that *Moone*; this *Martlet*, and that *Mound*;
This counterchange of *Perle* and *Diamond*.
What joy can *Clun* have in that Coat, or this,
When as his owne still out at elboes is?

Upon Cupid

LOVE, like a Beggar, came to me
With Hose and Doublet torne:
His Shirt bedangling from his knee,
With Hat and Shooes out-worne.

He askt an almes; I gave him bread,
And meat too, for his need:
Of which, when he had fully fed,
He wisht me all *Good speed*.

Away he went, but as he turn'd
(In faith I know not how)
He toucht me so, as that I burn'd,
And am tormented now.

Love's silent flames, and fires obscure
Then crept into my heart;
And though I saw no Bow, I'm sure,
His finger was the dart.

Upon Blisse

B*LISSE* (last night drunk) did kisse his mothers knee:
Where he will kisse (next drunk) conjecture ye.

3.11 burn'd] burn *48*

Upon Burr

B*URR* is a smell-feast, and a man alone,
That (where meat is) will be a hanger on.

Upon Megg

M*EGG* yesterday was troubled with a Pose,
Which, this night hardned, sodders up her nose.

An Hymne to Love

I *WILL* confesse
With Cheerfulnesse,
Love is a thing so likes me,
That let her lay
On me all day,
Ile kiss the hand that strikes me.

2.   I will not, I,
Now blubb'ring, cry,
It (Ah!) too late repents me,
That I did fall   10
To love at all,
Since love so much contents me.

3.   No, no, Ile be
In fetters free;
While others they sit wringing
Their hands for paine;
Ile entertaine
The wounds of love with singing.

4.   With Flowers and Wine,
And Cakes Divine,   20
To strike me I will tempt thee:
Which done; no more
Ile come before
Thee and thine Altars emptie.

To his honoured and most Ingenious friend
*M*ʳ. Charles Cotton

FOR brave comportment, wit without offence,
 Words fully flowing, yet of influence:
Thou art that man of men, the man alone,
Worthy the Publique Admiration:
Who with thine owne eyes read'st what we doe write,
And giv'st our Numbers *Euphonie*, and weight.
Tel'st when a Verse springs high, how understood
To be, or not borne of the Royall-blood.
What State above, what *Symmetrie* below,
Lines have, or sho'd have, thou the best canst show.   10
For which (my *Charles*) it is my pride to be,
Not so much knowne, as to be lov'd of thee.
Long may I live so, and my wreath of *Bayes*,
Be lesse anothers *Laurell*, then thy praise.

Women uselesse

WHAT need we marry Women, when
 Without their use we may have men?
And such as will in short time be,
For murder fit, or mutinie;
As *Cadmus* once a new way found,
By throwing teeth into the ground:
(From which poore seed, and rudely sown)
Sprung up a War-like Nation.
So let us Yron, Silver, Gold,
Brasse, Leade or Tinne, throw into th'mould;   10
And we shall see in little space
Rise up of men, a fighting race.
If this can be, say then, what need
Have we of Women or their seed?

Love is a sirrup

LOVE *is a sirrup*; and who er'e we see
 Sick and surcharg'd with this sacietie:
Shall by this pleasing trespasse quickly prove,
Ther's loathsomnesse e'en in the sweets of love.

297

Leven

LOVE is a Leven, and a loving kisse
The Leven of a loving sweet-heart is.

Repletion

PHYSITIANS say Repletion springs
More from the sweet then sower things.

On Himselfe

WEEPE for the dead, for they have lost this light:
And weepe for me, lost in an endlesse night.
Or mourne, or make a Marble Verse for me,
Who writ for many. *Benedicite.*

No man without Money

No man such rare parts hath, that he can swim,
If favour or occasion helpe not him.

On Himselfe

LOST to the world; lost to my selfe; alone
Here now I rest under this Marble stone:
In depth of silence, heard, and seene of none.

To M. Leonard Willan his
peculiar friend

I WILL be short, and having quickly hurl'd
This line about, live Thou throughout the world;
Who art a man for all Sceanes; unto whom
(What's hard to others) nothing's troublesome.
Can'st write the *Comick, Tragick* straine, and fall
From these to penne the pleasing Pastorall:
Who fli'st at all heights: Prose and Verse run'st through;
Find'st here a fault, and mend'st the trespasse too:
For which I might extoll thee, but speake lesse,
Because thy selfe art comming to the Presse: 10
And then sho'd I in praising thee be slow,
Posterity will pay thee what I owe.

To his worthy friend M. John Hall,
Student of Grayes-Inne

TELL me young man, or did the Muses bring
  Thee lesse to taste, then to drink up their spring;
That none hereafter sho'd be thought, or be
A Poet, or a Poet-like but Thee.
What was thy Birth, thy starre that makes thee knowne,
At twice ten yeares, a prime and publike one?
Tell us thy Nation, kindred, or the whence
Thou had'st, and hast thy *mighty influence,*
That makes thee lov'd, and of the men desir'd,
And no lesse prais'd, then of the maides admir'd.   10
Put on thy Laurell then; and in that trimme
Be thou *Apollo,* or the type of him:
Or let the *Unshorne God* lend thee his Lyre,
And next to him, be Master of the Quire.

To Julia

OFFER thy gift; but first the Law commands
  Thee *Julia,* first, to *sanctifie* thy hands:
Doe that my *Julia* which the rites require,
Then boldly give thine incense to the fire.

To the most comely and proper
M. Elizabeth Finch

HANSOME you are, and Proper you will be
  Despight of all your infortunitie:
Live long and lovely, but yet grow no lesse
In that your owne prefixed comelinesse:
Spend on that stock: and when your life must fall,
Leave others Beauty, to set up withall.

Upon Ralph

RALPH pares his nayles, his warts, his cornes, and *Raph*
  In sev'rall tills, and boxes keepes 'em safe;
Instead of Harts-horne (if he speakes the troth)
To make a lustie-gellie for his broth.

To his Booke

IF hap it must, that I must see thee lye
  Absyrtus-like all torne confusedly:
With solemne tears, and with much grief of heart,
Ile recollect thee (weeping) part by part;
And having washt thee, close thee in a chest
With spice; that done, Ile leave thee to thy rest.

TO THE KING,

Upon his welcome to Hampton-Court

Set and Sung

WELCOME, *Great Cesar*, welcome now you are,
  As dearest Peace, after destructive Warre:
Welcome as slumbers; or as beds of ease
After our long, and peevish sicknesses.
O *Pompe of Glory!* Welcome now, and come
To re-possess once more your long'd-for home.
A thousand Altars smoake; a thousand thighes
Of Beeves here ready stand for Sacrifice.
Enter and prosper; while our eyes doe waite
For an *Ascendent* throughly *Auspicate*:   10
Under which signe we may the former stone
Lay of our safeties new foundation:
That done; O *Cesar*, live, and be to us,
Our *Fate*, our *Fortune*, and our *Genius*;
To whose free knees we may our temples tye
As to a still protecting Deitie.
That sho'd you stirre, we and our Altars too
May (*Great Augustus*) *goe along with You.*
Chor. Long live the King; and to accomplish this,
We'l from our owne, adde far more years to his.   20

Ultimus Heroum:
OR,
To the most learned, and to the right Honourable,
Henry, Marquesse of Dorchester

AND as time past when Cato the Severe
Entred the circumspacious Theater;
In reverence of his person, every one
Stood as he had been turn'd from flesh to stone:
E'ne so my numbers will astonisht be
If but lookt on; struck dead, if scan'd by Thee.

To his Muse, another to the same

TELL that Brave Man, fain thou wo'dst have access
To kiss his hands, but that for fearfullness;
Or else because th'art like a modest Bride,
Ready to blush to death, sho'd he but chide.

Upon Vineger

VINEGER is no other I define,
Then the dead Corps, or carkase of the Wine.

Upon Mudge

MUDGE every morning to the Postern comes,
(His teeth all out) to rince and wash his gummes.

To his learned friend M. Jo. Harmar, Phisitian
to the Colledge of Westminster

WHEN first I find those Numbers thou do'st write;
To be most soft, terce, sweet, and perpolite:
Next, when I see Thee towring in the skie,
In an expansion no less large, then high;
Then, in that compass, sayling here and there,
And with Circumgyration every where;
Following with love and active heate thy game,
And then at last to truss the Epigram;
I must confess, distinction none I see
Between Domitians Martiall then, and Thee.   10
But this I know, should Jupiter agen
Descend from heaven, to re-converse with men;
The Romane Language full, and superfine,
If Iove wo'd speake, he wo'd accept of thine.

Upon his Spaniell Tracie

Now thou art dead, no eye shall ever see,
For shape and service, *Spaniell* like to thee.
This shall my love doe, give thy sad death one
Teare, that deserves of me a million.

The deluge

Drowning, drowning, I espie
Coming from my *Julia's* eye:
'Tis some solace in our smart,
To have friends to beare a part:
I have none; but must be sure
Th'inundation to endure.
Shall not times hereafter tell
This for no meane *miracle*;
When the waters by their fall
Threatn'd ruine unto all?   10
Yet the deluge here was known,
Of a world to drowne but One.

Upon Lupes

Lupes for the outside of his suite has paide;
But for his heart, he cannot have it made:
The reason is, his credit cannot get
The inward carbage for his cloathes as yet.

Raggs

What are our patches, tatters, raggs, and rents,
But the base dregs and lees of vestiments?

Strength to support Soveraignty

Let Kings and Rulers, learne this line from me;
Where power is weake, unsafe is Majestie.

Upon Tubbs

For thirty yeares, *Tubbs* has been proud and poor,
'Tis now his habit, which he can't give ore.

Crutches

T HOU seest me *Lucia* this year droope,
  Three *Zodiaks* fill'd more I shall stoope;
Let Crutches then provided be
To shore up my debilitie.
Then while thou laugh'st; Ile, sighing, crie,
A *Ruine underpropt* am I:
Do'n will I then my *Beadsmans* gown,
And when so feeble I am grown,
As my weake shoulders cannot beare
The burden of a *Grashopper*:   10
Yet with the bench of aged sires,
When I and they keep tearmly fires;
With my weake voice Ile sing, or say
Some Odes I made of *Lucia*:
Then will I heave my wither'd hand
To *Jove* the Mighty for to stand
Thy faithfull friend, and to poure downe
Upon thee many a *Benizon*.

To Julia

H OLY waters hither bring
  For the sacred sprinkling:
Baptize me and thee, and so
Let us to the Altar go.
And (ere we our rites commence)
Wash our hands in innocence.
Then I'le be the *Rex Sacrorum*,
Thou the Queen of *Peace and Quorum*.

Upon Case

C *ASE* is a Lawyer, that near pleads alone,
  But when he hears the like confusion,
As when the disagreeing Commons throw
About their House, their clamorous I, or No:
Then *Case*, as loud as any *Serjant* there,
Cries out (my Lord, my Lord) the Case is clear:
But when all's husht, *Case* then a fish more mute,
Bestirs his Hand, but starves in hand the Suite.

To Perenna

I A *Dirge* will pen for thee;
Thou a *Trentall* make for me:
That the Monks and Fryers together,
Here may sing the rest of either:
Next, I'm sure, the Nuns will have
Candlemas to grace the Grave.

To his Sister in Law, M. Susanna Herrick

THE Person crowns the Place; your lot doth fall
Last, yet to be with These a Principall.
How ere it fortuned; know for Truth, I meant
You a fore-leader in this Testament.

Upon the Lady Crew

THIS Stone can tell the storie of my life,
What was my Birth, to whom I was a Wife:
In teeming years, how soon my Sun was set,
Where now I rest, these may be known by *Jet.*
For other things, my many Children be
The best and truest *Chronicles* of me.

On Tomasin Parsons

GROW up in Beauty, as thou do'st begin,
And be of all admired, *Tomasin.*

Ceremony upon Candlemas Eve

DOWN with the Rosemary, and so
Down with the Baies, & misletoe:
Down with the Holly, Ivie, all,
Wherewith ye drest the Christmas Hall:
That so the superstitious find
No one least Branch there left behind:
For look how many leaves there be
Neglected there (maids trust to me)
So many *Goblins* you shall see.

Suspicion makes secure

H E that will live of all cares dispossest,
Must shun the bad, I, and suspect the best.

Upon Spokes

S *POKES* when he sees a rosted Pig, he swears
Nothing he loves on't but the chaps and ears:
But carve to him the fat flanks; and he shall
Rid these, and those, and part by part eat all.

To his kinsman M. Tho: Herrick, *who desired to be in his Book*

W ELCOME to this my Colledge, and though late
Tha'st got a place here (standing candidate)
It matters not, since thou art chosen one
Here of my great and good foundation.

A Bucolick betwixt Two: Lacon *and* Thyrsis

Lacon. F OR a kiss or two, confesse,
What doth cause this pensiveness?
Thou most lovely Neat-heardesse:
Why so lonely on the hill?
Why thy pipe by thee so still,
That ere while was heard so shrill?

Tell me, do thy kine now fail
To fulfill the milkin-paile?
Say, what is't that thou do'st aile?

Thyr. None of these; but out, alas!   10
A mischance is come to pass,
And I'le tell thee what it was:
See mine eyes are weeping ripe,
Lacon. Tell, and I'le lay down my Pipe.

Thyr. I have lost my lovely steere,
That to me was far more deer
Then these kine, which I milke here.
Broad of fore-head, large of eye,
Party colour'd like a Pie;
Smooth in each limb as a die;   20

Clear of hoof, and clear of horn;
Sharply pointed as a thorn:
With a neck by yoke unworn.
From the which hung down by strings,
Balls of Cowslips, Daisie rings,
Enterplac't with ribbanings.
Faultless every way for shape;
Not a straw co'd him escape;
Ever gamesome as an ape:
But yet harmless as a sheep.   30
(Pardon, *Lacon* if I weep)
Tears will spring, where woes are deep.
Now (ai me) (ai me.) Last night
Came a mad dog, and did bite,
I, and kil'd my dear delight.

Lacon. Alack for grief!
Thyr. But I'le be brief,

Hence I must, for time doth call
Me, and my sad Play-mates all,
To his Ev'ning Funerall.   40
Live long, *Lacon*, so *adew.*
Lacon. Mournfull maid farewell to you;
Earth afford ye flowers to strew.

Upon Sapho

LOOK upon *Sapho's* lip, and you will swear,
There is a love-like-leven rising there.

Upon Faunus

WE read how *Faunus*, he the shepheards *God,*
His wife to death whipt with a *Mirtle Rod.*
The Rod (perhaps) was better'd by the name;
But had it been of Birch, the death's the same.

The Quintell

UP with the Quintill, that the Rout,
May fart for joy, as well as shout:
Either's welcome, Stinke or Civit,
If we take it, as they give it.

A Bachanalian Verse

DRINKE up
Your Cup,
But not spill Wine;
For if you
Do,
'Tis an ill signe;
2.   That we
Foresee,
You are cloy'd here,
If so, no
Hoe,
But avoid here.

Care a good keeper

CARE keepes the Conquest; 'tis no lesse renowne,
To keepe a Citie, then to winne a Towne.

Rules for our reach

MEN must have Bounds how farre to walke; for we
Are made farre worse, by lawless liberty.

To Biancha

AH *Biancha!* now I see,
It is Noone and past with me:
In a while it will strike one;
Then *Biancha*, I am gone.
Some *effusions* let me have,
Offer'd on my holy Grave;
Then, *Biancha*, let me rest
With my face towards the East.

To the handsome Mistresse Grace Potter

AS is your name, so is your comely face,
Toucht every where with such diffused grace,
As that in all that *admirable round*,
There is not one least *solecisme* found;
And as that part, so every portion else,
Keepes line for line with *Beauties Parallels*.

Anacreontike

I MUST
Not trust
Here to any;
Bereav'd,
Deceiv'd
By so many:
As one
Undone
By my losses;
Comply   10
Will I
With my crosses.
Yet still
I will
Not be grieving;
Since thence
And hence
Comes relieving.
But this
Sweet is   20
In our mourning;
Times bad
And sad
Are a turning:
And he
Whom we
See dejected;
Next day
Wee may
See erected.   30

More modest, more manly

'TIS still observ'd, those men most valiant are,
That are most modest ere they come to warre.

Not to covet much where little is the charge

WHY sho'd we covet much, when as we know,
W'ave more to beare our charge, then way to go?

Anacrontick Verse

B RISK methinks I am, and fine,
    When I drinke my capring wine:
Then to love I do encline;
When I drinke my wanton wine:
And I wish all maidens mine,
When I drinke my sprightly wine:
Well I sup, and well I dine,
When I drinke my frolick wine:
But I languish, lowre, and Pine,
When I want my fragrant wine.   10

Upon Pennie

B ROWN bread *Tom Pennie* eates, and must of right,
    Because his stock will not hold out for white.

Patience in Princes

K *INGS must not use the Axe for each offence*:
    Princes cure some faults by their patience.

Feare gets force

D *ESPAIRE takes heart, when ther's no hope to speed:*
    The Coward then takes Armes, and do's the deed.

Parcell-gil't-Poetry

L ET'S strive to be the best; the Gods, we know it,
    Pillars and men, hate an indifferent Poet.

Upon Love, by way of question and answer

I BRING ye love, *Quest.* What will love do?
    Ans. Like, and dislike ye:
I bring ye love: *Quest.* What will love do?
    Ans. Stroake ye to strike ye.
I bring ye love: *Quest.* What will Love do?
    Ans. Love will be-foole ye:
I bring ye love: *Quest.* What will love do?
    Ans. Heate ye to coole ye:

I bring ye love: *Quest.* What will love do?
    Ans. Love gifts will send ye: 10
I bring ye love: *Quest.* What will love do?
    Ans. Stock ye to spend ye:
I bring ye love: *Quest.* What will love do?
    Ans. Love will fulfill ye:
I bring ye love: *Quest.* What will love do?
    Ans. Kisse ye, to kill ye.

To the Lord Hopton, *on his fight in* Cornwall

Go on brave *Hopton*, to effectuate that
  Which wee, and times to come, shall wonder at.
Lift up thy Sword; next, suffer it to fall,
And by that *One blow* set an end to all.

His Grange

How well contented in this private *Grange*
  Spend I my life (that's subject unto change:)
Under whose Roofe with *Mosse-worke* wrought, there I
Kisse my *Brown wife*, and *black Posterity*.

Leprosie in houses

When to a House I come, and see
  The *Genius* wastefull, more then free:
The servants *thumblesse*, yet to eat,
With lawlesse tooth the floure of wheate:
The Sonnes to suck the milke of Kine,
More then the teats of Discipline:
The Daughters wild and loose in dresse;
Their cheekes unstain'd with shamefac'tnesse:
The Husband drunke, the Wife to be
A Baud to incivility: 10
I must confesse, I there descrie,
A House spred through with *Leprosie*.

Good manners at meat

This rule of manners I will teach my guests,
  To come with their own bellies unto feasts:
Not to eat equall portions; but to rise
Farc't with the food, that may themselves suffice.

Anthea's *Retractation*

A^{NTHEA} laught, and fearing lest excesse
Might stretch the cords of civill comelinesse:
She with a dainty blush rebuk't her face;
And cal'd each line back to his *rule* and *space*.

Comforts in Crosses

B^E not dismaide, though crosses cast thee downe;
Thy fall is but the rising to a Crowne.

Seeke and finde

A^{TTEMPT} *the end, and never stand to doubt;*
Nothing's so hard, but search will find it out.

Rest

O^N with thy worke, though thou beest hardly prest;
Labour is held up, by the hope of rest.

Leprosie in Cloathes

W^{HEN} flowing garments I behold
Enspir'd with *Purple*, *Pearle*, and *Gold*;
I think no other but I see
In them a glorious leprosie
That do's infect, and make the rent
More mortall in the vestiment.
As flowrie vestures doe descrie
The wearers rich immodestie;
So plaine and simple cloathes doe show
Where vertue walkes, not those that flow.   10

Upon Buggins

B^{UGGINS} is Drunke all night, all day he sleepes;
This is the Levell-coyle that *Buggins* keeps.

Great Maladies, long Medicines

To an old soare a long cure must goe on;
Great faults require great satisfaction.

His Answer to a friend

You aske me what I doe, and how I live?
And (Noble friend) this answer I must give:
Drooping, I draw on to the vaults of death,
Or'e which you'l walk, when I am laid beneath.

The Begger

Shall I a daily Begger be,
For loves sake asking almes of thee?
Still shall I crave, and never get
A hope of my desired bit?
Ah cruell maides! Ile goe my way,
Whereas (perchance) my fortunes may
Finde out a Threshold or a doore,
That may far sooner speed the poore:
Where thrice we knock, and none will heare,
Cold comfort still I'm sure lives there.   10

Bastards

Our Bastard-children are but like to Plate,
Made by the Coyners illegitimate.

His change

My many cares and much distress,
Has made me like a wilderness:
Or (discompos'd) I'm like a rude,
And all confused multitude:
Out of my comely manners worne;
And as in meanes, in minde all torne.

The Vision

ME thought I saw (as I did dreame in bed)
A crawling Vine about *Anacreon's* head:
Flusht was his face; his haires with oyle did shine;
And as he spake, his mouth ranne ore with wine.
Tipled he was; and tipling lispt withall;
And lisping reeld, and reeling like to fall.
A young *Enchantresse* close by him did stand
Tapping his plump thighes with a *mirtle* wand:
She smil'd; he kist; and kissing, cull'd her too;
And being cup-shot, more he co'd not doe.   10
For which (me thought) in prittie anger she
Snatcht off his Crown, and gave the wreath to me:
Since when (me thinks) my braines about doe swim,
And I am wilde and wanton like to him.

A vow to Venus

HAPPILY I had a sight
Of my dearest deare last night;
Make her this day smile on me,
And Ile Roses give to thee.

On his Booke

THE bound (almost) now of my book I see,
But yet no end of those therein or me:
Here we begin new life; while thousands quite
Are lost, and theirs, in everlasting night.

A sonnet of Perilla

THEN did I live when I did see
Perilla smile on none but me.
But (ah!) by starres malignant crost,
The life I got I quickly lost:
But yet a way there doth remaine,
For me embalm'd to live againe;
And that's to love me; in which state
Ile live as one *Regenerate*.

Bad may be better

M AN may at first transgress, but next do well:
Vice doth in some but lodge a while, not dwell.

Posting to Printing

L ET others to the Printing Presse run fast,
Since after death comes glory, *Ile not haste.*

Rapine brings Ruine

W HAT'S got by Justice is establisht sure;
No Kingdomes got by Rapine long endure.

Comfort to a youth that had lost his Love

W HAT needs complaints,
When she a place
Has with the race
Of Saints?
In endlesse mirth,
She thinks not on
What's said or done
In earth:
She sees no teares,
Or any tone   10
Of thy deep grone
She heares:
Nor do's she minde,
Or think on't now,
That ever thou
Wast kind.
But chang'd above,
She likes not there,
As she did here,
Thy Love.   20
Forbeare therefore,
And Lull asleepe
Thy woes and weep
No more.

314

Upon Boreman. *Epig.*

B*OREMAN* takes tole, cheats, flatters, lyes, yet *Boreman*,
For all the Divell helps, will be a poore man.

Saint Distaffs day, or the morrow after Twelfth day

PARTLY worke and partly play
Ye must on S. *Distaffs* day:
From the Plough soone free your teame;
Then come home and fother them.
If the Maides a spinning goe,
Burne the flax, and fire the tow:
Scorch their plackets, but beware
That ye singe no maiden-haire.
Bring in pailes of water then,
Let the Maides bewash the men.   10
Give S. *Distaffe* all the right,
Then bid Christmas sport *good-night*.
And next morrow, every one
To his owne vocation.

Sufferance

IN the hope of ease to come,
Let's endure one Martyrdome.

His tears to Thamasis

I SEND, I send here my supremest kiss
To thee my *silver-footed Thamasis*.
No more shall I reiterate thy Strand,
Whereon so many Stately Structures stand:
Nor in the summers sweeter evenings go,
To bath in thee (as thousand others doe.)
No more shall I a long thy christall glide,
In Barge (with boughes and rushes beautifi'd)
With soft-smooth Virgins (for our chast disport)
To *Richmond*, *Kingstone*, and to *Hampton-Court:*   10
Never againe shall I with Finnie-Ore

3.2 one] (?) our (see note on 207, l. 61)

Put from, or draw unto the faithfull shore:
And Landing here, or safely Landing there,
Make way to my *Beloved Westminster:*
Or to the *Golden-cheap-side*, where the earth
Of *Julia Herrick* gave to me my Birth.
May all clean *Nimphs* and curious water Dames,
With Swan-like-state, flote up & down thy streams:
No drought upon thy wanton waters fall
To make them Leane, and languishing at all.   20
No ruffling winds come hither to discease
Thy pure, and *Silver-wristed Naides.*
Keep up your state ye streams; and as ye spring,
Never make sick your Banks by surfeiting.
Grow young with Tydes, and though I see ye never,
Receive this vow, *so fare-ye-well for ever.*

Pardons

T*HOSE* ends in *War* the best contentment bring,
    Whose Peace is made up with a Pardoning.

Peace not Permanent

G*REAT* Cities seldome rest: *If there be none*
    T'invade from far: They'l finde worse foes at home.

Truth and Errour

T*WIXT* Truth and Errour, *there's this difference known,*
    Errour is fruitfull, Truth is onely one.

Things mortall still mutable

T*HINGS* are uncertain, *and the more we get,*
    The more on ycie pavements we are set.

Studies to be supported

S*TUDIES* themselves will languish and decay,
    When either price, or praise is ta'ne away.

Wit punisht, prospers most

DREAD not the shackles: on with thine intent;
Good wits get more fame by their punishment.

Twelfe night, or King *and* Queene

Now, now the mirth comes
    With the cake full of plums,
Where Beane's the *King* of the sport here;
    Beside we must know,
    The Pea also
Must revell, as *Queene,* in the Court here.

    Begin then to chuse,
    (This night as ye use)
Who shall for the present delight here,
    Be a *King* by the lot,   10
    And who shall not
Be Twelfe-day *Queene* for the night here.

    Which knowne, let us make
    Joy-sops with the cake;
And let not a man then be seen here,
    Who unurg'd will not drinke
    To the base from the brink
A health to the King and the Queene here.

    Next crowne the bowle full
    With gentle lambs-wooll;   20
Adde sugar, nutmeg and ginger,
    With store of ale too;
    And thus ye must doe
To make the wassaile a swinger.

    Give then to the King
    And Queene wassailing;
And though with ale ye be whet here;
    Yet part ye from hence,
    As free from offence,
As when ye innocent met here.   30

His desire

GIVE me a man that is not dull,
    When all the world with rifts is full:
But unamaz'd dares clearely sing,
When as the roof's a tottering:
And, though it falls, continues still
Tickling the *Citterne* with his quill.

Caution in Councell

KNOW when to speake; for many times it brings
    Danger to give the best advice to Kings.

Moderation

LET moderation on thy passions waite
    Who loves too much, too much the lov'd will hate.

Advice the best actor

*STILL take advice; though counsels when they flye
    At randome, sometimes hit most happily.*

Conformity is comely

*CONFORMITY gives comelinesse to things.
    And equall shares exclude all murmerings.*

Lawes

WHO violates the Customes, hurts the Health,
    Not of one man, but all the Common-wealth.

The meane

TIS much among the filthy to be clean;
    Our heat of youth can hardly keep the mean.

Like loves his like

LIKE will to like, each Creature loves his kinde;
Chaste words proceed still from a bashfull minde.

His hope or sheat-Anchor

AMONG these Tempests great and manifold
My Ship has here one only Anchor-hold;
That is my hope; which if that slip, I'm one
Wildred in this vast watry *Region*.

Comfort in Calamity

TIS no discomfort in the world to fall,
When the great Crack not Crushes one, but all.

Twilight

THE Twi-light is no other thing (we say)
Then Night now gone, and yet not sprung the Day.

False Mourning

HE who wears Blacks, and mournes not for the Dead,
Do's but deride the Party buried.

The will makes the work, or consent
makes the Cure

NO grief is grown so desperate, but the ill
Is halfe way cured, if the party will.

Diet

IF wholsome Diet can re-cure a man,
What need of Physick, or Physitian?

Smart

STRIPES justly given yerk us (with their fall)
But causelesse whipping smarts the most of all.

The Tinkers Song

ALONG, come along,
   Let's meet in a throng
      Here of Tinkers;
And quaffe up a Bowle
As big as a Cowle
      To Beer Drinkers.
The pole of the Hop
Place in the Ale-shop
      to Bethwack us;
If ever we think   10
So much as to drink
      Unto *Bacchus.*
Who frolick will be,
For little cost he
      Must not vary,
From Beer-broth at all,
So much as to call
      For Canary.

His Comfort

THE only comfort of my life
   Is, that I never yet had wife;
Nor will hereafter; since I know
Who Weds, ore-buyes his weal with woe.

Sincerity

WASH clean the Vessell, lest ye soure
   What ever Liquor in ye powre.

To Anthea

SICK is *Anthea,* sickly is the spring,
   The Primrose sick, and sickly every thing:
The while my deer *Anthea* do's but droop,
The *Tulips, Lillies, Daffadills* do *stoop*;
But when again sh'as got her healthfull houre,
Each bending then, will rise a proper flower.

Nor buying or selling

Now, if you love me, tell me,
For as I will not sell ye,
So not one cross to buy thee
Ile give, if thou deny me.

To his peculiar friend M. Jo: Wicks

Since shed or Cottage I have none,
I sing the more, that thou hast one;
To whose glad threshold, and free door
I may a Poet come, though poor;
And eat with thee a savory bit,
Paying but common thanks for it.
Yet sho'd I chance, (my *Wicks*) to see
An over-leven-looke in thee,
To soure the Bread, and turn the Beer
To an exalted vineger;   10
Or sho'dst thou prize me as a Dish
Of thrice-boyl'd-worts, or third dayes fish;
I'de rather hungry go and come,
Then to thy house be Burdensome;
Yet, in my depth of grief, I'de be
One that sho'd drop his *Beads* for thee.

The more mighty, the more mercifull

Who may do most, do's least: The bravest will
Shew mercy there, where they have power to kill.

After Autumne, Winter

Die ere long I'm sure, I shall;
After leaves, the tree must fall.

A good death

For truth I may this sentence tell,
No man dies ill, that liveth well.

2.8 looke] looks *48*

Recompence

W HO plants an Olive, but to eate the Oile?
Reward, we know, is the chiefe end of toile.

On Fortune

T HIS is my comfort, when she's most unkind,
She can but spoile me of my Meanes, not Mind.

To Sir George Parrie, *Doctor of the Civill Law*

I HAVE my Laurel Chaplet on my head,
If 'mongst these many Numbers to be read,
But one by you be hug'd and cherished.

Peruse my Measures thoroughly, and where
Your judgement finds a guilty Poem, there
Be you a Judge; but not a Judge severe.

The meane passe by, or over, none contemne;
The good applaud: the peccant lesse condemne,
Since *Absolution* you can give to them.

Stand forth Brave Man, here to the publique sight;   10
And in my Booke now claim a two-fold right:
The first as *Doctor*, and the last as *Knight*.

Charmes

T HIS Ile tell ye by the way,
Maidens when ye Leavens lay,
Crosse your Dow, and your dispatch,
Will be better for your Batch.

Another

I N the morning when ye rise
Wash your hands, and cleanse your eyes.
Next be sure ye have a care,
To disperse the water farre.
For as farre as that doth light,
So farre keepes the evill Spright.

Another

IF ye feare to be affrighted
When ye are (by chance) benighted:
In your Pocket for a trust,
Carrie nothing but a Crust:
For that holy piece of Bread,
Charmes the danger, and the dread.

Upon Gorgonius

UNTO *Pastillus* ranke *Gorgonius* came,
To have a tooth twitcht out of's native frame.
Drawn was his tooth; but stanke so, that some say,
The Barber stopt his Nose, and ranne away.

Gentlenesse

THAT Prince must govern with a gentle hand,
Who will have love comply with his command.

A Dialogue betwixt himselfe and Mistresse Eliza: Wheeler, *under the name of* Amarillis

MY dearest Love, since thou wilt go,
And leave me here behind thee;
For love or pitie let me know
The place where I may find thee.

Amaril. In country Meadowes pearl'd with Dew,
And set about with Lillies;
There filling Maunds with Cowslips, you
May find your *Amarillis.*

Her. What have the Meades to do with thee,
Or with thy youthfull houres?
Live thou at Court, where thou mayst be
The *Queen* of men, not flowers.

Let Country wenches make 'em fine
With Poesies, since 'tis fitter
For thee with richest Jemmes to shine,
And like the Starres to glitter.

Amaril. You set too high a rate upon
    A Shepheardess so homely;
 Her. Believe it (dearest) ther's not one
    I'th'Court that's halfe so comly.   20

  I prithee stay. (*Am.*) I must away,
    Lets kiss first, then we'l sever.
 Ambo. And though we bid adieu to day,
    Wee shall not part for ever.

To Julia

HELP me, *Julia*, for to pray,
 Mattens sing, or Mattens say:
This I know, the Fiend will fly
Far away, if thou beest by.
Bring the Holy-water hither;
Let us wash, and pray together:
When our Beads are thus united,
Then the Foe will fly affrighted.

To Roses in Julia's *Bosome*

ROSES, you can never die,
 Since the place wherein ye lye,
Heat and moisture mixt are so,
As to make ye ever grow.

To the Honoured, Master
Endimion Porter

WHEN to thy Porch I come, and (ravisht) see
 The State of Poets there attending Thee:
Those *Bardes*, and I, all in a *Chorus* sing,
We are Thy *Prophets Porter*; *Thou our King.*

Speake in season

WHEN times are troubled, then forbeare; but speak,
 When a cleare day, out of a Cloud do's break.

Obedience

THE Power of Princes rests in the Consent
Of onely those, who are obedient:
Which if away, proud Scepters then will lye
Low, and of Thrones the Ancient *Majesty*.

Another on the same

NO man so well a Kingdome Rules, as He,
Who hath himselfe obaid the Soveraignty.

Of Love

1. INSTRUCT me now, what love will do;
2. 'Twill make a tongless man to wooe.
1. Inform me next, what love will do;
2. 'Twill strangely make a one of too.
1. Teach me besides, what love wil do;
2. 'Twill quickly mar, & make ye too.
1. Tell me, now last, what love will do;
2. 'Twill hurt and heal a heart pierc'd through.

Upon Trap

TRAP, of a Player turn'd a Priest now is;
Behold a suddaine *Metamorphosis*.
If Tythe-pigs faile, then will he shift the scean,
And, from a Priest, turne Player once again.

Upon Grubs

GRUBS loves his Wife and Children, while that they
Can live by love, or else grow fat by Play:
But when they call or cry on *Grubs* for meat;
Instead of Bread, *Grubs* gives them stones to eat.
He raves, he rends, and while he thus doth tear,
His Wife and Children fast to death for fear.

Upon Dol

NO question but *Dols* cheecks wo'd soon rost dry,
Were they not basted by her either eye.

Upon Hog

H OG has a place i'th'Kitchen, and his share
The flimsie Livers, and blew Gizzards are.

The School or Perl of Putney, the Mistress of all singular manners, Mistresse Portman

W HETHER I was my selfe, or else did see
Out of my self that *Glorious Hierarchie*!
Or whether those (in orders rare) or these
Made up One State of *Sixtie Venuses*;
Or whether *Fairies, Syrens, Nymphes* they were,
Or *Muses*, on their mountaine sitting there;
Or some enchanted Place, I do not know
(Or *Sharon*, where eternall Roses grow.)
This I am sure; I Ravisht stood, as one
Confus'd in utter Admiration.   10
Me thought I saw them stir, and gently move,
And look as all were capable of Love:
And in their motion smelt much like to flowers
Enspir'd by th'Sun-beams after dews & showers.
There did I see the *Reverend Rectresse* stand,
Who with her eyes-gleam, or a glance of hand,
Those spirits rais'd; and with like precepts then
(As with a *Magick*) laid them all agen:
(*A happy Realme! When no compulsive Law,*
Or fear of it, but Love keeps all in awe.)   20
Live you *great Mistresse* of your Arts, and be
A nursing Mother so to Majesty;
As those your Ladies may in time be seene,
For Grace and Carriage, every one a Queene.
One Birth their Parents gave them; but their new,
And better Being, they receive from You.
Mans former Birth is grace-lesse; but the state
Of life comes in, when he's Regenerate.

To Perenna

THOU say'st I'm dull; if edge-lesse so I be,
Ile whet my lips, and sharpen Love on thee.

On himselfe

LET me not live, if I not love,
Since I as yet did never prove,
Where Pleasures met; at last, doe find,
All Pleasures meet in Woman-kind.

On Love

THAT love 'twixt men do's ever longest last
Where War and Peace the Dice by turns doe cast.

Another on Love

LOVE'S of it self, too sweet; the best of all
Is, when loves hony has a dash of gall.

Upon Gut

SCIENCE puffs up, sayes *Gut*, when either Pease
Make him thus swell, or windy Cabbages.

Upon Chub

WHEN *Chub* brings in his harvest, still he cries,
Aha my boyes! heres wheat for Christmas Pies!
Soone after, he for beere so scores his wheat,
That at the tide, he has not bread to eate.

Pleasures Pernicious

WHERE Pleasures rule a Kingdome, never there
Is sober virtue, seen to move her sphere.

On himself

A WEARIED Pilgrim, I have wandred here
  Twice five and twenty (bate me but one yeer)
Long I have lasted in this world; (tis true)
But yet those yeers that I have liv'd, but few.
Who by his gray Haires, doth his lusters tell,
Lives not those yeers, but he that lives them well.
One man has reatch't his sixty yeers, but he
Of all those three-score, has not liv'd halfe three:
He lives, who lives to virtue: men who cast
Their ends for Pleasure, do not live, but last.   10

To *M*. Laurence Swetnaham

R EAD thou my Lines, my *Swetnaham*, if there be
  A fault, tis hid, if it be voic't by thee.
Thy mouth will make the sourest numbers please;
How will it drop pure hony, speaking these?

His *Covenant or Protestation to* Julia

W HY do'st thou wound, & break my heart?.
  As if we sho'd for ever part?
Hast thou not heard an Oath from me,
After a day, or two, or three,
I wo'd come back and live with thee?
Take, if thou do'st distrust that Vowe;
This second Protestation now.
Upon thy cheeke that spangel'd Teare,
Which sits as Dew of Roses there:
That Teare shall scarce be dri'd before   10
Ile kisse the Threshold of thy dore.
Then weepe not sweet; but thus much know,
I'm halfe return'd before I go.

On himselfe

I WILL no longer kiss,
  I can no longer stay;
The way of all Flesh is,
That I must go this day:
Since longer I can't live,
My frolick Youths adieu;
My Lamp to you Ile give,
And all my troubles too.

3.6 distrust] distrust, *48*

To the most accomplisht Gentleman Master
Michael Oulsworth

NOR thinke that Thou in this my Booke art worst,
Because not plac't here with the midst, or first.
Since Fame that sides with these, or goes before
Those, that must live with Thee for evermore.
That Fame, and Fames rear'd Pillar, thou shalt see
In the next sheet *Brave Man* to follow Thee.
Fix on That Columne then, and never fall;
Held up by Fames *eternall Pedestall*.

To his Girles who would have him sportfull

ALAS I can't, for tell me how
Can I be gamesome (aged now)
Besides ye see me daily grow
Here Winter-like, to Frost and Snow.
And I ere long, my Girles, shall see,
Ye quake for cold to looke on me.

Truth and falsehood

TRUTH *by her own simplicity is known,*
Falsehood by Varnish and Vermillion.

His last request to Julia

I HAVE been wanton, and too bold I feare,
To chafe o're much the Virgins cheek or eare:
Beg for my Pardon *Julia*; *He doth winne*
Grace with the Gods, who's sorry for his sinne.
That done, my *Julia*, dearest *Julia*, come,
And go with me to chuse my Buriall roome:
My Fates are ended; when thy *Herrick* dyes,
Claspe thou his Book, then close thou up his Eyes.

On himselfe

ONE Eare tingles; some there be,
That are snarling now at me:
Be they those that *Homer* bit,
I will give them thanks for it.

2.5 Girles, *ed.*: Girles *48*

Upon Kings

KINGS must be dauntlesse: Subjects will contemne
Those, who want Hearts, and weare a Diadem.

To his Girles

WANTON Wenches doe not bring
For my haires black colouring:
For my Locks (Girles) let 'em be
Gray or white, all's one to me.

Upon Spur

SPUR jingles now, and sweares by no meane oathes,
He's double honour'd, since h'as got gay cloathes:
Most like his Suite, and all commend the Trim;
And thus they praise the Sumpter; but not him:
As to the Goddesse, people did conferre
Worship, and not to'th'Asse that carried her.

To his Brother Nicolas Herrick

WHAT others have with cheapnesse seene, and ease,
In Varnisht maps; by'th'helpe of Compasses:
Or reade in Volumes, and those Bookes (with all
Their large Narrations, *Incanonicall*)
Thou hast beheld those seas, and Countries farre;
And tel'st to us, what once they were, and are.
So that with bold truth, thou canst now relate
This Kingdomes fortune, and that Empires fate:
Canst talke to us of *Sharon*; where a spring
Of Roses have an endlesse flourishing.   10
Of *Sion, Sinai, Nebo*, and with them,
Make knowne to us the now *Jerusalem*.
The Mount of *Olives*; *Calverie*, and where
Is (and hast seene) *thy Saviours Sepulcher*.
So that the man that will but lay his eares,
As *Inapostate*, to the thing he heares,
Shall by his hearing quickly come to see
The truth of Travails lesse in bookes then Thee.

4.17 by] be *48*

The Voice and Violl

RARE is the voice it selfe; but when we sing
To'th Lute or Violl, then 'tis ravishing.

Warre

IF Kings and kingdomes, once distracted be,
The sword of war must trie the Soveraignty.

A King and no King

THAT Prince, who may doe nothing but what's just,
Rules but by leave, and takes his Crowne on trust.

Plots not still prosperous

ALL are not ill Plots, that doe sometimes faile;
Nor those false vows, which oft times don't prevaile.

Flatterie

WHAT is't that wasts a Prince? example showes,
'Tis flatterie spends a King, more then his foes.

Upon Rumpe

RUMPE is a Turne-broach, yet he seldome can
Steale a swolne sop out of the Dripping pan.

Upon Shopter

OLD Widow *Shopter*, when so ere she cryes,
Lets drip a certain Gravie from her eyes.

Upon Deb

IF felt and heard, (unseen) thou dost me please;
If seen, thou lik'st me, *Deb*, in none of these.

Excesse

EXCESSE is sluttish: keepe the meane; for why?
Vertue's clean Conclave is sobriety.

Upon Croot

ONE silver spoon shines in the house of *Croot*;
Who cannot buie, or steale a second to't.

The soul is the salt

THE body's salt, the soule is; which when gon,
The flesh soone sucks in putrifaction.

Upon Flood, *or a thankfull man*

FLOOD, if he has for him and his a bit,
He sayes his fore and after Grace for it:
If meate he wants, then Grace he sayes to see
His hungry belly borne by Legs *Jaile-free.*
Thus have, or have not, all alike is good,
To this our poore, yet ever patient *Flood.*

Upon Pimpe

WHEN *Pimpes* feet sweat (as they doe often use)
There springs a sope-like-lather in his shoos.

Upon Luske

IN Den'-shire Kerzie *Lusk* (when he was dead)
Wo'd shrouded be, and therewith buried.
When his Assignes askt him the reason why?
He said, because he got his wealth thereby.

Foolishnesse

IN's *Tusc'lanes, Tullie* doth confesse,
No plague ther's like to foolishnesse.

Upon Rush

RUSH saves his shooes, in wet and snowie wether;
And feares in summer to weare out the lether:
This is strong thrift that warie *Rush* doth use
Summer and Winter still to save his shooes.

Abstinence

AGAINST diseases here the strongest fence
Is the defensive vertue, Abstinence.

No danger to men desperate

WHEN feare admits no hope of safety, then
Necessity makes dastards valiant men.

Sauce for sorrowes

ALTHOUGH our suffering meet with no reliefe,
An equall mind is the best sauce for griefe.

To Cupid

I HAVE a leaden, thou a shaft of gold;
Thou kil'st with heate, and I strike dead with cold.
Let's trie of us who shall the first expire;
Or thou by frost, or I by quenchlesse fire:
Extreames are fatall, where they once doe strike,
And bring to'th'heart destruction both alike.

Distrust

WHAT ever men for Loyalty pretend,
'Tis Wisdomes part to' doubt a faithfull friend.

The Hagg

THE staffe is now greas'd,
    And very well pleas'd,
She cockes out her Arse at the parting,
    To an old Ram Goat,
    That rattles i'th'throat,
Halfe choakt with the stink of her farting.

    In a dirtie Haire-lace
    She leads on a brace
Of black-bore-cats to attend her;
    Who scratch at the Moone,   10
    And threaten at noone
Of night from Heaven for to rend her.

4.4 by frost] be frost *48*

333

A hunting she goes;
A crackt horne she blowes;
At which the hounds fall a bounding;
While th'Moone in her sphere
Peepes trembling for feare,
And night's afraid of the sounding.

The mount of the Muses

AFTER thy labour take thine ease,
Here with the sweet *Pierides*.
But if so be that men will not
Give thee the Laurell Crowne for lot;
Be yet assur'd, thou shalt have one
Not subject to corruption.

On Himselfe

IL'E write no more of Love; but now repent
Of all those times that I in it have spent.
Ile write no more of life; but wish twas ended,
And that my dust was to the earth commended.

To his Booke

GOE thou forth my booke, though late;
Yet be timely fortunate.
It may chance good-luck may send
Thee a kinsman, or a friend,
That may harbour thee, when I,
With my fates neglected lye.
If thou know'st not where to dwell,
See, the fier's by: *Farewell*.

The end of his worke

PART of the worke remaines; one part is past:
And here my ship rides having Anchor cast.

To Crowne it

MY wearied Barke, O Let it now be Crown'd!
The Haven reacht to which I first was bound.

On Himselfe

THE worke is done: young men, and maidens set
   Upon my curles the *Mirtle Coronet*,
Washt with sweet ointments; Thus at last I come
To suffer in the Muses *Martyrdome:*
But with this comfort, if my blood be shed,
The Muses will weare blackes, when I am dead.

The pillar of Fame

FAMES pillar here, at last, we set,
  Out-during *Marble*, *Brasse*, or *Jet*,
    Charm'd and enchanted so,
    As to withstand the blow
      Of   overthrow:
      Nor shall the seas,
      Or OUTRAGES
      Of storms orebear
      What we up-rear,
      Tho Kingdoms fal,   10
    This pillar never shall
    Decline or waste at all;
  But stand for ever by his owne
  Firme and well fixt foundation.

To his Book's end this last line he'd have plac't,
Jocond his Muse was; *but his Life was chast.*

FINIS.

HIS
NOBLE NUMBERS:
O R,
HIS PIOUS PIECES,

Wherein (amongſt other things)

he ſings the Birth of his CHRIST:
and ſighes for his *Saviours* ſuffe-
ring on the *Croſſe.*

HESIOD.

Ἴδμθμ ψϵύδεα πολλὰ λέγϵιν ἐτύμοισιν ὁμοῖα.
Ἴδμθμ δ᾽, εὖτ᾽ ἐθέλωμθμ, ἀληθέα μυθήσαϑ.

LONDON,
Printed for *John Williams,* and *Francis Eglesfield.*
1647.

HIS
Noble Numbers:
OR,
His pious Pieces

His Confession

LOOK how our foule Dayes do exceed our faire;
    And as our bad, more then our good Works are:
Ev'n so those Lines, pen'd by my wanton Wit,
Treble the number of these good I've writ.
Things precious are least num'rous: Men are prone
To do ten Bad, for one Good Action.

His Prayer for Absolution

FOR Those my unbaptized Rhimes,
    Writ in my wild unhallowed Times;
For every sentence, clause and word,
That's not inlaid with Thee, (my Lord)
Forgive me God, and blot each Line
Out of my Book, that is not Thine.
But if, 'mongst all, thou find'st here one
Worthy thy Benediction;
That One of all the rest, shall be
The Glory of my Work, and Me.

To finde God

WEIGH me the Fire; or, canst thou find
    A way to measure out the Wind;
Distinguish all those Floods that are
Mixt in that watrie Theater;
And tast thou them as saltlesse there,
As in their Channell first they were.

Tell me the People that do keep
Within the Kingdomes of the Deep;
Or fetch me back that Cloud againe,
Beshiver'd into seeds of Raine;   10
Tell me the motes, dust, sands, and speares
Of Corn, when Summer shakes his eares;
Shew me that world of Starres, and whence
They noiselesse spill their Influence:
This if thou canst; then shew me Him
That rides the glorious *Cherubim*.

What God is

G OD is above the sphere of our esteem,
And is the best known, not defining Him.

Upon God

G OD is not onely said to be
An *Ens*, but *Supraentitie*.

Mercy and Love

G OD hath two wings, which He doth ever move,
The one is Mercy, and the next is Love:
Under the first the Sinners ever trust;
And with the last he still directs the Just.

Gods Anger without Affection

G OD when He's angry here with any one,
His wrath is free from perturbation;
And when we think His looks are sowre and grim,
The alteration is in us, not Him.

God not to be comprehended

'T IS hard to finde God, but to comprehend
Him, as He is, is labour without end.

Gods part

PRAYERS and Praises are those spotlesse two
Lambs, by the Law, which God requires as due.

Affliction

GOD n'ere afflicts us more then our desert,
Though He may seem to over-act His part:
Somtimes He strikes us more then flesh can beare;
But yet still lesse then Grace can suffer here.

Three fatall Sisters

THREE fatall Sisters wait upon each sin;
First, Fear and Shame without, then Guilt within.

Silence

SUFFER thy legs, but not thy tongue to walk:
God, the most Wise, is sparing of His talk.

Mirth

TRUE mirth resides not in the smiling skin:
The sweetest solace is to act no sin.

Loading and unloading

GOD loads, and unloads, (thus His work begins)
To load with blessings, and unload from sins.

Gods Mercy

GODS boundlesse mercy is (to sinfull man)
Like to the ever-wealthy Ocean:
Which though it sends forth thousand streams, 'tis ne're
Known, or els seen to be the emptier:
And though it takes all in, 'tis yet no more
Full, and fild-full, then when full-fild before.

Prayers must have Poise

GOD He rejects all Prayers that are sleight,
And want their Poise: words ought to have their weight.

To God: an Anthem, sung in the Chappell at
White-Hall, before the King

Verse.   MY God, I'm wounded by my sin,
            And sore without, and sick within:
Ver. Chor. I come to Thee, in hope to find
            Salve for my body, and my mind.
Verse.   In *Gilead* though no Balme be found,
            To ease this smart, or cure this wound;
Ver. Chor. Yet, Lord, I know there is with Thee
            All saving health, and help for me.
Verse.   Then reach Thou forth that hand of Thine,
            That powres in oyle, as well as wine.   10
Ver. Chor. And let it work, for I'le endure
            The utmost smart, so Thou wilt cure.

Upon God

GOD is all fore-part; for, we never see
Any part backward in the Deitie.

Calling, and correcting

GOD is not onely mercifull, to call
Men to repent, but when He strikes withall.

No escaping the scourging

GOD scourgeth some severely, some He spares;
But all in smart have lesse, or greater shares.

The Rod

GODS Rod doth watch while men do sleep; & then
The Rod doth sleep, while vigilant are men.

God has a twofold part

GOD when for sin He makes His Children smart,
His own He acts not, but anothers part:
But when by stripes He saves them, then 'tis known,
He comes to play the part that is His own.

God is One

GOD, as He is most Holy knowne;
So He is said to be most One.

Persecutions profitable

AFFLICTIONS they most profitable are
To the beholder, and the sufferer:
Bettering them both, but by a double straine,
The first by patience, and the last by paine.

To God

DO with me, God! as Thou didst deal with *Iohn*,
(Who writ that heavenly *Revelation*)
Let me (like him) first cracks of thunder heare;
Then let the Harps inchantments strike mine eare;
Here give me thornes; there, in thy Kingdome, set
Upon my head the golden coronet;
There give me day; but here my dreadfull night:
My sackcloth here; but there my *Stole* of white.

Whips

GOD has his whips here to a twofold end,
The bad to punish, and the good t'amend.

Gods Providence

IF all transgressions here should have their pay,
What need there then be of a reckning day:
If God should punish no sin, here, of men,
His Providence who would not question then?

343

Temptation

THOSE Saints, which God loves best,
The Devill tempts not least.

His Ejaculation to God

MY God! looke on me with thine eye
Of pittie, not of scrutinie;
For if thou dost, thou then shalt see
Nothing but loathsome sores in mee.
O then! for mercies sake, behold
These my irruptions manifold;
And heale me with thy looke, or touch:
But if thou wilt not deigne so much,
Because I'me odious in thy sight,
Speak but the word, and cure me quite.   10

Gods gifts not soone granted

GOD heares us when we pray, but yet defers
His gifts, to exercise Petitioners:
And though a while He makes Requesters stay,
With Princely hand He'l recompence delay.

Persecutions purifie

GOD strikes His Church, but 'tis to this intent,
To make, not marre her, by this punishment:
So where He gives the bitter Pills, be sure,
'Tis not to poyson, but to make thee pure.

Pardon

GOD pardons those, who do through frailty sin;
But never those that persevere therein.

An Ode of the Birth of our Saviour

1. IN Numbers, and but these few,
   I sing Thy Birth, Oh JESU!
   Thou prettie Babie, borne here,
   With sup'rabundant scorn here:
   Who for Thy Princely Port here,
         Hadst for Thy place
         Of Birth, a base
   Out-stable for thy Court here.

2. Instead of neat Inclosures
   Of inter-woven Osiers;   10
   Instead of fragrant Posies
   Of Daffadills, and Roses;
   Thy cradle, Kingly Stranger,
         As Gospell tells,
         Was nothing els,
   But, here, a homely manger.

3. But we with Silks, (not Cruells)
   With sundry precious Jewells,
   And Lilly-work will dresse Thee;
   And as we dispossesse thee   20
   Of clouts, wee'l make a chamber,
         Sweet Babe, for Thee,
         Of Ivorie,
   And plaister'd round with Amber.

4. The Jewes they did disdaine Thee,
   But we will entertaine Thee
   With Glories to await here
   Upon Thy Princely State here,
   And more for love, then pittie.
         From yeere to yeere   30
         Wee'l make Thee, here,
   A Free-born of our Citie.

Lip labour

IN the old Scripture I have often read,
The calfe without meale n'ere was offered;
To figure to us, nothing more then this,
Without the heart, lip-labour nothing is.

        1.29 pittie.] (?) pittie

The Heart

IN Prayer the Lips ne're act the winning part,
Without the sweet concurrence of the Heart.

Eare-rings

WHY wore th'Egyptians Jewells in the Eare?
But for to teach us, all the grace is there,
When we obey, by acting what we heare.

Sin seen

WHEN once the sin has fully acted been,
Then is the horror of the trespasse seen.

Upon Time

TIME was upon
The wing, to flie away;
And I cal'd on
Him but a while to stay;
But he'd be gone,
For ought that I could say.

He held out then,
A Writing, as he went;
And askt me, when
False man would be content   10
To pay agen,
What God and Nature lent.

An houre-glasse,
In which were sands but few,
As he did passe,
He shew'd, and told me too,
Mine end near was,
And so away he flew.

His Petition

IF warre, or want shall make me grow so poore.
As for to beg my bread from doore to doore;
Lord! let me never act that beggars part,
Who hath thee in his mouth, not in his heart.
He who asks almes in that so sacred Name,
Without due reverence, playes the cheaters game.

To God

THOU hast promis'd, Lord, to be
With me in my miserie;
Suffer me to be so bold,
As to speak, Lord, say and hold.

His Letanie, to the Holy Spirit

1. IN the houre of my distresse,
When temptations me oppresse,
And when I my sins confesse,
        Sweet Spirit comfort me!

2. When I lie within my bed,
Sick in heart, and sick in head,
And with doubts discomforted,
        Sweet Spirit comfort me!

3. When the house doth sigh and weep,
And the world is drown'd in sleep,   10
Yet mine eyes the watch do keep;
        Sweet Spirit comfort me!

4. When the artlesse Doctor sees
No one hope, but of his Fees,
And his skill runs on the lees;
        Sweet Spirit comfort me!

5. When his Potion and his Pill,
His, or none, or little skill,
Meet for nothing, but to kill;
        Sweet Spirit comfort me!   20

3.18 His] Has *editors*

347

6. When the passing-bell doth tole,
   And the Furies in a shole
   Come to fright a parting soule;
      Sweet Spirit comfort me!

7. When the tapers now burne blew,
   And the comforters are few,
   And that number more then true;
      Sweet Spirit comfort me!

8. When the Priest his last hath praid,
   And I nod to what is said,   30
   'Cause my speech is now decaid;
      Sweet Spirit comfort me!

9. When (God knowes) I'm tost about,
   Either with despaire, or doubt;
   Yet before the glasse be out,
      Sweet Spirit comfort me!

10. When the Tempter me pursu'th
    With the sins of all my youth,
    And halfe damns me with untruth;
       Sweet Spirit comfort me!   40

11. When the flames and hellish cries
    Fright mine eares, and fright mine eyes,
    And all terrors me surprize;
       Sweet Spirit comfort me!

12. When the Judgment is reveal'd,
    And that open'd which was seal'd,
    When to Thee I have appeal'd;
       Sweet Spirit comfort me!

Thanksgiving

THANKSGIVING for a former, doth invite
God to bestow a second benefit.

Cock-crow

BELL-MAN of Night, if I about shall go
For to denie my Master, do thou crow.
Thou stop'st S. *Peter* in the midst of sin;
Stay me, by crowing, ere I do begin;
Better it is, premonish'd, for to shun
A sin, then fall to weeping when 'tis done.

All things run well for the Righteous

ADVERSE and prosperous Fortunes both work on
Here, for the righteous mans salvation:
Be he oppos'd, or be he not withstood,
All serve to th'Augmentation of his good.

Paine ends in Pleasure

AFFLICTIONS bring us joy in times to come,
When sins, by stripes, to us grow wearisome.

To God

I'LE come, I'le creep, (though Thou dost threat)
Humbly unto Thy Mercy-seat:
When I am there, this then I'le do,
Give Thee a Dart, and Dagger too;
Next, when I have my faults confest,
Naked I'le shew a sighing brest;
Which if that can't Thy pittie wooe,
Then let Thy Justice do the rest,
        And strike it through.

A Thanksgiving to God, for his House

LORD, Thou hast given me a cell
        Wherein to dwell;
And little house, whose humble Roof
        Is weather-proof;
Under the sparres of which I lie
        Both soft, and drie;
Where Thou my chamber for to ward
        Hast set a Guard

Of harmlesse thoughts, to watch and keep
    Me, while I sleep.   10
Low is my porch, as is my Fate,
    Both void of state;
And yet the threshold of my doore
    Is worn by'th poore,
Who thither come, and freely get
    Good words, or meat:
Like as my Parlour, so my Hall
    And Kitchin's small:
A little Butterie, and therein
    A little Byn,   20
Which keeps my little loafe of Bread
    Unchipt, unflead:
Some brittle sticks of Thorne or Briar
    Make me a fire,
Close by whose living coale I sit,
    And glow like it.
Lord, I confesse too, when I dine,
    The Pulse is Thine,
And all those other Bits, that bee
    There plac'd by Thee;   30
The Worts, the Purslain, and the Messe
    Of Water-cresse,
Which of Thy kindnesse Thou hast sent;
    And my content
Makes those, and my beloved Beet,
    To be more sweet.
'Tis thou that crown'st my glittering Hearth
    With guiltlesse mirth;
And giv'st me Wassaile Bowles to drink,
    Spic'd to the brink.   40
Lord, 'tis thy plenty-dropping hand,
    That soiles my land;
And giv'st me, for my Bushell sowne,
    Twice ten for one:
Thou mak'st my teeming Hen to lay
    Her egg each day:
Besides my healthfull Ewes to beare
    Me twins each yeare:
The while the conduits of my Kine
    Run Creame, (for Wine.)   50

All these, and better Thou dost send
      Me, to this end,
That I should render, for my part,
      A thankfull heart;
Which, fir'd with incense, I resigne,
      As wholly Thine;
But the acceptance, that must be,
      My Christ, by Thee.

To God

MAKE, make me Thine, my gracious God,
  Or with thy staffe, or with thy rod;
And be the blow too what it will,
Lord, I will kisse it, though it kill:
Beat me, bruise me, rack me, rend me,
Yet, in torments, I'le commend Thee:
Examine me with fire, and prove me
To the full, yet I will love Thee:
Nor shalt thou give so deep a wound,
But I as patient will be found.   10

Another, to God

    LORD, do not beat me,
Since I do sob and crie,
And swowne away to die,
    Ere Thou dost threat me.

    Lord, do not scourge me,
If I by lies and oaths
Have soil'd my selfe, or cloaths,
    But rather purge me.

None truly happy here

HAPPY'S that man, to whom God gives
  A stock of Goods, whereby he lives
Neer to the wishes of his heart:
No man is blest through ev'ry part.

To his ever-loving God

CAN I not come to Thee, my God, for these
    So very-many-meeting hindrances,
That slack my pace; but yet not make me stay?
Who slowly goes, rids (in the end) his way.
Cleere Thou my paths, or shorten Thou my miles,
Remove the barrs, or lift me o're the stiles:
Since rough the way is, help me when I call,
And take me up; or els prevent the fall.
I kenn my home; and it affords some ease,
To see far off the smoaking Villages.   10
Fain would I rest; yet covet not to die,
For feare of future-biting penurie:
No, no, (my God) Thou know'st my wishes be
To leave this life, not loving it, but Thee.

Another

THOU bidst me come; I cannot come; for why,
    Thou dwel'st aloft, and I want wings to flie.
To mount my Soule, she must have pineons given;
For, 'tis no easie way from Earth to Heaven.

To Death

THOU bidst me come away,
    And I'le no longer stay,
Then for to shed some teares
For faults of former yeares;
And to repent some crimes,
Done in the present times:
And next, to take a bit
Of Bread, and Wine with it:
To d'on my robes of love,
Fit for the place above;   10
To gird my loynes about
With charity throughout;
And so to travaile hence
With feet of innocence:
These done, I'le onely crie
God mercy; and so die.

Neutrality loathsome

GOD will have all, or none; serve Him, or fall
Down before *Baal*, *Bel*, or *Belial:*
Either be hot, or cold: God doth despise,
Abhorre, and spew out all Neutralities.

Welcome what comes

WHATEVER comes, let's be content withall:
Among Gods Blessings, there is no one small.

To his angrie God

THROUGH all the night
    Thou dost me fright,
And hold'st mine eyes from sleeping;
    And day, by day,
    My Cup can say,
My wine is mixt with weeping.

    Thou dost my bread
    With ashes knead,
Each evening and each morrow:
    Mine eye and eare   10
    Do see, and heare
The coming in of sorrow.

    Thy scourge of steele,
    (Ay me!) I feele,
Upon me beating ever:
    While my sick heart
    With dismall smart
Is disacquainted never.

    Long, long, I'm sure,
    This can't endure;   20
But in short time 'twill please Thee,
    My gentle God,
    To burn the rod,
Or strike so as to ease me

Patience, or Comforts in Crosses

ABUNDANT plagues I late have had,
Yet none of these have made me sad:
For why, my Saviour, with the sense
Of suffring gives me patience.

Eternitie

1 O YEARES! and Age! Farewell:
        Behold I go,
        Where I do know
Infinitie to dwell.

2 And these mine eyes shall see
        All times, how they
        Are lost i'th'Sea
Of vast Eternitie.

3 Where never Moone shall sway
        The Starres; but she,   10
        And Night, shall be
Drown'd in one endlesse Day.

To his Saviour, a Child; a Present, by a child

GO prettie child, and beare this Flower
Unto thy little Saviour;
And tell Him, by that Bud now blown,
He is the *Rose of Sharon* known:
When thou hast said so, stick it there
Upon his Bibb, or Stomacher:
And tell Him, (for good handsell too)
That thou hast brought a Whistle new,
Made of a clean strait oaten reed,
To charme his cries, (at time of need:)   10
Tell Him, for Corall, thou hast none;
But if thou hadst, He sho'd have one;
But poore thou art, and knowne to be
Even as monilesse, as He.
Lastly, if thou canst win a kisse
From those mellifluous lips of his;
Then never take a second on,
To spoile the first impression.

354

The New-yeeres Gift

LET others look for Pearle and Gold,
  Tissues, or Tabbies manifold:
One onely lock of that sweet Hay
Whereon the blessed Babie lay,
Or one poore Swadling-clout, shall be
The richest New-yeeres Gift to me.

To God

IF any thing delight me for to print
  My Book, 'tis this; that *Thou, my God, art in't.*

God, and the King

HOW am I bound to Two! God, who doth give
  The mind; the King, the meanes whereby I live.

Gods mirth, Mans mourning

WHERE God is merry, there write down thy fears:
What He with laughter speaks, heare thou with tears.

Honours are hindrances

GIVE me Honours: what are these,
  But the pleasing hindrances?
Stiles, and stops, and stayes, that come
In the way 'twixt me, and home:
Cleer the walk, and then shall I
To my heaven lesse run, then flie.

The Parasceve, or Preparation

TO a Love-Feast we both invited are:
  The figur'd Damask, or pure Diaper,
Over the golden Altar now is spread,
With Bread, and Wine, and Vessells furnished;
The *sacred Towell,* and the *holy Eure*
Are ready by, to make the Guests all pure:
Let's go (my *Alma*) yet e're we receive,
Fit, fit it is, we have our *Parasceve.*
Who to that *sweet Bread* unprepar'd doth come
Better he starv'd, then but to tast one crumme.   10

To God

GOD gives not onely corne, for need,
But likewise sup'rabundant seed;
Bread for our service, bread for shew;
Meat for our meales, and fragments too:
He gives not poorly, taking some
Between the finger, and the thumb;
But, for our glut, and for our store,
Fine flowre prest down, and running o're.

A will to be working

ALTHOUGH we cannot turne the fervent fit
Of sin, we must strive 'gainst the streame of it:
And howsoe're we have the conquest mist;
'Tis for our glory, that we did resist.

Christs part

CHRIST, He requires still, wheresoere He comes,
To feed, or lodge, to have the best of Roomes:
Give Him the choice; grant Him the nobler part
Of all the House: the best of all's the Heart.

Riches and Poverty

GOD co'd have made all rich, or all men poore;
But why He did not, let me tell wherefore:
Had all been rich, where then had Patience been?
Had all been poore, who had His Bounty seen?

Sobriety in Search

TO seek of God more then we well can find,
Argues a strong distemper of the mind.

Almes

GIVE, if thou canst, an Almes; if not, afford,
Instead of that, a sweet and gentle word:
God crowns our goodnesse, where so ere He sees,
On our part, wanting all abilities.

To his Conscience

CAN I not sin, but thou wilt be
 My private *Protonotarie*?
Can I not wooe thee to passe by
A short and sweet iniquity?
I'le cast a mist and cloud, upon
My delicate transgression,
So utter dark, as that no eye
Shall see the hug'd impietie:
Gifts blind the wise, and bribes do please,
And winde all other witnesses: 10
And wilt not thou, with gold, be ti'd
To lay thy pen and ink aside?
That in the mirk and tonguelesse night,
Wanton I may, and thou not write?
It will not be: And, therefore, now,
For times to come, I'le make this Vow,
From aberrations to live free;
So I'le not feare the Judge, or thee.

To his Saviour

LORD, I confesse, that Thou alone art able
 To purifie this my *Augean* stable:
Be the Seas water, and the Land all Sope,
Yet if Thy Bloud not wash me, there's no hope.

To God

GOD is all-sufferance here; here He doth show
 No Arrow nockt, onely a stringlesse Bow:
His Arrowes flie; and all his stones are hurl'd
Against the wicked, in another world.

His Dreame

I DREAMT, last night, Thou didst transfuse
 Oyle from Thy Jarre, into my creuze;
And powring still, Thy wealthy store,
The vessell full, did then run ore:

Me thought, I did Thy bounty chide,
To see the waste; but 'twas repli'd
By Thee, Deare God, God gives man seed
Oft-times for wast, as for his need.
Then I co'd say, that house is bare,
That has not bread, and some to spare.   10

Gods Bounty

GODS Bounty, that ebbs lesse and lesse,
As men do wane in thankfulnesse.

To his sweet Saviour

NIGHT hath no wings, to him that cannot sleep;
And Time seemis then, not for to flie, but creep;
Slowly her chariot drives, as if that she
Had broke her wheele, or crackt her axeltree.
Just so it is with me, who list'ning, pray
The winds, to blow the tedious night away;
That I might see the cheerfull peeping day.
Sick is my heart; O Saviour! do Thou please
To make my bed soft in my sicknesses:
Lighten my candle, so that I beneath   10
Sleep not for ever in the vaults of death:
Let me Thy voice betimes i'th morning heare;
Call, and I'le come; say Thou, the when, and where:
Draw me, but first, and after Thee I'le run,
And make no one stop, till my race be done.

His Creed

I DO believe, that die I must,
And be return'd from out my dust:
I do believe, that when I rise,
Christ I shall see, with these same eyes:
I do believe, that I must come,
With others, to the dreadfull Doome:
I do believe, the bad must goe
From thence, to everlasting woe:

I do believe, the good, and I,
Shall live with Him eternally: 10
I do believe, I shall inherit
Heaven, by Christs mercies, not my merit:
I do believe, the One in Three,
And Three in perfect Unitie:
Lastly, that JESUS is a Deed
Of Gift from God: *And heres my Creed.*

Temptations

TEMPTATIONS hurt not, though they have accesse:
Satan o'recomes none, but by willingnesse.

The Lamp

WHEN a mans Faith is frozen up, as dead;
Then is the Lamp and oyle extinguished.

Sorrowes

SORROWES our portion are: Ere hence we goe,
Crosses we must have; or, hereafter woe.

Penitencie

A MANS transgression God do's then remit,
When man he makes a Penitent for it.

The Dirge of Jephthahs Daughter: sung by the Virgins

1 O THOU, the wonder of all dayes!
O Paragon, and Pearle of praise!
O Virgin-martyr, ever blest
                              Above the rest
Of all the Maiden-Traine! We come,
And bring fresh strewings to thy Tombe.

2 Thus, thus, and thus we compasse round
Thy harmlesse and unhaunted Ground;
And as we sing thy Dirge, we will
                              The Daffadill,   10
And other flowers, lay upon
(The Altar of our love) thy Stone.

3 Thou wonder of all Maids, li'st here,
 Of Daughters all, the Deerest Deere;
 The eye of Virgins; nay, the Queen
     Of this smooth Green,
 And all sweet Meades; from whence we get
 The Primrose, and the Violet.

4 Too soon, too deere did *Jephthah* buy,
 By thy sad losse, our liberty: 20
 His was the Bond and Cov'nant, yet
     Thou paid'st the debt,
 Lamented Maid! he won the day,
 But for the conquest thou didst pay.

5 Thy Father brought with him along
 The Olive branch, and Victors Song:
 He slew the Ammonites, we know,
     But to thy woe;
 And in the purchase of our Peace,
 The Cure was worse then the Disease.   30

6 For which obedient zeale of thine,
 We offer here, before thy Shrine,
 Our sighs for Storax, teares for Wine;
     And to make fine,
 And fresh thy Herse-cloth, we will, here,
 Foure times bestrew thee ev'ry yeere.

7 Receive, for this thy praise, our teares:
 Receive this offering of our Haires:
 Receive these Christall Vialls fil'd
     With teares, distil'd   40
 From teeming eyes; to these we bring,
 Each Maid, her silver Filleting,

8 To guild thy Tombe; besides, these Caules,
 These Laces, Ribbands, and these Faules,
 These Veiles, wherewith we use to hide
     The Bashfull Bride,
 When we conduct her to her Groome:
 All, all we lay upon thy Tombe.

9 No more, no more, since thou art dead,
 Shall we ere bring coy Brides to bed;   50

No more, at yeerly Festivalls
                    We Cowslip balls,
Or chaines of Columbines shall make,
For this, or that occasions sake.

10 No, no; our Maiden-pleasures be
Wrapt in the winding-sheet, with thee:
'Tis we are dead, though not i'th grave:
                    Or, if we have
One seed of life left, 'tis to keep
A Lent for thee, to fast and weep.   60

11 Sleep in thy peace, thy bed of Spice;
And make this place all Paradise:
May Sweets grow here! & smoke from hence,
                    Fat Frankincense:
Let Balme, and Cassia send their scent
From out thy Maiden-Monument.

12 May no Wolfe howle, or Screech-Owle stir
A wing about thy Sepulcher!
No boysterous winds, or stormes, come hither,
                    To starve, or wither   70
Thy soft sweet Earth! but (like a spring)
Love keep it ever flourishing.

13 May all shie Maids, at wonted hours,
Come forth, to strew thy Tombe with flow'rs:
May Virgins, when they come to mourn,
                    Male-Incense burn
Upon thine Altar! then return,
And leave thee sleeping in thy Urn.

To God, on his sicknesse

WHAT though my Harp, and Violl be
Both hung upon the Willow-tree?
What though my bed be now my grave,
And for my house I darknesse have?
What though my healthfull dayes are fled,
And I lie numbred with the dead?
Yet I have hope, by Thy great power,
To spring; though now a wither'd flower.

Sins loath'd, and yet lov'd

SHAME *checks our first attempts; but then 'tis prov'd,*
Sins first dislik'd, are after that belov'd.

Sin

SIN leads the way, but as it goes, it feels
The following plague still treading on his heels.

Upon God

GOD when He takes my goods and chattels hence,
Gives me a portion, giving patience:
What is in God is God; if so it be,
He patience gives; He gives himselfe to me.

Faith

WHAT here we hope for, we shall once inherit:
By Faith we all walk here, not by the Spirit.

Humility

HUMBLE we must be, if to Heaven we go:
High is the roof there; but the gate is low:
When e're thou speak'st, look with a lowly eye:
Grace is increased by humility.

Teares

OUR present Teares here (not our present laughter)
Are but the handsells of our joyes hereafter.

Sin and Strife

AFTER true sorrow for our sinnes, our strife
Must last with Satan, to the end of life.

An Ode, or Psalme, to God

DEER God,
 If thy smart Rod
Here did not make me sorrie,
 I sho'd not be
 With Thine, or Thee,
In Thy eternall Glorie.

 But since
 Thou didst convince
My sinnes, by gently striking;
 Add still to those   10
 First stripes, new blowes,
According to Thy liking.

 Feare me,
 Or scourging teare me;
That thus from vices driven,
 I may from Hell
 Flie up, to dwell
With Thee, and Thine in Heaven.

Graces for Children

WHAT God gives, and what we take,
 'Tis a gift for Christ His sake:
Be the meale of Beanes and Pease,
God be thank'd for those, and these:
Have we flesh, or have we fish,
All are Fragments from His dish.
He His Church save, and the King,
And our Peace here, like a Spring,
Make it ever flourishing.

God to be first serv'd

HONOUR thy Parents; but good manners call
Thee to adore thy God, the first of all.

Another Grace for a Child

Here a little child I stand,
Heaving up my either hand;
Cold as Paddocks though they be,
Here I lift them up to Thee,
For a Benizon to fall
On our meat, and on us all. *Amen.*

A Christmas Caroll, *sung to the King in the Presence at* White-Hall

Chor. What sweeter musick can we bring,
Then a Caroll, for to sing
The Birth of this our heavenly King?
Awake the Voice! Awake the String!
Heart, Eare, and Eye, and every thing
Awake! the while the active Finger
Runs division with the Singer.

From the Flourish they came to the Song.

1 Dark and dull night, flie hence away,
And give the honour to this Day,
That sees *December* turn'd to *May.*   10

2 If we may ask the reason, say;
The why, and wherefore all things here
Seem like the Spring-time of the yeere?

3 Why do's the chilling Winters morne
Smile, like a field beset with corne?
Or smell, like to a Meade new-shorne,
Thus, on the sudden? 4. Come and see
The cause, why things thus fragrant be:
'Tis He is borne, whose quickning Birth
Gives life and luster, publike mirth,   20
To Heaven, and the under-Earth.

Chor. We see Him come, and know him ours,
Who, with His Sun-shine, and His showers,
Turnes all the patient ground to flowers.

1 The Darling of the world is come,
  And fit it is, we finde a roome
  To welcome Him. 2. The nobler part
  Of all the house here, is the heart,

Chor. Which we will give Him; and bequeath
  This Hollie, and this Ivie Wreath,   30
  To do Him honour; who's our King,
  And Lord of all this Revelling.

The Musicall Part was composed by
M. Henry Lawes.

The New-yeeres Gift, or Circumcisions Song, sung to the King in the Presence at White-Hall

1 P REPARE for Songs; He's come, He's come;
    And be it sin here to be dumb,
  And not with Lutes to fill the roome.

2 Cast Holy Water all about,
  And have a care no fire gos out,
  But 'cense the porch, and place throughout.

3 The Altars all on fier be;
  The Storax fries; and ye may see,
  How heart and hand do all agree,
To make things sweet. *Chor.* Yet all less sweet then He.   10

4 Bring Him along, most pious Priest,
  And tell us then, when as thou seest
  His gently-gliding, Dove-like eyes,
  And hear'st His whimp'ring, and His cries;
  How canst thou this Babe circumcise?

5 Ye must not be more pitifull then wise;
  For, now unlesse ye see Him bleed,
  Which makes the Bapti'me; 'tis decreed,
The Birth is fruitlesse: *Chor.* Then the *work God speed.*

365

1 Touch gently, gently touch; and here   20
  Spring Tulips up through all the yeere;
  And from His sacred Bloud, here shed,
May Roses grow, to crown His own deare Head.

Chor. Back, back again; each thing is done
    With zeale alike, as 'twas begun;
    Now singing, homeward let us carrie
    The Babe unto His Mother *Marie*;
    And when we have the Child commended
To her warm bosome, then our Rites are ended.

          Composed by M. *Henry Lawes.*

Another New-yeeres Gift, or Song for the Circumcision

1 HENCE, hence prophane, and none appeare
    With any thing unhallowed, here:
  No jot of Leven must be found
  Conceal'd in this most holy Ground:

2 What is corrupt, or sowr'd with sin,
  Leave that without, then enter in;
Chor. But let no Christmas mirth begin
  Before ye purge, and circumcise
  Your hearts, and hands, lips, eares, and eyes.

3 Then, like a perfum'd Altar, see   10
  That all things sweet, and clean may be:
  For, here's a Babe, that (like a *Bride*)
  Will *blush to death*, if ought be spi'd
  Ill-scenting, or unpurifi'd.

Chor. The room is cens'd: help, help t'invoke
  Heaven to come down, the while we choke
  The Temple, with a cloud of smoke.

4 Come then, and gently touch the Birth
  Of Him, who's Lord of Heav'n and Earth;

5 And softly handle Him: y'ad need,   20
  Because the *prettie Babe* do's bleed.
  Poore-pittied Child! who from Thy Stall
  Bring'st, in Thy Blood, a Balm, that shall
  Be the best New-yeares Gift to all.

1 Let's blesse the Babe: And, as we sing
  His praise; so let us blesse the King:

Chor. Long may He live, till He hath told
  His New-yeeres trebled to His old:
  And, when that's done, to re-aspire
A new-borne *Phœnix* from His own chast fire.   30

Gods Pardon

WHEN I shall sin, pardon my trespasse here;
  For, once in hell, none knowes Remission there.

Sin

SIN once reacht up to Gods eternall Sphere,
  And was committed, not remitted there.

Evill

EVILL no Nature hath; the losse of good
  Is that which gives to sin a livelihood.

The Star-Song: A Caroll to the King; sung at White-Hall

The Flourish of Musick: then followed the Song.

1 TELL us, thou cleere and heavenly Tongue,
    Where is the Babe but lately sprung?
  Lies He the Lillie-banks among?

2 Or say, if this new Birth of ours
  Sleeps, laid within some Ark of Flowers,
  Spangled with deaw-light; thou canst cleere
  All doubts, and manifest the where.

3 Declare to us, bright Star, if we shall seek
  Him in the Mornings blushing cheek,
  Or search the beds of Spices through,   10
  To find him out?
Star. No, this ye need not do;
  But only come, and see Him rest
  A Princely Babe in's Mothers Brest.

Chor. He's seen, He's seen, why then a Round,
    Let's kisse the sweet and holy ground;
    And all rejoyce, that we have found
    A King, before conception crown'd.

4 Come then, come then, and let us bring
    Unto our prettie *Twelfth-Tide King*,   20
    Each one his severall offering;

Chor. And when night comes, wee'l give Him wassailing:
And that His treble Honours may be seen,
Wee'l chuse Him King, and make His Mother Queen.

To God

WITH golden Censers, and with Incense, here,
    Before Thy Virgin-Altar I appeare,
To pay Thee that I owe, since what I see
In, or without; all, all belongs to Thee:
Where shall I now begin to make, for one
Least loane of Thine, half Restitution?
Alas! I cannot pay a jot; therefore
I'le kisse the Tally, and confesse the score.
Ten thousand Talents lent me, Thou dost write:
'Tis true, my God; *but I can't pay one mite.*   10

To his deere God

I'LE hope no more,
For things that will not come;
And, if they do, they prove but cumbersome;
    Wealth brings much woe:
    And, since it fortunes so;
    'Tis better to be poore,
    Then so t'abound,
    As to be drown'd,
Or overwhelm'd with store.

    Pale care, avant,   10
    I'le learn to be content
With that small stock, Thy Bounty gave or lent.
    What may conduce
    To my most healthfull use,

Almighty God me grant;
But that, or this,
That hurtfull is,
Denie Thy suppliant.

To God, his good will

GOLD I have none, but I present my need,
O Thou, that crown'st the will, where wants the deed.
Where Rams are wanting, or large Bullocks thighs,
There a poor Lamb's a plenteous sacrifice.
Take then his Vowes, who, if he had it, would
Devote to Thee, both incense, myrrhe, and gold,
Upon an Altar rear'd by Him, and crown'd
Both with the *Rubie*, *Pearle*, and *Diamond*.

On Heaven

PERMIT mine eyes to see
Part, or the whole of Thee,
O happy place!
Where all have Grace,
And Garlands shar'd,
For their reward;
Where each chast Soule
In long white stole,
And Palmes in hand,
Do ravisht stand;   10
So in a ring,
The praises sing
Of Three in One,
That fill the Throne;
While Harps, and Violls then
To Voices, say, *Amen.*

The Summe, and the Satisfaction

LAST night I drew up mine Account,
And found my Debits to amount
To such a height, as for to tell
How I sho'd pay,'s impossible:
Well, this I'le do; my mighty score
Thy mercy-seat I'le lay before;

But therewithall I'le bring the Band,
Which, in full force, did daring stand,
Till my Redeemer (on the Tree)
Made void for millions, as for me.   10
Then, if Thou bidst me pay, or go
Unto the prison, I'le say, no;
Christ having paid, I nothing owe:
For, this is sure, the Debt is dead
By Law, the Bond once *cancelled*.

Good men afflicted most

GOD makes not good men wantons, but doth bring
  Them to the field, and, there, to skirmishing;
With trialls those, with terrors these He proves,
And hazards those most, whom the most He loves:
For *Sceva*, darts; for *Cocles*, dangers; thus
He finds a fire for mighty *Mutius*;
Death for stout *Cato*; and besides all these,
A poyson too He has for *Socrates*;
Torments for high *Attilius*; and, with want,
Brings in *Fabricius* for a Combatant: 10
But, bastard-slips, and such as He dislikes,
He never brings them once to th'push of Pikes.

Good Christians

PLAY their offensive and defensive parts,
  Till they be hid o're with a wood of darts.

The Will the cause of Woe

WHEN man is punisht, he is plagued still,
  Not for the fault of Nature, but of will.

To Heaven

OPEN thy gates
To him, who weeping waits,
    And might come in,
But that held back by sin.
    Let mercy be
So kind, to set me free,
    And I will strait
Come in, or force the gate.

The Recompence

ALL I have lost, that co'd be rapt from me;
  And fare it well: yet *Herrick*, if so be
Thy Deerest Saviour renders thee but one
Smile, that one smile's full restitution.

To God

PARDON me God, (once more I Thee intreat)
  That I have plac'd Thee in so meane a seat,
Where round about Thou seest but all things vaine,
Uncircumcis'd, unseason'd, and prophane.
But as Heavens publike and immortall Eye
Looks on the filth, but is not soil'd thereby;
So Thou, my God, may'st on this impure look,
But take no tincture from my sinfull Book:
Let but one beame of Glory on it shine,
And that will make me, and my Work divine.   10

To God

LORD, I am like to *Misletoe*,
  Which has no root, and cannot grow,
Or prosper, but by that same tree
It clings about; so I by Thee.
What need I then to feare at all,
So long as I about Thee craule?
But if that Tree sho'd fall, and die,
Tumble shall heav'n, and down will I.

His wish to God

I WOULD to God, that mine old age might have
  Before my last, but here a living grave,
Some one poore Almes-house; there to lie, or stir,
Ghost-like, as in my meaner sepulcher;
A little piggin, and a pipkin by,
To hold things fitting my necessity;
Which, rightly us'd, both in their time and place,
Might me excite to fore, and after-grace.
Thy Crosse, my *Christ*, fixt 'fore mine eyes sho'd be,
Not to adore that, but to worship Thee.   10
So, here the remnant of my dayes I'd spend,
Reading Thy Bible, and my Book; *so end.*

Satan

WHEN we 'gainst Satan stoutly fight, the more
  He teares and tugs us, then he did before;
Neglecting once to cast a frown on those
Whom ease makes his, without the help of blowes.

Hell

HELL is no other, but a soundlesse pit,
  Where no one beame of comfort peeps in it.

The way

WHEN I a ship see on the Seas,
  Cuft with those watrie savages,
And therewithall, behold, it hath
In all that way no beaten path;
Then, with a wonder, I confesse,
Thou art our way i'th wildernesse:
And while we blunder in the dark,
Thou art our candle there, or spark.

Great grief, great glory

THE lesse our sorrowes here and suffrings cease,
  The more our Crownes of Glory there increase.

Hell

HELL is the place where whipping-cheer abounds,
  But no one Jailor there to wash the wounds.

The Bell-man

ALONG the dark, and silent night,
  With my Lantern, and my Light,
And the tinkling of my Bell,
Thus I walk, and this I tell:

Death and dreadfulnesse call on,
To the gen'rall Session;
To whose dismall Barre, we there
All accompts must come to cleere:
Scores of sins w'ave made here many,
Wip't out few, (God knowes) if any.   10
Rise ye Debters then, and fall
To make paiment, while I call.
Ponder this, when I am gone;
By the clock 'tis almost *One.*

The goodnesse of his God

WHEN Winds and Seas do rage,
   And threaten to undo me,
Thou dost their wrath asswage,
   If I but call unto Thee.

A mighty storm last night
   Did seek my soule to swallow,
But by the peep of light
   A gentle calme did follow.

What need I then despaire,
   Though ills stand round about me;   10
Since mischiefs neither dare
   To bark, or bite, without Thee?

The *Widdowes teares: or, Dirge* of Dorcas

1. COME pitie us, all ye, who see
      Our Harps hung on the Willow-tree:
   Come pitie us, ye Passers by,
   Who see, or heare poor Widdowes crie:
   Come pitie us; and bring your eares,
   And eyes, to pitie Widdowes teares.
      Chor. And when you are come hither;
            Then we will keep
            A Fast, and weep
         Our eyes out all together.   10

373   B b

2. For *Tabitha*, who dead lies here,
   Clean washt, and laid out for the Beere;
   O modest Matrons, weep and waile!
   For now the Corne and Wine must faile:
   The Basket and the Bynn of Bread,
   Wherewith so many soules were fed
     Chor. Stand empty here for ever:
           And ah! the Poore,
           At thy worne Doore,
       Shall be releeved never.   20

3. Woe worth the Time, woe worth the day,
   That reav'd us of thee *Tabitha!*
   For we have lost, with thee, the Meale,
   The Bits, the Morsells, and the deale
   Of gentle Paste, and yeelding Dow,
   That Thou on Widdowes didst bestow.
     Chor. All's gone, and Death hath taken
           Away from us
           Our Maundie; thus,
       Thy Widdowes stand forsaken.   30

4. Ah *Dorcas, Dorcas!* now adieu
   We bid the Creuse and Pannier too:
   I and the flesh, for and the fish,
   Dol'd to us in That Lordly dish.
   We take our leaves now of the Loome,
   From whence the house-wives cloth did come:
     Chor. The web affords now nothing;
           Thou being dead,
           The woosted thred
       Is cut, that made us clothing.   40

5. Farewell the Flax and Reaming wooll,
   With which thy house was plentifull.
   Farewell the Coats, the Garments, and
   The Sheets, the Rugs, made by thy hand.
   Farewell thy Fier and thy Light,
   That ne're went out by Day or Night:
     Chor. No, or thy zeale so speedy,
           That found a way
           By peep of day,
       To feed and cloth the Needy.   50

374

6. But, ah, alas! the Almond Bough,
   And Olive Branch is wither'd now.
   The Wine Presse now is ta'ne from us,
   The Saffron and the Calamus.
   The Spice and Spiknard hence is gone,
   The Storax and the Cynamon,
      Chor. The Caroll of our gladnesse
             Ha's taken wing,
             And our late spring
         Of mirth is turn'd to sadnesse.   60

7. How wise wast thou in all thy waies!
   How worthy of respect and praise!
   How Matron-like didst thou go drest!
   How soberly above the rest
   Of those that prank it with their Plumes;
   And jet it with their choice purfumes.
      Chor. Thy vestures were not flowing:
             Nor did the street
             Accuse thy feet
         Of mincing in their going.   70

8. And though thou here li'st dead, we see
   A deale of beauty yet in thee.
   How sweetly shewes thy smiling face,
   Thy lips with all diffused grace!
   Thy hands (though cold) yet spotlesse, white,
   And comely as the Chrysolite.
      Chor. Thy belly like a hill is,
             Or as a neat
             Cleane heap of wheat,
         All set about with Lillies.   80

9. Sleep with thy beauties here, while we
   Will shew these garments made by thee;
   These were the Coats, in these are read
   The monuments of *Dorcas* dead.
   These were thy Acts, and thou shalt have
   These hung, as honours o're thy Grave,
      Chor. And after us (distressed)
             Sho'd fame be dumb;
             Thy very Tomb
         Would cry out, *Thou art blessed.*   90

To God, in time of plundering

RAPINE has yet tooke nought from me;
 But if it please my God, I be
Brought at the last to th'utmost bit,
God make me thankfull still for it.
I have been gratefull for my store:
Let me say grace when there's no more.

To his Saviour. The New yeers gift

THAT little prettie bleeding part
 Of Foreskin send to me:
And Ile returne a bleeding Heart,
 For New-yeers gift to thee.

Rich is the Jemme that thou did'st send,
 Mine's faulty too, and small:
But yet this Gift Thou wilt commend,
 Because I send Thee *all*.

Doomes-Day

LET not that Day Gods Friends and Servants scare:
 The Bench is then their place; and not the Barre.

The Poores Portion

THE sup'rabundance of my store,
 That is the portion of the poore:
Wheat, Barley, Rie, or Oats; what is't
But he takes tole of ? all the Griest.
Two raiments have I: *Christ* then makes
This Law; that He and I part stakes.
Or have I two loaves; then I use
The poore to cut, and I to chuse.

The white Island: or place of the Blest

IN this world (the *Isle of Dreames*)
 While we sit by sorrowes streames,
Teares and terrors are our theames
 Reciting:

But when once from hence we flie,
More and more approaching nigh
Unto young Eternitie
          Uniting:

In that *whiter Island*, where
Things are evermore sincere;   10
Candor here, and lustre there
          Delighting:

There no monstrous fancies shall
Out of hell an horrour call,
To create (or cause at all)
          Affrighting.

There in calm and cooling sleep
We our eyes shall never steep;
But eternall watch shall keep,
          Attending   20

Pleasures, such as shall pursue
Me immortaliz'd, and you;
And fresh joyes, as never too
          Have ending.

To Christ

I CRAWLE, I creep; my *Christ*, I come
  To Thee, for curing *Balsamum:*
Thou hast, nay more, Thou art the Tree,
Affording salve of Soveraigntie.
My mouth I'le lay unto Thy wound
Bleeding, that no Blood touch the ground:
For, rather then one drop shall fall
To wast, my JESU, I'le take all.

To God

G OD! to my little meale and oyle,
  Add but a bit of flesh, to boyle:
And Thou my Pipkinnet shalt see,
Give a *wave-offring* unto Thee.

Free Welcome

GOD He refuseth no man; but makes way
For All that now come, or hereafter may.

Gods Grace

GODS Grace deserves here to be daily fed,
That, thus increast, it might be perfected.

Coming to Christ

To him, who longs unto his CHRIST to go,
Celerity even it self is slow.

Correction

GOD had but one Son free from sin; but none
Of all His sonnes free from correction.

Gods Bounty

GOD, as He's potent, so He's likewise known,
To give us more then Hope can fix upon.

Knowledge.

SCIENCE in God, is known to be
A Substance, not a Qualitie.

Salutation

CHRIST, I have read, did to His Chaplains say,
Sending them forth, *Salute no man by'th way:*
Not, that He taught His Ministers to be
Unsmooth, or sowre, to all civilitie;
But to instruct them, to avoid all snares
Of tardidation in the Lords Affaires.
Manners are good: but till his errand ends,
Salute we must, nor Strangers, Kin, or Friends.

Lasciviousnesse

LASCIVIOUSNESSE is known to be
The sister to saturitie.

Teares

GOD from our eyes all teares hereafter wipes,
And gives His Children kisses then, not stripes.

Gods Blessing

IN vain our labours are, whatsoe're they be,
Unlesse God gives the *Benedicite*.

God, and Lord

GOD, is His Name of Nature; but that word
Implies His Power, *when He's cal'd the LORD*.

The Iudgment-Day

GOD hides from man the reck'ning Day, that He
May feare it ever for uncertaintie:
That being ignorant of that one, he may
Expect the coming of it ev'ry day.

Angells

ANGELLS are called Gods; yet of them, none
Are Gods, but by *participation*:
As Just Men are intitled Gods, yet none
Are Gods, of them, but by Adoption.

Long life

THE longer thred of life we spin,
The more occasion still to sin.

Teares

THE teares of Saints more sweet by farre,
Then all the songs of sinners are.

Manna

THAT Manna, which God on His people cast,
Fitted it self to ev'ry Feeders tast.

Reverence

TRUE rev'rence is (as *Cassiodore* doth prove)
The feare of God, commixt with cleanly love.

Mercy

MERCY, the wise Athenians held to be
Not an Affection, but a *Deitie*.

Wages

AFTER this life, the wages shall
Not shar'd alike be unto all.

Temptation

GOD tempteth no one (as S. *Aug'stine* saith)
For any ill; but, for the proof of Faith:
Unto temptation God exposeth some;
But none, of purpose, to be overcome.

Gods hands

GODS Hands are round, & smooth, that gifts may fall
Freely from them, and hold none back at all.

Labour

LABOUR we must, and labour hard
I'th *Forum* here, or *Vineyard*.

Mora Sponsi, *the stay of the Bridegroome*

THE time the Bridegroom stayes from hence,
Is but the time of penitence.

Roaring

ROARING is nothing but a weeping part,
Forc'd from the mighty dolour of the heart.

The Eucharist

H<small>E</small> *that is hurt seeks help:* sin is the wound;
The salve for this i'th Eucharist is found.

Sin severely punisht

G<small>OD</small> in His own Day will be then severe,
To punish great sins, who small faults whipt here.

Montes Scripturarum, *the Mounts of the Scriptures*

T<small>HE</small> Mountains of the Scriptures are (some say)
Moses, and *Iesus,* called *Ioshua:*
The *Prophets* Mountains of the 'Old are meant;
Th' *Apostles* Mounts of the *New Testament.*

Prayer

A P<small>RAYER</small>, that is said alone,
Starves, having no companion.
Great things ask for, when thou dost pray,
And those great are, which ne're decay.
Pray not for silver, rust eats this;
Ask not for gold, which metall is:
Nor yet for houses, which are here
But earth: *such vowes nere reach Gods eare.*

Christs sadnesse

C<small>HRIST</small> was not sad, i'th garden, for His own
Passion, but for His sheeps dispersion.

God heares us

G<small>OD</small>, who's in Heav'n, will hear from thence;
If not to'th sound, yet, to the sense.

God

G<small>OD</small> (as the learned *Damascen* doth write)
A *Sea of Substance* is, *Indefinite.*

Clouds

HE that ascended in a cloud, shall come
In clouds, descending to the publike *Doome*.

Comforts in contentions

THE same, who crownes the Conquerour, will be
A Coadjutor in the Agonie.

Heaven

HEAV'N is most faire; but fairer He
That made that fairest Canopie.

God

IN God there's nothing, but 'tis known to be
Ev'n God Himself, in perfect *Entitie*.

His Power

GOD can do all things, save but what are known
For to imply a contradiction.

Christs words on the Crosse, My God, My God

CHRIST, when He hung the dreadfull Crosse upon,
Had (as it were) a *Dereliction*;
In this regard, in those great terrors He
Had no one *Beame* from Gods sweet Majestie.

JEHOVAH

JEHOVAH, as *Boëtius* saith,
No number of the *Plurall* hath.

Confusion of face

GOD then confounds mans face, when He not hears
The Vowes of those, who are Petitioners.

Another

THE shame of mans face is no more
Then prayers repel'd, (sayes *Cassiodore*.)

Beggars

JACOB Gods Beggar was; and so we wait
(Though ne're so rich) all beggars at His Gate.

Good, and bad

THE Bad among the Good are here mixt ever:
The Good without the Bad are here plac'd never.

Sin

SIN *no Existence; Nature none it hath,*
Or Good at all, (as learn'd *Aquinas* saith.)

Martha, Martha

THE repetition of the name made known
No other, then *Christs* full Affection.

Youth, and Age

GOD on our Youth bestowes but little ease;
But on our Age most sweet *Indulgences*.

Gods Power

GOD is so potent, as His Power can
Draw out of *bad* a soveraigne *good* to man.

Paradise

PARADISE is (as from the Learn'd I gather)
A quire of blest Soules circling in the Father.

Observation

THE Jewes, when they built Houses (I have read)
   One part thereof left still unfinished:
To make them, thereby, mindfull of their own
Cities most sad and dire destruction.

The Asse

GOD did forbid the Israelites, to bring
   An Asse unto Him, for an *offering*:
Onely, by this dull creature, to expresse
His detestation to all slothfulnesse.

Observation

THE Virgin-Mother stood at distance (there)
   From her Sonnes Crosse, not shedding once a teare:
Because the Law forbad to sit and crie
For those, who did as malefactors die.
So she, to keep her mighty woes in awe,
Tortur'd her love, not to transgresse the Law.
Observe we may, how *Mary Joses* then,
And th'other *Mary* (*Mary Magdalen*)
Sate by the Grave; and sadly sitting there,
Shed for their Master many a bitter teare: 10
But 'twas not till their *dearest Lord* was dead;
And then to weep they both were licensed.

Tapers

THOSE Tapers, which we set upon the grave,
   In fun'rall pomp, but this importance have;
That soules departed are not put out quite;
But, as they walk't here in their *vestures* white,
So live in Heaven, in everlasting light.

Christs Birth

ONE Birth our Saviour had; the like none yet
   Was, or will be a *second* like to it.

The *Virgin* Mary

TO work a *wonder*, God would have her shown,
   At once, a Bud, and yet a *Rose full-blowne*.

384

Another

As Sun-beames pierce the glasse, and streaming in,
No crack or Schisme leave i'th subtill skin:
So the Divine Hand work't, and brake no thred,
But, in a *Mother*, kept a *maiden-head*.

God

GOD, in the *holy Tongue*, they call
The Place that filleth *All in all*.

Another of God

GOD's said to leave this place, and for to come
Nearer to that place, then to other some:
Of locall motion, in no least respect,
But only by impression of effect.

Another

GOD is *Jehovah* cal'd; which name of His
Implies or *Essence*, or the *He* that Is.

Gods presence

GOD's evident, and may be said to be
Present with just men, to the veritie:
But with the wicked if He doth comply,
'Tis (as S. *Bernard* saith) but seemingly.

Gods Dwelling

GOD's said to dwell there, wheresoever He
Puts down some prints of His high Majestie:
As when to man He comes, and there doth place
His *holy Spirit*, or doth plant His *Grace*.

The *Virgin* Mary

THE *Virgin Marie* was (as I have read)
The *House of God*, by *Christ* inhabited;
Into the which He enter'd: but, the Doore
Once shut, was never to be open'd more.

To God

GOD's undivided, *One* in *Persons Three*;
And *Three* in *Inconfused Unity*:
Originall of Essence there is none
'Twixt God the *Father, Holy Ghost*, and *Sonne:*
And though the *Father* be the first of *Three*,
'Tis but by *Order*, not by *Entitie.*

Upon *Woman and* Mary

SO long (it seem'd) as *Maries* Faith was small,
Christ did her *Woman*, not her *Mary* call:
But no more *Woman*, being strong in Faith;
But *Mary* cal'd then (as S. *Ambrose* saith.)

North and South

THE *Jewes* their beds, and offices of ease,
Plac't *North* and *South*, for these cleane purposes;
That mans uncomely froth might not molest
Gods wayes and walks, which lie still East and West.

Sabbaths

SABBATHS are threefold, (as S. *Austine* sayes:)
The first of Time, or Sabbath here of Dayes;
The second is a Conscience trespasse-free;
The last the *Sabbath of Eternitie.*

The Fast, or Lent

NOAH the first was (as Tradition sayes)
That did ordaine the Fast of forty Dayes.

Sin

THERE is no evill that we do commit,
But hath th'extraction of some good from it:
As when we sin; God, the great *Chymist*, thence
Drawes out th'*Elixar* of true penitence.

God

GOD is more here, then in another place,
Not by His *Essence*, but commerce of *Grace*.

This, and the next World

GOD hath this world for many made; 'tis true:
But He hath made the world to come for few.

Ease

GOD gives to none so absolute an Ease,
As not to know, or feel some *Grievances*.

Beginnings and Endings

PAUL, he began ill, but he ended well;
Judas began well, but he foulely fell:
In godlinesse, not the beginnings, so
Much as the ends are to be lookt unto.

Temporall goods

THESE temp'rall goods God (the most Wise) commends
To th'good and bad, in common, for two ends:
First, that these goods none here may o're esteem,
Because the wicked do partake of them:
Next, that these ills none cowardly may shun;
Being, oft here, the just mans portion.

Hell fire

THE fire of Hell this strange condition hath,
To burn, not shine (as learned *Basil* saith.)

Abels *Bloud*

SPEAK, did the Bloud of *Abel* cry
To God for vengeance? yes say I;
Ev'n as the sprinkled bloud cal'd on
God, for an expiation.

Another

THE bloud of *Abel* was a thing
   Of such a rev'rend reckoning,
As that the old World thought it fit,
Especially to sweare by it.

A Position in the Hebrew Divinity

ONE man repentant is of more esteem
With God, then one, that never sin'd 'gainst Him.

Penitence

THE Doctors, in the Talmud, say,
   That in this world, one onely day
In true repentance spent, will be
More worth, then Heav'ns Eternitie.

Gods presence

GOD's present ev'ry where; but most of all
   Present by Union *Hypostaticall:*
God, He is there, where's nothing else (Schooles say)
And nothing else is there, *where He's away.*

The Resurrection possible, and probable

FOR each one Body, that i'th earth is sowne,
   There's an up-rising but of one for one:
But for each Graine, that in the ground is thrown,
Threescore or fourescore spring up thence for one:
So that the wonder is not halfe so great,
Of ours, as is the rising of the wheat.

Christs suffering

JUSTLY our *dearest Saviour* may abhorre us,
   Who hath more suffer'd by us farre, then for us.

Sinners

SINNERS confounded are a twofold way,
   Either as when (the learned Schoolemen say)
Mens sins destroyed are, when they repent;
Or when, for sins, men suffer punishment.

Temptations

No man is tempted so, but may o'recome,
If that he has a will to Masterdome.

Pittie, and punishment

God doth embrace the good with love; & gaines
The good by mercy, as the bad by paines.

Gods price, and mans price

God bought man here with his hearts blood expence;
And man sold God here for base *thirty pence.*

Christs Action

Christ never did so great a work, but there
His humane Nature did, in part, appeare:
Or, ne're so meane a peece, but men might see
Therein some beames of His Divinitie:
So that, in all He did, there did combine
His Humane Nature, and His Part Divine.

Predestination

Predestination is the Cause alone
Of many standing, but of fall to none.

Another

Art thou not destin'd? then, with hast, go on
To make thy faire *Predestination:*
If thou canst change thy life, God then will please
To change, or call back, His past *Sentences.*

Sin

Sin never slew a soule, unlesse there went
Along with it some tempting blandishment.

Another

Sin is an act so free, that if we shall
Say, 'tis not free, 'tis then no sin at all.

Another

SIN is the cause of death; and sin's alone
The cause of Gods *Predestination:*
And from Gods *Prescience* of mans sin doth flow
Our *Destination* to eternall woe.

Prescience

GODS *Prescience makes none sinfull;* but th'offence
Of man's the chief cause of Gods *Prescience.*

Christ

To all our wounds, here, whatsoe're they be,
Christ is the one sufficient *Remedie.*

Christs Incarnation

CHRIST took our Nature on Him, not that He
'Bove all things lov'd it, for the puritie:
No, but He drest Him with our humane Trim,
Because our flesh stood most in need of Him.

Heaven

HEAVEN is not given for our good works here:
Yet it is given to the *Labourer.*

Gods keyes

GOD has *foure keyes,* which He reserves alone;
The first of *Raine,* the key of *Hell* next known:
With the third key He opes and shuts the wombe;
And with the *fourth key* He unlocks the tombe.

Sin

THERE'S no constraint to do amisse,
Whereas but one enforcement is.

Almes

G IVE unto all, lest he, whom thou deni'st,
May chance to be no other man, but *Christ.*

Hell fire

O NE onely fire has Hell; but yet it shall,
Not after one sort, there excruciate all:
But look, how each transgressor onward went
Boldly in sin, shall feel more punishment.

To keep a true Lent

1 I s this a Fast, to keep
  The Larder leane?
   And cleane
From fat of Veales, and Sheep?

2 Is it to quit the dish
  Of Flesh, yet still
   To fill
The platter high with Fish?

3 Is it to fast an houre,
  Or rag'd to go,
   Or show   10
A down-cast look, and sowre?

4 No: 'tis a Fast, to dole
  Thy sheaf of wheat,
   And meat,
Unto the hungry Soule.

5 It is to fast from strife,
  From old debate,
   And hate;
To circumcise thy life.   20

6 To shew a heart grief-rent;
  To sterve thy sin,
   Not Bin;
And that's to keep thy Lent.

No time in Eternitie

B Y houres we all live here, in Heaven is known
No spring of Time, or Times succession.

His Meditation upon Death

B E those few hours, which I have yet to spend,
Blest with the Meditation of my end:
Though they be few in number, I'm content;
If otherwise, I stand indifferent:
Nor makes it matter, *Nestors* yeers to tell,
If man lives long, and if he live not well.
A multitude of dayes still heaped on,
Seldome brings order, but confusion.
Might I make choice, long life sho'd be with-stood;
Nor wo'd I care how short it were, if good: 10
Which to effect, let ev'ry passing Bell
Possesse my thoughts, next comes my dolefull knell:
And when the night perswades me to my bed,
I'le thinke I'm going to be buried:
So shall the Blankets which come over me,
Present those Turfs, which once must cover me:
And with as firme behaviour I will meet
The sheet I sleep in, as my Winding-sheet.
When sleep shall bath his body in mine eyes,
I will believe, that then my body dies: 20
And if I chance to wake, and rise thereon,
I'le have in mind my Resurrection,
Which must produce me to that *Gen'rall Doome*,
To which the Pesant, so the Prince must come,
To heare the Judge give sentence on the Throne,
Without the least hope of affection.
Teares, at that day, shall make but weake defence;
When Hell and Horrour fright the Conscience.
Let me, though late, yet at the last, begin
To shun the least Temptation to a sin;   30
Though to be tempted be no sin, untill
Man to th'alluring object gives his will.
Such let my life assure me, when my breath
Goes theeving from me, I am safe in death;
Which is the height of comfort, when I fall,
I rise triumphant in my Funerall.

Cloaths for Continuance

THOSE Garments lasting evermore,
  Are works of mercy to the poore,
Which neither Tettar, Time, or Moth
Shall fray that silke, or fret this cloth.

To God

COME to me God; but do not come
  To me, as to the gen'rall Doome,
In power; or come Thou in that state,
When Thou Thy Lawes didst promulgate,
When as the Mountaine quak'd for dread,
And sullen clouds bound up his head.
No, lay thy stately terrours by,
To talke with me familiarly;
For if Thy thunder-claps I heare,
I shall lesse swoone, then die for feare.   10
Speake thou of love and I'le reply
By way of *Epithalamie*,
Or sing of *mercy*, and I'le suit
To it my Violl and my Lute:
Thus let Thy lips but love distill,
Then come my God, and hap what will.

The Soule

WHEN once the Soule has lost her way,
  O then, how restlesse do's she stray!
And having not her God for light,
How do's she erre in endlesse night!

The Judgement day

IN doing justice, God shall then be known,
  Who shewing mercy here, few priz'd, or none.

Sufferings

WE merit all we suffer, and by far
  More stripes, then God layes on the sufferer.

2.5 Mountaine *Pollard*: Mountains *48* (see Exod. xix. 18)

Paine and pleasure

GOD suffers not His Saints, and Servants deere,
To have continuall paine, or pleasure here:
But look how night succeeds the day, so He
Gives them by turnes their grief and jollitie.

Gods presence

GOD is *all-present* to what e're we do,
And as *all-present*, so *all-filling* too.

Another

THAT there's a God, we all do know,
But what God is, we cannot show.

The poore mans part

TELL me rich man, for what intent
Thou load'st with gold thy vestiment?
When as the poore crie out, to us
Belongs all gcld superfluous.

The right hand

GOD has a Right Hand, but is quite bereft
Of that, which we do nominate the Left.

The Staffe and Rod

TWO instruments belong unto our God;
The one a *Staffe* is, and the next a *Rod*:
That if the twig sho'd chance too much to smart,
The staffe might come to play the friendly part.

God sparing in scourging

GOD still rewards us more then our desert:
But when He strikes, He quarter-acts His part.

Confession

CONFESSION twofold is (as *Austine* sayes,)
The first of *sin* is, and the next of *praise:*
If ill it goes with thee, thy faults confesse:
If well, then chant Gods praise with cheerfulnesse.

Gods descent

GOD is then said for to descend, when He
Doth, here on earth, some thing of novitie;
As when, in humane nature He works more
Then ever, yet, the like was done before.

No coming to God without Christ

GOOD *and great God!* How sho'd I feare
To come to Thee, if *Christ* not there!
Co'd I but think, He would not be
Present, to plead my cause for me;
To Hell I'd rather run, then I
Wo'd see Thy Face, and He not by.

Another, to God

THOUGH Thou beest all that *Active Love,*
Which heats those ravisht Soules above;
And though all joyes spring from the glance
Of Thy most winning countenance;
Yet sowre and grim Thou'dst seem to me;
If through my *Christ* I saw not Thee.

The Resurrection

THAT *Christ* did die, the *Pagan* saith;
But that He rose, that's *Christians* Faith.

Coheires

WE are Coheires with *Christ*; nor shall His own
Heire-ship be lesse, by our adoption:
The number here of Heires, shall from the state
Of His great *Birth-right* nothing derogate.

The number of two

GOD hates the *Duall Number*; being known
The lucklesse number of division:
And when He blest each sev'rall Day, whereon
He did His *curious operation*;
'Tis never read there (as the Fathers say,)
God blest His work done on the *second day*:
Wherefore two prayers ought not to be said,
Or by our selves, or from the Pulpit read.

Hardning of hearts

GOD'S said our hearts to harden then,
When as His grace not supples men.

The Rose

BEFORE Mans fall, the Rose was born
(S. *Ambrose* sayes) without the Thorn:
But, for Mans fault, then was the Thorn,
Without the fragrant Rose-bud, born;
But ne're the Rose without the Thorn.

Gods time must end our trouble

GOD doth not promise here to man, that He
Will free him quickly from his miserie;
But in His own time, and when He thinks fit,
Then He will give a happy end to it.

Baptisme

THE strength of *Baptisme*, that's within;
It saves the soule, by drowning sin.

Gold and Frankincense

GOLD serves for Tribute to the King;
The *Frankincense* for Gods Offring.

To God

GOD, who me gives a will for to repent,
Will add a power, to keep me innocent;
That I shall ne're that trespasse recommit,
When I have done true Penance here for it.

The chewing the Cud

WHEN well we speak, & nothing do that's good,
We not divide the *Hoof*, but chew the *Cud*:
But when good words, by good works, have their proof,
We then both chew the *Cud*, and cleave the *Hoof*.

Christs twofold coming

THY former coming was to cure
My soules most desp'rate *Calenture*;
Thy second *Advent*, that must be
To heale my Earths infirmitie.

To God, his gift

As my little Pot doth boyle,
We will keep this *Levell-Coyle*;
That a *Wave*, and I will bring
To my God, a *Heave-offering*.

Gods Anger

GOD can't be wrathfull; but we may conclude,
Wrathfull He may be, by similitude:
God's wrathfull said to be, when He doth do
That without *wrath*, which wrath doth *force us* to.

Gods Commands

IN Gods Commands, ne're ask the reason why;
Let thy *obedience* be the best Reply.

To God

IF I have plaid the *Truant*, or have here
Fail'd in my part; O! Thou that art my *deare*,
My *mild*, my *loving Tutor, Lord and God!*
Correct my errors gently with Thy Rod.
I know, that faults will many here be found,
But where sin swells, there let Thy grace abound.

To God

THE work is done; now let my *Lawrell* be
Given by none, but by Thy selfe, to me:
That done, with Honour Thou dost me create
Thy *Poet*, and Thy *Prophet Lawreat*.

Good Friday: Rex Tragicus, *or Christ going to His Crosse*

PUT off Thy Robe of *Purple*, then go on
To the sad place of execution:
Thine houre is come; and the Tormentor stands
Ready, to pierce Thy tender Feet, and Hands.
Long before this, the base, the dull, the rude,
Th'inconstant, and unpurged Multitude
Yawne for Thy coming; some e're this time crie,
How He deferres, how loath He is to die!
Amongst this scumme, the Souldier, with his speare,
And that sowre Fellow, with his *vineger*,   10
His *spunge*, and *stick*, do ask why Thou dost stay?
So do the *Skurfe* and *Bran* too: Go Thy way,
Thy way, Thou guiltlesse man, and satisfie
By Thine approach, each their beholding eye.
Not as a thief, shalt Thou ascend the mount,
But like a Person of some high account:
The *Crosse* shall be Thy *Stage*; and Thou shalt there
The spacious field have for Thy *Theater*.
Thou art that *Roscius*, and that markt-out man,
That must this day act the Tragedian,   20
To wonder and affrightment: Thou art He,

Whom all the flux of Nations comes to see;
Not those poor Theeves that act their parts with Thee:
Those act without regard, when once a *King*,
And *God*, as Thou art, comes to suffering.
No, No, this *Scene* from Thee takes life and sense,
And soule and spirit, plot, and excellence.
Why then begin, great King! ascend Thy Throne,
And thence proceed, to act Thy Passion
To such an height, to such a period rais'd,   30
As Hell, and Earth, and Heav'n may stand amaz'd.
God, and good Angells guide Thee; and so blesse
Thee in Thy severall parts of bitternesse;
That those, who see Thee nail'd unto the Tree,
May (though they scorn Thee) praise and pitie Thee.
And we (Thy Lovers) while we see Thee keep
The Lawes of Action, will both sigh, and weep;
And bring our Spices, to embalm Thee dead;
That done, wee'l see Thee sweetly buried.

His words to Christ, going to the Crosse

WHEN Thou wast taken, Lord, I oft have read,
All Thy Disciples Thee forsook, and fled.
Let their example not a pattern be
For me to flie, but now to follow Thee.

Another, to his Saviour

IF Thou beest taken, *God* forbid,
I flie from Thee, as others did:
But if Thou wilt so honour me,
As to accept my companie,
I'le follow Thee, hap, hap what shall,
Both to the *Judge*, and *Judgment-Hall*:
And, if I see Thee posted there,
To be all-flayd with whipping-cheere,
I'le take my share; or els, my God,
Thy stripes I'le kisse, or burn the *Rod*.   10

l. 27 spirit, *ed*.: spirit *48*

399

His Saviours words, going to the Crosse

HAVE, have ye no regard, all ye
  Who passe this way, to pitie me,
Who am a man of miserie!

A man both bruis'd, and broke, and one
Who suffers not here for mine own,
But for my friends *transgression!*

Ah! *Sions Daughters*, do not feare
The *Crosse*, the *Cords*, the *Nailes*, the *Speare*,
The *Myrrhe*, the *Gall*, the *Vineger:*

For *Christ*, your loving Saviour, hath   10
Drunk up the wine of Gods fierce wrath;
Onely, there's left a little froth,

Lesse for to tast, then for to shew,
What bitter cups had been your due,
Had He not drank them up for *you*.

His Anthem, to Christ on the Crosse

WHEN I behold Thee, almost slain,
  With one, and all parts, full of pain:
When I Thy gentle Heart do see
Pierc't through, and dropping bloud, for me,
I'le call, and cry out, Thanks to Thee.

Vers. But yet it wounds my soule, to think,
That for my sin, Thou, Thou must drink,
Even Thou alone, the *bitter cup*
Of *furie*, and of *vengeance* up.

Chor. Lord, I'le not see Thee to drink all   10
The *Vineger*, the *Myrrhe*, the *Gall*:

Ver. Chor. But I will sip a little wine;
Which done, Lord say, *The rest is mine.*

400

This   Crosse-Tree   here
Doth   JESUS   beare,
Who   sweet'ned   first,
The   Death   accurs't.
Here all things ready are, make hast, make hast away;
For, long this work wil be, & very short this Day.
Why then, go on to act: Here's wonders to be done,
Before the last least sand of Thy ninth houre be run;
Or e're dark Clouds do dull, or dead the Mid-dayes Sun.

Act when Thou wilt,   10
Bloud will be spilt;
Pure Balm, that shall
Bring Health to All.
Why   then,   Begin
To powre first in
Some Drops of Wine,
In   stead of Brine,
To search the Wound,
So   long   unsound:
And, when that's done,   20
Let Oyle, next, run,
To cure   the   Sore
Sinne made before.
And O! Deare Christ,
E'en as Thou di'st,
Look down, and see
Us weepe for Thee.
And tho (Love knows)
Thy dreadfull Woes
Wee   cannot   ease;   30
Yet doe Thou please,
Who   Mercie   art,
T'accept each Heart,
That   gladly   would
Helpe, if it could.
Meane while, let mee,
Beneath this Tree,
This Honour have,
To make my grave.

To his Saviours Sepulcher: his Devotion

Haile holy, and all-honour'd Tomb,
By no ill haunted; here I come,
With shoes put off, to tread thy Roome.
I'le not prophane, by soile of sin,
Thy Doore, as I do enter in:
For I have washt both hand and heart,
This, that, and ev'ry other part;
So that I dare, with farre lesse feare,
Then full affection, enter here.
Thus, thus I come to kisse Thy Stone   10
With a warm lip, and solemne one:
And as I kisse, I'le here and there
Dresse Thee with flowrie Diaper.
How sweet this place is! as from hence
Flow'd all *Panchaia's* Frankincense;
Or rich *Arabia* did commix,
Here, all her rare *Aromaticks*.
Let me live ever here, and stir
No one step from this *Sepulcher*.
Ravisht I am! and down I lie,   20
Confus'd, in this brave Extasie.
Here let me rest; and let me have
This for my *Heaven*, that was Thy *Grave:*
And, coveting no higher sphere,
I'le my Eternitie spend here.

His Offering, with the rest, at the Sepulcher

To joyn with them, who here confer
Gifts to my Saviours Sepulcher;
Devotion bids me hither bring
Somwhat for my Thank-Offering.
Loe! Thus I give a Virgin-Flower,
To dresse my Maiden-Saviour.

His coming to the Sepulcher

HENCE they have born my Lord: Behold! the Stone
Is rowl'd away; and my sweet Saviour's gone!
Tell me, white Angell; what is now become
Of Him, we lately seal'd up in this Tombe?
Is He, from hence, gone to the shades beneath,
To vanquish Hell, as here He conquer'd Death?
If so; I'le thither follow, without feare;
And live in Hell, if that my *Christ* stayes there.

OF all the good things whatsoe're we do,
God is the APXH, and the TEΛOΣ too.

ADDITIONAL POEMS

(The text of each poem is based on the specified source, corrected where necessary by other sources as detailed in OET *Herrick*, 1956, &c., pp. 492–7. Titles of poems from manuscripts are italicized whether underlined in the manuscript or not; titles in square brackets are editorial. Manuscript contractions are expanded.)

A. INCLUDED IN PREVIOUS MODERN EDITIONS

The Descripcion: of a Woman

WHOSE head befringed with bescattered tresses
    Seemes like Apollo's when the morne he blesses
Or like vnto Aurora when shee setts
her long disheuel'd rose=crown'd tramaletts
Her forehead smooth full polisht bright and high
bares in it selfe a gracefull maiestye
Vnder the which twoe crawling eyebrowes twine
like to the tendrells of a flattring vine
Vnder whose shades Twoe starry sparkling eyes
are beawtifi'd with faire fring'd canopies   10
Her comly nose with vniformall grace
like purest white stands in the middle place
Parting the paire as wee may well suppose
each cheeke resembling still a damaske rose
Which like a garden manifestly showe
how roses lillies and carnations grow
which sweetly mixed both with white and redd
like rose leaues, white and redd seeme mingled
Ther nature for a sweet allurement setts
twoe smelling swelling bashful Cherriletts   20
The which with ruby rednes being tipt
doe speake a virgin merry cherry=lip't
Over the which a meet sweet skin is drawne
Which makes them shewe like roses vnder lawne
These be the Ruby portalls and devine
Which ope themselves to shewe an holy shrine
Whose breath is rich perfume, that to the sence
smells like the burnt Sabæan ffrankinsense
In which the tongue, though but a member small
stands garded with a rosy hilly wall   30

From Bodleian MS. Rawlinson poet. 160, f. 105. Bodl. MS. Ashmole 38 appends: finis Robt Herick

And her white teeth which in the gumms are sett
Like pearle and gold make one rich Carcenett
Next doth her chinne with dimpled beawty striue
ffor his plumpe white and smooth prerogatiue
At whose faire topp to please the sight there growes
the blessed Image of a blushing rose
mou'd by the chinne whose motion causeth this
That both her lipps doe part doe meete doe kisse.
Her eares which like twoe Laborinths are plac'd
on either side with rich rare Jewells grac'd   40
mooving a question whether that by them
the Jem is grac'd? or they grac'd by the Jemme
But the foundacion of this Architect
is the swan=stayning faire rare stately neck
which with ambitious humblenes stands vnder
bearing aloft this rich round world of wonder
In which the veynes ymplanted seeme to lye
like loving vines hid vnder Ivorye
Soe full of clarrett that whoe soe pricks a vine
may see it sprout forth streames of muscadine   50
Her brest (a place for beawtyes throne most fitt)
beares vp twoe globes where loue and pleasure sitt
Which headed with twoe rich round rubies showe
like wanton rose buds growing out of snowe
And in the milky vally that's betweene
sits Cupid kissing of his mother Queene
Fingring the paps that feele like sleeded silke
And prest a little they will weepe new milke
Then comes the belly seated next belowe
like a faire mountaine of Riphean snowe   60
Where nature in a whitenes without spott
hath in the middle ty'de a Gordian knott
Or ells that she on that white waxen hill
hath seal'd the promise of her vtmost skill
But now my muse hath spi'de a darke descent
from this soe peereles pretious prominent,
A milky high waye that direction yeilds
Vnto the port mouth of th'Elisian feilds
A place desir'd of all but got by theis
whome loue admitts to this Hesperides   70
Heres golden fruit that farre exceeds all price
growing in this loue garded paradice

Aboue the entrance there is written this
this is the portall to the bowre of bliss
Through mid'st thereof a christall stream there flowes
passing the sweet sweet of a musky rose
Now loue invites me to survey her thighes
swelling in likenes like twoe christall skyes
With plumpe soft flesh of mettle pure & fine
Resembling sheilds both smooth and christalline   80
Hence rise those twoe ambitious hills that looke
into the middle moste sight pleasing crooke
Which for the better beawtifying shrowdes
its humble selfe twixt twoe aspiring cloudes
Which to the knees by nature fastned on
deriue their ever well grac'd motion
her leggs with twoe cleire calues like silver tride
Kindly swell vp with little pretty pride
Leaving a distance for the beawtious small
to beawtify the legg and foote withall   90
Then lowly yet most louely stand the feete
Round short and cleire, like pounded spices sweete
And whatsoever thing they tread vpon
They make it scent like bruized Cinnamon
The lovely shoulders now allure the eye
To see two tablets of pure Ivory
from which two armes like branches seem to spread
With tender ryne and silver coloured,
With little hands & fingers long and small
To grace a Lute a vyall Virginall.   100
In length each finger doth his next excell
Each richly headed with a pearly shell
Richer then that faire pretious virtuos horne
That armes the forehead of the Vnicorne
Thus every part in contrariety
Meets in the whole and maks a harmony
As divers strings do singly disagree
But form'd by number make sweet melody
Vnto the Idoll of the work devine
I consecrate this loving work of mine   110
Bowing my lips vnto that stately root
Whence beawty springs, and thus I kisse thy foot

·   ·   ·   ·   ·   ·   ·   ·   ·

Mr Hericke his daughter's Dowrye

ERE I goe hence and bee noe more
  Seene to the world, Ile giue the skore
I owe vnto A female Child,
And that is this, A uerse Instylde
My daughters Dowrye; haueing which
Ile leaue thee then Compleatly riche
Insteade of gould *Pearle Rubies Bonds*
Longe forfaite pawnèd diamonds
Or Antique pledges, House or Lande
I giue thee this that shall with stande   10
The blow of Ruine and of Chance
Theis hurte not thyne Inheritance
for tis ffee simple, and noe rent
Thou *Fortune* ow'st for tenèment
how euer after tymes will praise,
This Portion my Prophetique Bayes
Cannot deliuer vpp to'th rust
Yett I keepe peacefull in my dust
As for thy birth, and better seeds
(Those which must growe to *Vertuous deeds*)   20
Thou didst deriue from that old steem
(*Loue*, *Peace*, and *Mercie*, cherrish them)
which like a *Vestall Virgine* ply
with holye fier least that itt dye
Growe vpp with Mylder Lawes to knowe
Att what tyme to say I, or noe,
Lett Manners teach the whear to bee
More Comely flowing: where les free
Theis bringe thy husband, like to those
Old Coynes and Meddals, wee expose   30
To'th shew, but Neuer part with; next
As In a more Conspicuous Text
(Thy fore=head) lett therin bee sign'd
The Mayden Candour of thy Mynde:

From Bodl. MS. Ashmole 38, p. 94.

And vnder it two Chast borne spyes
To barr out, bolde Adulteryes
ffor through those Optickes, fly the dartes
Of Lust, which setts on fier our hartes
On eyther side of theis, quicke Eares
Ther must bee plac'd, for season'd feares   40
which sweeten Loue, yett ner'e come nighe
The Plague of wilder Jelousie
Then lett each Cheeke of thyne intice
his soule as to a bedd of spice
wheare hee may roule, and loose his sence
As in a bedd of Frankensence
A Lipp Inkyndled with that Coale
with which Loue Chafes and warmes the soule
Bringe to hym next, and in it shew
Loues Cherries from such fyers growe   50
And haue their haruest, which must stand
The Gathering of the Lipp: not hand
Then vnto theis, bee it thy Care
To cloath thy words in gentle Ayre
That smooth as Oyle, sweet softe and Cleane
As is the Childish Bloome of Beane
Thay may fall downe and stroake as the
Beames of the sunn, the peacefull sea
White handes as smooth, as Mercies, bring
hym for his better Cherrishing   60
That when thou doest his necke Insnare
Or with thy wrist or flattering Hayre
hee may (a prisoner) ther discrye
Bondage more Loued then Lybertye
A Nature, soe well form'd, soe wrought
Too Calme A tempest lett bee brought
with thee; that should hee but Inclyne
To Roughnes, Claspe hym lyke a Vine
Or lyke as woole meetes steele, giue way
Vnto the passion, not to stay;   70
Wrath yf resisted ouer boyles
Iff not, it dyes, or eles recoyles
And Lastly, see thou bring to hym
Somewhat peculiar to each lymm

And I charge thee to bee knowne
By n' other Face, but by thyne owne,
Lett itt (in Loues name) bee keept sleeke
Yett to bee found when hee shall seeke
It, and not Instead of Saint
Giue vpp his worshipp to the painte   80
ffor (trust me Girle) shee ouer-does
who by a double Proxie woes
But Least I should forgett his bedd
Bee sure thou bringe A Mayden head
That is *A Margarite*, which Lost
Thou bring'st vnto his bedd A frost
Or A colde Poyson, which his blood
Benummes like the forgettfull floode
Now for some Jewells to supplye
The Wante of Eare rings brauerye   90
ffor puplike Eyes, take onlye theis
Ne're trauylde for beyonde the Seas,
Theyre Nobly=home=bread, yett haue price
beyound the fare-fetch Marchandize
Obedience, *Wise=Distrust*, *Peace*; shey
Distance, and sweet *Vrbanitie*
Safe Modestie, *Lou'd Patience*, *feare*
Of offending, *Temperance*, *Deare*
Constancie, *Bashfullnes*, and all
The *Vertues Lesse*, or *Cardinall*   100
Take with my blessinge; and goe forth
In Jewelld, with thy Natiue worthe,
And now yf ther A man bee founde
That Lookes for such prepared grownd
Lett hym but with indifferent skill
Soe good a soile bee=stocke and till
   Hee may ere longe haue such a wyfe
   Nourish in's breast, a Tree of Life

finis   Robt: Hericke

Mr *Robert Hericke his farwell vnto Poetrie*

I HAVE behelde two louers in a night
(Hatch't o're with Moone=shine, from their stolen delight)
When this to that, and That, to This, had giuen
A kisse to such a Jewell of the heauen:
Or while that each from other's breath, did drincke
Healthes to the Rose, the Violet, or Pinke,
Call'd on the suddayne by the Jealouse Mother
Some strickter Mistris or suspitious other
Vrging diuorcement (worse then death to Theis)
By the soone gingling of some sleepy keyes   10
Parte with a hastye kisse; and in that shew
how stay thay would, yet forc't thay are to goe:
Euen such are wee; and in our parting, doe
Noe otherwise then as those former, two
Natures, like ours, wee who haue spent our tyme
Both from the Morning to the Euening Chyme;
Nay tell the Bell-man of the Night had tould
past Noone of night, yett weare the howers not old
Nor dull'd with Iron sleepe; but haue out-worne
The fresh and fayrest flourish of the Morne   20
With Flame, and Rapture; drincking to the ode
Number of Nyne, which makes vs full with God
And In that Misticke frenzie, wee haue hurl'de
(As with a Tempest) Nature through the worlde
And In a Whirl=wynd twirld her home, agast
Att that which in her extasie had past;
Thus Crownd with Rose Budds, Sacke, thou mad'st mee flye
Like fier-drakes, yett did'st mee no harme therby.
O thou Allmightye Nature, who did'st giue
True heate, whear with humanitie doth Liue   30
Beyond its stinted Circle; giueing foode
(While Fame) and Resurrection to the Good
Soaring them vpp, boue Ruyne, till the doome
(The generall Aprill of the world dothe Come)

From Bodl. MS. Ashmole 38, p. 106.

That makes all æquall, manye thowsands should
(wert not for thee) haue Crumbled Into Mould
And with thayr Ceareclothes rotted, not to shew
whether the world such Sperritts had or noe
whear as by Thee, Those, and A Million since
Nor Fate, nor Enuye, cann theyr Fames Conuince,　　40
Homer, Musæus, Ouid, Maro, more
Of those god-full Prophetts longe before
Holde there Eternall fiers; and ours of Late
(Thy Mercie helping) shall resist stronge fate
nor stoope to'th Center, but suruiue as Longe
As Fame or Rumour, hath or Trumpe or Tongue
But vnto mee, bee onlye hoarse, since now
(Heauen and my soule beare Record of my Vowe)
I, my desires screw from thee, and directe
Them and my Thoughts to that sublim'd respecte　　50
And Conscience vnto Preist-hood, tis not Need
(The skarcrow vnto Mankinde) that doth breed
Wiser Conclusions in mee, since I knowe
I'aue more to beare my Chardge, then way to goe
Or had I not, I'de stopp the spreading itch
Off craueing more: soe In Conceipt bee ritch,
But tis the god of Nature, who Intends
And shaps my Functions for more glorious ends
Guesse, soe departe; yett stay A while too see
The Lines of Sorrowe, that lye drawne in mee　　60
In speach, in Picture; noe otherwise then when
(Judgment and Death, denounc'd gainst Guilty men)
Each takes A weeping farwell, rackt in mynde
With Joyes before, and Pleasures left behind:
Shakeing the head, whilst each, to each dothe mourne
With thought thay goe, whence thay must ner returne
Soe with like lookes, as once the *Ministrell*
Cast, leading his *Euredice* through hell
I stricke thy loues, and greedyly persue
Thee, with myne Eyes, or in, or out, of View　　70
Soe look't the Grecian Oratour when sent
ffroms Natiue Cuntrye, in to Banishment
Throwing his eye balls backward, to suruaye
The smoake of his beloued *Attica*

Soe Tullye look't, when from the Brest's of Rome
The sad soule went, not with his Loue, but doome;
Shooting his Eye-darts 'gainst it, to surprise
It, or to drawe the Cittie to his Eyes
Such is my parting with thee; and to proue
Ther was not Varnish (only) in my loue   80
But substance, to! receaue this Pearlye Teare
ffrozen with Greife; and place it in thyne eare
Then Parte in name of peace; & softely on
With Numerous feete to Hoofy Helicon
And when thou art vppon that forked Hill
Amongest the thrice, three, sacred Virgins, fill
A full brimm'd bowle of Furye and of rage
And quafe it to the Prophets of our Age;
when drunck with Rapture; Curse the blind & lame
Base Ballad=mongers, who vsurpe thy name   90
And fowle thy Altar, Charme some Into froggs
Some to bee Ratts, and others to bee hoggs:
Into the Loathsomst shapps, thou Canst deuise
To make ffooles hate them, onlye by disguise;
Thus with a kisse of warmth, and loue, I parte
Not soe, but that some Relique In my Harte
Shall stand for euer, though I doe addresse
Cheifelye my selfe to what I must proffess:
Knowe yet (rare soule) when my diuiner Muse
Shall want a Hand-mayde, (as she ofte will vse)   100
Bee readye, thou In mee, to wayte vppon her
Thoughe as a seruant, yet a Mayde of Honor
   The Crowne of dutye is our dutye; well
   Doing's, the Fruite of Doinge well,   Farwell

finis   Mr Robt Herricke

A Charroll presented to D^r: Williams Bp. of Lincolne as a Newyears guift

F LY hence Pale Care, noe more remember
  Past Sorrowes with the fled December
But let each present Cheeke appeare
Smooth as the Childhood of the yeare
     And sing a Caroll here.
T'was braue, t'was braue could we comand the hand
Of Youths swift watch to stand
As yow haue done your day
Then should we not decay
But all we wither & our Light   10
Is spilt in euerlasting night'
When as your Sight
Shewes like the Heavens aboue the Moone
Like an Eternall Noone
That sees noe setting Sunn.

Keepe vp those flames, & though you shroud
A while your forehead in a Cloude
Doe it like the Sun to write
I'th ayre, a greater Text of light
Welcome to all our vowes   20
And since you pay
To vs the day
Soe longe desir'd
See we haue fyr'd
Our holy Spicknard & ther's none
But brings his stick of Cynamon
His eager Eye, or Smoother Smyle
And layes it gently on the Pyle
Which thus enkindled we invoke
Your name amidst the sacred smoke.   30

Chorus

Come then greate Lord
And see our Alter burne
With Loue of your Returne
And not a man here but consumes
His soule to glad you in perfumes.

                      Rob: Herrick.

From Bodl. MS. Ashmole 36–37, f. 298.

His Mistris to him at his farwell

Y OU may vow Ile not forgett
  To pay the debt,
Which to thy Memorie stands as due
  As faith can seale It you
Take then tribute of my teares
  So long as I haue feares
  To prompt mee, I shall euer
Languish and looke but thy returne see neuer
  Oh then to lessen my dispaire
  Prin: thy lips Into the ayre   10
    So by this
Meanes I may kisse thy kisse
  When as some kinde
    winde
Shall hither waft it and In leiu
My lipps shall send a 1000 back to you

        Ro: herrick.

Vpon parting

G OE hence away, and in thy parting know
 tis not my voice, but heauens, that bidds thee goe;
Spring hence thy faith, nor thinke it ill desert
I finde in thee, that makes me thus to part,
But voice of fame, and voice of heauen haue thunderd
we both were lost, if both of us not sunderd;
fould now thine armes, and in thy last looke reare
one Sighe of loue, and coole it with a teare;
Since part we must Let's kisse, that done retire
with as cold frost, as erst we mett with fire; 10
With such white vowes as fate can nere dissever
but truth knitt fast; and so farewell for euer.
        R: Herrick:

  1 From Brit. Mus. Add. MS. 11811, f. 37.
  2 From Brit. Mus. MS. Harl. 6917, f. 82ᵛ.

Upon Master FLETCHERS
Incomparable Playes

APOLLO sings, his harpe resounds; give roome,
For now behold the golden Pompe is come,
Thy Pompe of Playes which thousands come to see,
With admiration both of them and thee,
O Volume worthy leafe, by leafe and cover
To be with juice of Cedar washt all over;
Here's words with lines, and lines with Scenes consent,
To raise an Act to full astonishment;
Here melting numbers, words of power to move
Young men to swoone, and Maides to dye for love.   10
Love lyes a bleeding here, *Evadne* there
Swells with brave rage, yet comely every where,
Here's a *mad lover*, there that high designe
Of *King and no King* (and the rare Plott thine)
So that when 'ere wee circumvolve our Eyes,
Such rich, such fresh, such sweet varietyes,
Ravish our spirits, that entranc't wee see
None writes lov's passion in the world, like Thee.

ROB. HERRICK.

From *Comedies and Tragedies*, 1647, by Beaumont and Fletcher, f. e.

The New Charon,

Upon the death of *Henry* Lord *Hastings*

The Musical part being set by M. Henry Lawes

The Speakers,

Charon and Eucosmeia

Euc. Charon, O *Charon*, draw thy Boat to th' shore,
      And to thy many, take in one soul more.
Cha. Who calls? who calls? *Euc.* One overwhelm'd with ruth;
      Have pity either on my Tears or Youth,
      And take me in, who am in deep Distress;
      But first cast off thy wonted Churlishness.
Cha. I will be gentle as that Air which yeelds
      A breath of Balm along th'*Elizean* fields.
      Speak, what art thou? *Euc.* One, once that had a lover,
      Then which, thy self ne'er wafted sweeter over.   10
      He was—— *Cha.* Say what. *Eu.* Ay me, my woes are deep.
Cha. Prethee relate, while I give ear and weep.
Euc. He was an *Hastings*; and that one Name has
      In it all Good, that is, and ever was.
      He was my *Life*, my *Love*, my *Joy*; but di'd
      Some hours before I shou'd have been his Bride.
Chorus. *Thus, thus the Gods celestial still decree,*
      For Humane Joy, Contingent Misery.
Euc. The *hallowed Tapers* all prepared were,
      And *Hymen* call'd to bless the Rites. *Cha.* Stop there.   20
Euc. Great are my woes. *Cha.* And great must that Grief be,
      That makes grim *Charon* thus to pity thee.
      But now come in. *Euc.* More let me yet relate.
Cha. I cannot stay; more souls for waftage wait,
      And I must hence. *Eu.* Yet let me thus much know,
      Departing hence, where Good and Bad souls go.

From *Lachrymae Musarum*, 1649, p. 38.

Cha. Those souls which ne'er were drencht in pleasures stream,
    The Fields of *Pluto* are reserv'd for them;
    Where, drest with garlands, there they walk the ground,
    Whose blessed Youth with endless flow'rs is crown'd.   30
    But such as have been drown'd in this wilde *Sea*,
    For those is kept the Gulf of *Hecate*;
    Where, with their own contagion they are fed;
    And there do punish, and are punished.
    This known, the rest of thy sad story tell,
    When on the Flood that nine times circles Hell
Chorus. *We sail along, to visit mortals never;*
    But there to live, where Love shall last for ever.

ROB. HERRICK.

Vpon a Cherrystone sent to the tip of the Lady Jemmonia Walgraves eare

LADY I intreate yow weare
    this little pendant on your eare
Tis noe Jewell of great prize
Or in respect of Merchandize
But deepe mistery not the stone
gives it estimation.
Take it then and in a veiwe
See th'Epitomè of yow
ffor what life and death confines
Looks through the passage of theis lines   10
Whose incarvements doe descrye
A scripture how yow liue and dye
Read it then before your lipp
Comends it to your eares soft tipp
And the while yow doe surveye
this Janus looking double waye
With a tearè yow may compare
to that yow must be; what yow are
know time past this cherrystone
had a sweet complexion   20

From Bodl. MS. Rawl. poet. 160, f. 28.

417

Skynne and colour flesh and blood
daintye tast for ladyes food
All's now fledd saue this alone
Poore relique of the beawty, bone
And that soe little we despaire
It ever dangling smil'd i'th'aire.
Soe must that faire face of yours
(As this looking=glasse assures)
ffaile and scarce leaue to be showne
there ever lived such a one   30
And when an other age shall bring
Your leane scalp to sensuring
though the Sextons truly sweare
Here Jemmonia's titles were
In this rag'd Escutcheon
most maye smile beleiue will none
Or there thought of faith may growe
But to this to think 'twas soe
This lesson you must pearse to'th'truth
And know (faire mistris) of your youth   40
death with it still walkes along
ffrom Mattins to the Euensong,
from the Pickaxe to the spade
To the tombe wher't must be layd
Whether in the morne of noone
Of your beawty death comes soone
And though his visage hung i'th'eare
doth not to the sight appeare
At each warning hees as much
know, to'th'hearing as the touch.   50
Place then this mirror to the veiw
.Of those virgins whose briske hew
Of lines and colours make them scorne
This livery which the *greeke hath worne
Let them read this booke and learne
their ayry coulors to discerne
Twixt this and them this Gorgon showne
Turnes the beholders into stone.

ffinis   R: Herricke:

l. 54. The asterisk marks an intended note which was not supplied.

*[Epitaph on the Tomb of Sir Edward Giles and his
wife in the South Aisle of Dean Prior Church]*

No trust to Metals nor to Marbles, when
    These have their Fate, and wear away as Men;
Times, Titles, Trophies, may be lost and Spent;
But Vertue Rears the eternal Monument.
What more than these can Tombs or Tomb-stones Say
But here's the Sun-set of a Tedious day:
These Two asleep are: I'll but be Vndrest
And so to Bed: Pray wish us all Good Rest.

B. NOT INCLUDED IN EDITIONS
PRIOR TO 1956

To a Mayd

1. Fayre Mayd, you did but cast your eyes erewhile
        your ripening eyes
  Upon a Banke of Camomile,
      And straight a blushing Birth
        of Strawberryes
          began to smile
      and all to gild the earth.

2. Would you have Cherry harvest here
      still last? then doe no more
      but kisse yon Sicamore   10
    that Mirtle, or that Bay;
      And Cherryes will appeare
  not onely ripe for that one day
      but dangling all the yeare.   Rob:
                         Herricke.

1 This is attributed to Herrick by John Prince, *Danmonii Orientales
Illustres*, 1701, p. 334.
2 From Brit. Mus. Add. MS. 33998, f. 82ᵛ.

Epitaph on a man who had a Scold to his Wife

1. NAY, read & spare not, Passenger,
      my sence is now past feeling,
   who to my Grave a wound did beare
      within, past Physicks healing.

2. But doe not, if thou be to wed,
      to read my story tarry;
   least thou envy me this cold Bed,
      rather then live to marry.

3. For a long strife with a leud Wife
      (worst of all Ills beside)   10
   made me grow weary of my life,
      so I fell sicke & dyde.   Rob:
                                 Herricke.

To his false Mistris

1. WHITHER are all her false oathes blowne,
      or in what region doe they live?
   I'me sure no place where faith is knowne
      dare any harbour to them give.

2. My withered heart, which Love did burne,
      shall venture one sigh with the wind,
   Oh may it never home returne
      till one of her false oathes it find.

3. Then lett them wrestle in the sky
      till they shall both one Lightning prove,   10
   and falling may they pierce her eye
      that was thus periurd in her love.   Rob:
                                           Herricke.

1 From Brit. Mus. Add. MS. 33998, f. 33^v.
2 From Brit. Mus. Add. MS. 33998, f. 82^v.

[To a disdaynefull fayre]

T HOU maist be proud and be thou so for me
    yet know there is a death for me & thee
when as poore souls our softer frailties must
be lost in blended dust,
That Charnell house that keepes us both shall signe
no neat distinction twixt thy bones & mine.

2. And when to Hell our two lean soules must come
Where that just iudge shall giue to each his doome
Think'st thou thy pride forme colour there can fee
Him not to censure thee   10
Know wretched soule a judge thou there shalt finde
Who not respects the body but the minde.

3. And for my plea in acorne cups Ile show
Those two last teares which from mine eyes did flow
And all my sighs through silke-worme bags shall sound
Thou gau'st me deadly wound.
Can Justice then when these haue sworne thy guilt,
Ah! not reuenge the blood that thou hast spilt.

Herick

[Orpheus and Pluto]

[Or.] H OWLE not you Ghosts & furies while I sing
        Accents of greife to your infernall King
    Pluto oh! Pluto pitty my sad teares!
[Pl.] What heavenly rapture this doth peirce our eares
    Hark hark what art that cal'st to Hell
[Or.] Orpheus the poore Thracian Minstrell
    What cam'st thou here for! [Or.] Justice. [Pl.] Whats
        thy plea
[Or.] To crave againe my deare Euridice
[Pl.] Com'st thou for her whom fates too hasty sheares
    cut of but in the blossome of her yeares   10
[Or.] for her I come [Pl.] fond man she's our's by fate
[Or.] Yet Love's intreaty never comes too Late
[Pl.] What should infernall Jove doe [Or.] Deigne to warne
    the fatall Sisters to retwist the yarne
    But oh! it is in Pluto's power to doe it

---

1 From Bodl. MS. Don. c. 57, f. 41, corrected by Bodl. MS. Eng. Poet.
c. 50, recently acquired by the Library. Title from Brit. Mus. Add. MS.
33998, f. 82ᵛ.   2 From Bodl. MS. Don. c. 57, f. 53ᵛ.

If he but nodd & put the Parcae to it
Let Love move Pluto let my greife tormenting
And jointly both move Pluto to repenting
[Pl.] Can we in justice do it [Or.] Jove may & who
    dares speak 'gainst that which Jove is pleased to doe   20
Call back her fate and give a new beginning
to the cut web & blesse the thread in spinning
[Pl.] Why then triumph go take her hence & tell
Thy Music fetch't Euridice from Hell.
Such are thy measures Musick such thy charmes
that it the Furies of their brands disarmes
Such were thy active numbers Musick then
when thou build'st Thebes & cast it downe agen.

Mᵣ Robt Ramsy
Mᵣ. Heyrick

Parkinsons shade to the house of mᵣ
Pallauicine takeing his death ill

WILL you still lament and rayse
      A shade from rest
doe you loue and will molest
      A harmles Ghost with Ayes
Babram, by my loue forbeare
      to shed A teare
or spend A groane, unless for Tombes
      youle haue me come to haunt your romes
        ah should I proue
A Goblin to the place I loue   10
      no, no rather lett me keepe
        my peacefull vrne
Then to the Comon light returne
and want my silken sleepe
I am ould and loue to bee
        mongst Auncestry
wher in charnels we compare
our Grandsires bones to those which are
        in theis dayes when
      the Age breeds boyes not men   20
but howsoeuer theyse defaults
      haue fate alike in uaults.

From Huntington Library MS. HM 198, p. 30.

this from the dead: prepare to come,
for me and you benignant Earth has rome
    meane while Gods benison and good mens vowes
    preuent your Acts, Peace guard this house
        Exit Parkenson:
                R: Herricke

[*The Showre of Roses*]

M Y Mistris blush'de, and therewithall,
   as that Rich Crimson Spred,
from either cheeke, A showre did fall,
   of blossoms whyte and Red.

2 the More she blush'de, the More the grace
   did Make the Softe bloomes grow,
which Guilded there, fell downe a pace,
   like flakes of winters snow.

3 had she not cast her Eye beneath
   and Seene a Realme of flowr's   10
Ah doubtles she had bloomde to death.
   with Rayninge Rosye showr's

4 but when she stopt A sent soe blest
   I Smelt, that I did sweare
that parradice had lefte the East
   to spend his spices there.

[*The Eclipse*]

V AILE thou thine eyes a while my Deare,
   and muffle vp those twins of light,
Suns which euery day appeare
surfeit the eye and dimne the sight
preserve those fyers
till vennom'd age shall me benight
of my desires
sights seene aloofe more strictly tye the sence
to due observance of their Excellence,

[1] From H. Lawes autograph MS., p. 139. First printed and attributed to Herrick by Willa M. Evans in her biography, *Henry Lawes*, 1941, pp.157–8.
[2] From Bodl. MS. Mus. b. 1, f. 110ᵛ.

423

The Lilly or the blushing rose   10
wrappt in a mantle of pure lawne
more gently strokes the sight of those
whose eyes by that Eclipse are drawne,
then should they lye
tendring themselv's a naked pawne
to every eye
Beauty still gaz'd on dyes, but somtimes hid
doth strike amazement & cheape eyes forbid

The farewell

SWEETEST Loue since wee must part
    by meere constraint, not heart,
stay a kissing while to know
what are my vowes, then goe:
Let that day when you goe hence
with other care dispence,
only busied to descrye
this happy Augury
that as she doth part us twaine
she will neuer meete againe: 10
Let the free, and gentle ayre
a teare or two declare,
and the sadd and passing Bell
bee dolefull Philomell;
to whose ruthfull tones wee'll weepe
that teares true time may keepe:
Let noe Churlish winde once dare
to awake the quiet ayre
as you ride, but still bee they
as to *Alcione*;   20
Let the stroaking sunne first aske
leaue of your vailing maske,
Ere his rayes through that Ecclipse
dare come to kisse your lipps:
Let the soft, the sweet the kinde
breath of the westerne winde
Calmely spire a kisse, not blowe
yet make your Tresses flowe
Like to Daphnes, when shee fledd

From Brit. Mus. MS. Harl. 6918, f. 50ᵛ.

the losse of maydenhead: 30
Let your steede noe other pace
haue, nor noe other grace
then the Bull that bare the sweete
Europa into Creete:
Let our parting still the scope
keepe of a meeting hope,
though not this day, or the next
A third may make loue vext,
yet a fourth may issue when
wee two shall meete againe;   40
Then faire mistrisse, though delayes
make two seeme twenty dayes,
Let truth number them in sport
our absence will bee short.

A Sonnet

ILE dote noe more, nor shall mine eyes
        againe
        maintaine
    my former Jealousies,
    If I can feare
        noe more her haire
to fetter mee, twill bee the best
the noblest Trophy I can reare
        unto my rest:
Thus perish in mee all my fire of Lust   10
        only a Just
    desire keepe heate in mee
        to bee
A looker on yet still Liue free.

[A Song]

LOOSE no time nor youth but be
  kinde to men as they to thee
the faire Lyllyes that now grow
in thy cheekes & purely show
the cherry & the rose that blow

1 From Brit. Mus. MS. Harl. 6918, f. 51ᵛ.
2 From Bodl. MS. Don. c. 57, f. 17ᵛ. Title from Bodl. MS. Mus. b. 1,
f. 39ᵛ.

if too long they hang & wast
winter comes & all will blast
thou art ripe full ripe for men
in thy sweet be gathred then.

[*Advice to a Maid*]

LOVE in thy youth fayre Mayde bee wise
    Ould time will make thee colder
and thoughe each Morneinge newe arise
    yett wee each daye growe oulder,

Thou as heauen art faire, and younge,
    thine Eyes like twynn Starrs shineinge,
but ere an other daye bee sprunge
    all theise will bee declineinge.

Then winter comes with all his feares,
    and all thy sweetes shall borrowe,   10
too Late then wilt thou showre thy teares,
    and I too Late shall sorrowe.

ffinis

[*Elegy*]

SINCE louely sweete, much like vnto a Dewe
  Of pearle thou art lost vnto our View
Or like a vanish't dreame, this ground
When wee haue pray'd and censt it, lett it round
In our wild eares, whether thou art gone
If to thine endlesse habitation,
Or to insoule some starre till that great yeare
Fills vp the motion of the Maister spheare
And to returne att All soules daye, when wee
Att that great Aprill shall reviue and bee   10
Those verie same wee are, or yf not soe
Yett lett thy shade enforme, that wee maie knowe
If in the Orient, or the spice'd West
Thou lyest conceal'd, rowl'd vp in a nest

---

1 From Brit. Mus. Add. MS. 25707, f. 149.
2 From Harvard MS. Eng. 626F, f. 36ᵛ, corrected by Bodl. MS. Eng.
Poet. c. 50.

Of Ladanum and spiknard, that some wind
Maie fann thine odours hither; soe to find
Thee, and fall downe to worshipp, like as when
That siluer candle lead those wiser men,
To that they sought for: soe lett some one thing
What e're it bee (soe true) guide vs and bring   20
Where wee may thinke and bee. this by my teare
And my late Primrose tell I charge thee where
Thou settlest thine abode: saye do'st thou looke
Nymph-like into some glibb, and pratling brooke
Hemm'd all about with lillies, or sowest reames
Amidds't the pibbly murmure of her streames?
Speake by thy purling accent, and make knowne
Thou liu'st a swann there, or some Halcion,
Or yf some Meadowe Nymph thou art, declare
Thy Goddhead in some flower, that wee may spare   30
The plucking to adore it; or if in
None of these shapes thou wilt bee worshipp't, spynne
This to our madd thoughts, thou art become
The Genius to some Cittie great, as Rome
Had hirs, whose onely but revealed name
Did overturne the very Fate and frame
Of all her Building, or if like some shield
Or fallne Palladium thou do'st sway and weild
Some farre Republique, wee dare name thee And
With reverence to our wellfare laye an hand   40
Of holy rigour on thee, and thy Powers
Charme forth, and soe reduce thee wholy ours
But thou art lost, and whether will th'excesse
Of hudwinkt passions lead vs? What Wi'ldernesse
Is this soe vast, soe boundlesse, in whose straye
Wee wind and looke, yett neuer find a waye
That leads vs to a Saboth, thou art lost
O thou art lost for ever, like a frost
Dissolu'd and fledd n'ere to bee found againe
Noe more then broaken blisters, dropps of raine   50
Rais'd to vndoe. whoe guides vs, where our eies
May on the tombe stone paie the sacrifice
Due to soe iust a greife, and there wee'le lie
Weeping our eies out dropp by dropp and die.

Finis

427

SELECT GLOSSARY OF UNCOMMON WORDS AND MEANINGS

(The first number is that of the page; the second that of the poem on that page; the third that of the line in that poem. '1' after the page-number always applies to the first poem to *begin* on that page, not to the continuation of a poem begun on a preceding page; such continuations are referred to by page and line-numbers only.

When the word or meaning occurs more than once the glossary usually records the first occurrence only. Proper names are generally excluded.)

Accesse (25. 2. 10). Coming.

Axeltree (239. 2. 8). Funeral cart.

Barly-Break (33. 3, title). A country game played by couples. One couple occupied a 'den' called Hell until they could catch other players.

Baudery (133, l. 54). Material dirt.

Benjamin (131. 1. 10). Benzoin.

Bestrutted (119. 1. 34). Swollen.

Bishop't (64. 2. 10). Confirmed.

Bore-cats (333. 6. 9). Tom-cats.

Box (211. 3. 2). Box-wood.

Bran (398. 3. 12). Common people.

Briefs (39. 1. 2). Licences to make a special collection.

Bruckel'd (91, l. 58). Grimy.

Burle (211. 2. 2). Smooth.

Calamus (375, l. 54). An eastern aromatic plant (Song of Sol. iv. 4).

Calenture (397. 3. 2). Fever.

Candidate (106. 1. 2). In a white sheet.

Candlemas (304. 1. 6). A display of candles.

Carbage (302. 3. 4). Padding, lining (cf. Garbage, 76. 2. 6).

Carkanet (14. 2, title). Necklace.

Cedar (45. 1. 36). Cedar-oil, used for preserving papyri.

Cess (33. 2. 3). Reckoning; ('from out the Cess', beyond one's supposed means).

Ceston (166, l. 37). Cestus, girdle.

Chamlets (47. 3. 11). Camlets; garments of silk, &c.

Chanters side (93, l. 125). Precentor's (cantoris) side in antiphonal singing.

Cherry-pit (19. 1, title). Game of throwing cherry-stones into a small hole.

Chev'rell (71. 2. 3). Kid-leather (purse).

Chick of Jove (108. 1. 8). Favourite child ('pullus Jovis').

Circular (134, l. 68). Unified.

Circum-crost (227. 1. 2). Crossed all over; sanctified.

Circummortall (96. 2. 2). Beyond or above mortal.

Circumstants (79, l. 85). By-standers.

Cockall (91, l. 59). Knuckle-bone; used in the game of cockal or dibs.

Codpeece (118. 3. 5). Appendage to front of breeches.

Compartiement (227. 2. 8). Decoration, design.

Comply (206, l. 40). Enfold.

Conclave (331. 9. 2). Dwelling-place.

Confirm'd (241. 2. 2). Sanctioned.

SELECT GLOSSARY

Conscripts of the Citie (176. 1. 6). City fathers.

Consonant (210. 3. 1). Agreeable.

Cross (321. 1. 3). Coin.

Crosse (101. 1. 21). Bestride.

Crosse and Pile (189. 3, title). Upper and lower side (of coins with cross on the obverse; pile = lower iron of minting machine).

Cup-shot (313. 1. 10). Drunk.

Dead (42. 2. 2). Kill, deaden.

Dead lift (256. 1. 13). Extremity.

Deaf (232. 4. 6). Empty, hollow.

Dew-locks (68, l. 24). Dewy hair.

Ding-thrift (160. 2. 3). Spendthrift.

Discruciate (239. 5. 2). Excruciate.

Distemper (148, l. 87). Intoxication.

Distraction (28. 1. 4). Displacement, divagation.

Draw Gloves (99. 2, title). A parlour-game involving a race to draw off gloves.

Excathedrated (64. 2. 4). Formally condemned.

Expansion. (3. 1. 4). Firmament.

Fan (45, 1. 23). Winnowing-fan; carried round in Bacchic festivals.

Fanes (102, l. 40). Winnowing-fans.

Farced (146. 1. 24). Stuffed.

Fasting-Spittle (93, l. 117). Saliva of a person fasting; supposed to have medicinal value.

Fatts (102, l. 40). Vats.

Feare (363. 1. 13). Frighten.

Fetuous (92, l. 68). Featous, elegant.

Fil'de (140. 2. 6). Recorded.

Fill-horse (101. 1. 21). Shaft-horse ('fill' is a variant of 'thill' = shaft).

Fillit (256. 2. 10). Head-band, diadem.

Foot-pace (93, l. 132). Altar platform.

Forked-fee (202, l. 25). Fee taken from both parties in a lawsuit.

Fox-i'th'hole (126. 3. 14). A kind of hopping-game.

Fuz-ball (119. 1. 29). Puff-ball (fungus).

Garbage (76. 2. 6). See Carbage.

Gentle-heart (114, l. 96). Plant not identified.

Gospel-tree (20. 2. 4). See Holy-oke.

Green (64. 1, title). Pale.

Green-gown (69, l. 51). Gown soiled by lying on grass.

Grounded (152. 4. 7). Established.

Grutch (115, l. 136). Complain.

Guesse (411, l. 59). Guest.

Heave-offering (397. 4. 4). Offering elevated by the priest (Num. xv. 20).

Heyes (192. 1. 30). Country dances.

Hock-cart (5. 1. 3). The cart carrying the last load (hock = harvest feast).

Hoe (307. 1. 11). Delay; 'no Hoe', forthwith.

Holy-Forum (106. 1. 2). Church.

Holy-oke (20. 2. 4). An oak at which the Gospel was read during 'beating the bounds'.

Hoofy (412, l. 84). Struck by hoof of Pegasus to create the fountain Hippocrene.

Hope-seed (52. 2. 8). ? Grain of hope.

Huckson (223. 3. 11). Hockshin, underside.

Hypostaticall (388. 4. 2). Substantial; referring to the Second Person of the Trinity, who has unity of substance (hypostasis) with the Godhead.

Inapostate (330. 4. 16). Believing, faithful.

Ingrost (190, l. 43). Made out in form.

Jets (257. 1. 8). Black marble monuments.

Jimmall (173. 5, title). Gimmal; ring divisible into two or three rings.

July-flower (5. 1. 2). Perversion of Gillyflower.

Justments (27. 1. 4). Due ceremonies; funeral rites.

SELECT GLOSSARY

Ladanum (181. 3. 4). A gum-resin used in fumigation.

Lady of the Lobster (93, l. 131). 'The calcareous structure in the stomach of a lobster . . . fancifully supposed to resemble. the outline of a seated female figure.' (OED.)

Lady-smock (114, l. 94). Cuckoo-flower.

Lations (47. 3. 4). Movements.

Lautitious (262. 2. 3). Sumptuous.

Lemster Ore (165. 1. 28). A fine wool associated with Leominster.

Levell-coyle (311. 6. 2). Noisy games; racket.

Leven (199. 1. 3). Batch, quality.

Lip (199. 1. 3). Language.

Lively-hood (152. 4. 8). Existence.

Luster (23. 1. 3). Lustrum; period of five years.

Lustie[-gellie] (299. 4. 4). Pleasant tasting.

Maiden[-Pomander] (145. 1. 26). Fresh, unspoilt.

Maidens-blush (114, l. 97). Light-pink rose.

Male perfume (277. 5. 4). A superior kind of incense.

Manch (295. 2. 5). Sleeve.

Mantle-tree (131. 3. 3). Beam across fireplace.

Mashes (282. 5. 6). Meshes, nets.

Maukin (101. 1. 9). Mop.

Maunds (261. 4. 8). Baskets.

Mell (143. 5. 4). Honey.

Mettle (406, l. 79). Substance.

Mew (144. 2. 2). Shed.

Miching (246. 1. 24). Pilfering.

Misterie (115, l. 123). Art.

Mop-ey'd (97. 3. 1). Short-sighted.

Mothering (236. 6. 2). The mid-Lent custom of visiting parents with gifts.

Mowes (179, l. 23). Stacks or heaps.

Nations (116, l. 158). Families.

Nectarell (20. 1. 4). Like nectar.

One (168. 3. 2). ? Owned.

Open Sceane (148, l. 76). ? Immodest play-acting.

O're-leven'd (7. 2. 2). Puffed-up.

Pannicles (242. 2. 4). Membranes of the brain.

Pean[-Gardens] (234. 3. 3). ? Belonging to Apollo (Paean).

Perpolite (301. 5. 2). Highly polished.

Piggin (371. 4. 5). Pail.

Pill (32. 3. 3). Plunder.

Platonick year (190, l. 47). Period of c. 30,000 years completing astronomical movements.

Pose (296. 2. 1). Catarrh.

Post and Paire (238. 5. 1). A gambling card-game.

Posterne-bribe (202, l. 25). Back-door.

Pounc't (67, l. 9). Sprinkled.

Praises-proof (150. 1. 11). Sign of admiration.

Prick-madam (114, l. 96). Houseleek.

Primates (272. 1. 4). Leaders.

Print (162. 1. 3). Proper style.

Prominent (405, l. 66). Eminence.

Protonotarie (357. 1. 2). Principal notary or recording clerk.

Purfling (206, l. 14). Embellishing.

Pushes (211. 2. 1). Pimples or boils.

Questions and Commands (215. 2. 8). A game in which absurd questions, &c., were put to each player.

Quintell (159. 1. 4). Quintain; a post used as a mark in tilting.

Ravell (134, l. 72). Disentangle.

Reaks (56, l. 117). Pranks, games.

Reames (427, l. 25). Foam.

Reaming (374, l. 41) Filamented; or ? frothy, creamy.

Religious (27. 1, title). Revered, sacred.

Repullulate (133, l. 23). Renew life.

Reprobate (209. 3. 8). Rejected.

Respasses (145. 1. 20). Raspberries.

Roster (256. 1. 15). Roast meat.

Ryne (406, l. 98). Skin (rind).

Saciety (297. 3. 2). Satiety.

Sagge (119. 1. 33). Sagging, pendent.

Saturitie (378. 8. 2). Repletion.

Scald (33. 1. 1). Scall; eruption.

Sceanes (76. 2. 8). Curtains, veils.

Sciography (139. 1. 2). Outline, rough draft.

Seale-work (91, l. 63). Ornamentation as on a seal.

Shots (13. 1. 2). Reckonings.

Sign'd (288. 2. 2). Ensured.

Signs (85. 3. 2). Omens.

Sir-reverence (200. 1. 6). Piece of excrement.

Skurfe (398. 3. 12). Scum of the people.

Slam (238. 5. 1). A gambling card-game.

Sleeded silk (405, l. 57). Silk separated into its filaments; floss-silk.

Snakie (206, l. 45). ? Venomous.

Sperrables (226. 5. 2). Headless nails.

State (8. 2. 5). Canopy. 185. 4. 5, 'tooke State'. Felt superior.

States (36, l. 85). Councils or courts.

Stool-ball (238. 2, title). A kind of cricket game, with stool used as wicket.

Sumpter (330. 3. 4). Cloth covering a pack-horse.

Tabbies (207. 1. 3). Mingled colours.

Tansie (238. 2. 3). A pudding or omelet flavoured with tansy.

Tap (79, l. 88). Tap-house or tap-room.

Tearce (291, l. 8). Tierce; one-third of a pipe.

Tearmly (303. 1. 12). Periodical.

Teaster (154. 1. 2). Tester; sixpence.

Teend (263. 3. 2). Ignite.

Throtle (187. 1. 4). Adulterate.

Thumblesse (310. 3. 3). Clumsy, helpless.

Tittyries (126. 3. 2). A brotherhood in London about 1623–4, who called themselves 'Tityre, tu's' (Virgil, *Ecl.* 1. 1.).

To (256. 2. 10). Before, or in succession to.

Topick (172, l. 8). Place.

Tost (79, l. 88). Toast; drinker (? collective for 'toasts').

Toucht (236. 3. 5). Tested.

Trentall (89. 1. 2). Set of 30 successive masses for the dead.

Truss (301. 5. 8). Tie neatly together.

Tucker (211. 2. 2). Fuller, cloth-finisher.

Turfe (79, l. 88). ? The commoner sort of people, clods.

Unflead (350, l. 22). Intact (unflayed).

Up tailes all (247. 2, title). Name of a song.

Watched (92, l. 73). Watchet; blue or green.

Wave-off'ring (377. 2. 4). Offering waved by the priest (Exod. xxix. 24).

Wheales (273. 4. 1). Pimples.

While (278. 3. 4). Until.

Whit-flaw (66. 1. 3). Whitlow.

Whorry (157. 3. 1). Obsolete form of Hurry.

Wimbling (282. 2. 6). Boring, hole-making.

INDEX OF TITLES

INDEX OF TITLES

INDEX OF TITLES

INDEX OF TITLES

INDEX OF TITLES

INDEX OF TITLES

447

INDEX OF FIRST LINES

INDEX OF FIRST LINES

INDEX OF FIRST LINES

PAGE

452

INDEX OF FIRST LINES

INDEX OF FIRST LINES

INDEX OF FIRST LINES

INDEX OF FIRST LINES

INDEX OF FIRST LINES

459

INDEX OF FIRST LINES

460

461

INDEX OF FIRST LINES

PAGE

INDEX OF FIRST LINES

INDEX OF FIRST LINES

INDEX OF FIRST LINES

H h

471

INDEX OF FIRST LINES

INDEX OF FIRST LINES

INDEX OF FIRST LINES

INDEX OF FIRST LINES

PRINTED IN GREAT BRITAIN
AT THE UNIVERSITY PRESS, OXFORD
BY VIVIAN RIDLER
PRINTER TO THE UNIVERSITY